"At a time when facile predictions about an Asian 21st century replacing the American 20th century as if it were an immutable law of nature, Vasuki Shastry provides a timely corrective, exposing the many complexities of "Asia" - itself a vast abstraction - will have to contend with if its promise is to be realised. Nothing is ever inevitable. Vasuki is in good company. In 1988, Deng Xiaoping told Rajiv Gandhi that he did not believe in the inevitability of an Asian century. It's a pity that the simple-minded promoters of the idea seem to have forgotten Deng's sage assessment. But they should at least read this book"

Bilahari Kausikan
Singapore's Ambassador-at-Large and
Chairman, Middle East Institute.

"Vasuki Shastry offers informative, readable sketches of the economic, social, political, and environmental challenges facing Asia as the region emerges from the grip of the pandemic"

Michael Vatikiotis
Regional Director - Asia, Centre for Humanitarian Dialogue and
author of "Blood and Silk: Power and Conflict in Modern Southeast Asia".

HAS ASIA LOST IT?

LOST IT?

Dynamic Past, Turbulent Future

HAS ASIA LOST IT?

Dynamic Past, Turbulent Future

Vasuki Shastry

World Scientific

NEW JERSEY · LONDON · SINGAPORE · BEIJING · SHANGHAI · HONG KONG · TAIPEI · CHENNAI · TOKYO

Published by

World Scientific Publishing Co. Pte. Ltd.

5 Toh Tuck Link, Singapore 596224

USA office: 27 Warren Street, Suite 401-402, Hackensack, NJ 07601

UK office: 57 Shelton Street, Covent Garden, London WC2H 9HE

British Library Cataloguing-in-Publication Data
A catalogue record for this book is available from the British Library.

HAS ASIA LOST IT?
Dynamic Past, Turbulent Future

ISBN 978-981-122-840-7 (hardcover)
ISBN 978-981-122-971-8 (paperback)
ISBN 978-981-122-841-4 (ebook for institutions)
ISBN 978-981-122-842-1 (ebook for individuals)

For any available supplementary material, please visit
https://www.worldscientific.com/worldscibooks/10.1142/12044#t=suppl

Desk Editor: Sandhya Venkatesh
Design and layout: Loo Chuan Ming

Printed in Singapore

To Uma, and to Bombay

CONTENTS

DYSUTOPIA

DYSUTOPIA

Chapter 1

Greatest Show on Earth

Every century gets the pandemic it deserves.

Ours arrived under mysterious circumstances in Wuhan, China sometime in the last quarter of 2019. In the memorable words of New York Governor Andrew Cuomo, the Covid-19 virus then "got on a plane" and became a super-spreading global pandemic in a matter of months. The human toll is devastating — over 80 million infected and over 1.7 million deaths as I write this. Over a century ago and during World War I no less, the world witnessed the devastating "Spanish flu" pandemic, which according to the U.S. Centres for Disease Control and Prevention infected 500 million people and killed over 50 million, with an estimated 20 million in Asia alone, although precise numbers are hard to come by. Pandemics are named pandemics because their human toll is on a global scale and devastating.

The origins of the current pandemic are largely unknown, on which there is fierce debate. What we know definitively is that Covid-19 and the world we live in, circa 2020, were a match made in heaven. Our hyper-globalised, super connected lives needed a biological reckoning of sorts. Habitat destruction placed us in ever so close contact with virus carriers in the wild. Nature struck back by delivering a Black Swan-like pandemic like no other. Even

> *These great strengths have now been shaken and stirred, both by the pandemic as well as pre-pandemic trends like the U.S.-China trade war which placed globalisation on reverse gear.*

before Covid-19, the winner-takes-all global economy was not working for everyone, certainly not in Asia. The prolonged lockdown has accelerated social distress and jealousies, and will force politicians to rethink our current economic order.

As the singular beneficiary of globalisation's munificence, Asia will not be insulated from tectonic changes to the global economy. True, the region has been the greatest show on earth for several decades and Asia's openness to trade and investment aligned perfectly with the tailwinds of globalisation. These great strengths have now been shaken and stirred, both by the pandemic as well as pre-pandemic trends like the U.S.–China trade war which placed globalisation on reverse gear. Some of Asia's problems, discussed in this book, are home grown and resolvable. These include the incompetence of political leaders, rising inequality, chronic gender gap, climate distress, and a rapacious billionaire class, which in many cases are acting against the public interest. The pandemic has also exposed the region's many shortcomings, which were glossed over due to high rates of economic growth. Asia's other challenges are outside the region's ability to control.

This surely includes the rise of China as a superpower and the new Cold War raging with America — which threatens to upend the global trading system and reorder supply chains, the secret sauce behind the region's phenomenal success. Asia's own reckoning was the subject of speculation before the pandemic. Covid-19 has perhaps made it inevitable.

But we are getting ahead of ourselves.

> *The pandemic has also exposed the region's many shortcomings, which were glossed over due to high rates of economic growth. Asia's other challenges are outside the region's ability to control.*

Model Continent

Let me start with my own story. I went to school in Southern India, a region famous for turning out nerdy students with exceptional grades. Unfortunately for my family, I was not one of them. Even in a class filled with "book worms," as most students were referred to, one of them stood out. Let's call him Ravi. In a class of high performers, he was the model student, whose academic rigour, studying habits, and commitment we all aspired to. He was every parent's favourite child — brilliant in the classroom, agile in the cricket field where he was a wily off-spinner, and an all-round nice guy. Ravi would go on to excel in higher education as well — with degrees in engineering, business, a doctorate in operations research, and also trained to be a Chartered Accountant. In short, he was simultaneously admired and despised by his classmates. When he entered a room, conversation would stop as anxious classmates waited for the smart man to say a few words of wisdom or encouragement.

If Ravi was a continent, he would be Asia. The model continent which in the economic and political literature *du jour* can do no wrong. There is an entire industry out there whom I would impolitely describe as Asian braggarts and boosters. The shelves of every bookstore in Asia have best-selling titles authored by this motley group — *Asia Rising, Asian Century, Asia's Rise and America's Decline*, etc. The authors of these august titles literally come from everywhere — multilateral institutions, international consulting firms, business, academia, and media — which I describe as the region's thought leadership mafia. I was a card-carrying member of this group for a number of years, even decades, buying into the proposition that Asia's time had come (which is true) and that the continent's many challenges can be easily overcome (which I now disagree with). I have become more disillusioned of late, which motivated me to write this book. The time has therefore come to deflate the Asian hype and bubble.

There is the undeniable fact, of course. Asia's emergence in the last seven decades from the depredations of colonialism, extreme poverty and conflict

> *Asia's emergence in the last seven decades from the depredations of colonialism, extreme poverty and conflict is shock and awe theatre.*

is shock and awe theatre. The continent's rise was not pre-ordained. In the early 1960s, Ghana's per capita income was about the same level as impoverished South Korea. Singapore's infrastructure was so creaky that much of its downtown was routinely flooded due to rains and its antiquated sewage system. And then there was chronic poverty — billions of poor people without it seemed a viable economic plan to lift them from penury.

The Asian rags-to-riches drama unfolded in the aftermath of World War II to a sceptical global audience. Europe's reconstruction and recovery were a dominant Western focus with the Marshall Plan delivering over $12 billion in American assistance, around $112 billion in today's dollars. Although aid did flow, Asia was regarded as a welfare child, forever doomed to low growth and slow reduction in poverty.

Nobel Prize winning economist Gunnar Myrdal, author of the *Asian Drama: An Inquiry into the Poverty of Nations* and a brilliant, thoughtful scholar, encapsulated this Western-centric world view when he wrote in 1958[1] that there is a "small group of countries which are quite well-off," referring to Europe and America, and a "much larger group" of extremely poor countries. He went on to say that countries in the former group are on the whole, "firmly settled in a pattern of continuing economic development, while in the latter group progress is slower; as many countries are in constant danger of not being able to lift themselves out of stagnation or even of losing ground so far as average income levels are concerned." Myrdal's primary research focus was South Asia, notably India. Economist Ravi Kanbur[2] wrote that

---

[1] Gunnar Myrdal: *Economic Theory and Underdeveloped Regions*, Published by Duckworth & Co, 1958.

[2] Ravi Kanbur, "Gunnar Myrdal and 'Asian Drama' in Context" VoxEU CEPR Policy Portal, March 2018.

it is this framing of more than a half-century ago which is "most at odds" with the Asian development experience of the last three decades "...with the explosive growth of China, India, Vietnam, and a host of other countries." He comments on Myrdal's book: "Although *Asian Drama* was focused primarily on South Asia, in the book China and other Asian countries were often painted with the same brush. Along with most others at the time, Myrdal did not foresee that the economies of India and China would come to rival the size of the U.S. economy in little more than half a century."

The most remarkable aspect of Asia's rise has been how *recent* the phenomenon has been. Europe has been gloriously wealthy from at least the 16th century, recovering smartly from multiple deadly wars and pestilence. America's growth trajectory and road to riches can be traced to the first globalisation era of the 1870s, which accelerated after World War II. In contrast, Asia is literally the new rich kid on the block. Japan was the continent's first miracle economy, whose grand economic and political revival was a 1950s and 1960s phenomenon, soon to be followed in lockstep during the 1970s and 1980s by the Asian Tigers — Korea, Taiwan, Hong Kong, and Singapore. The miracle virus soon spread to Southeast Asia with Indonesia, Malaysia, and Thailand also displaying Tiger-like characteristics of sustained economic growth and a fall in poverty. East Asia's phenomenal economic and social success was built on a familiar rather than exceptional set of public policies. "The research shows that most of East Asia's extraordinary growth is due to superior accumulation of physical and human capital," according to the World Bank in its famous and

> *The most remarkable aspect of Asia's rise has been how recent the phenomenon has been.*

> *The miracle virus soon spread to Southeast Asia with Indonesia, Malaysia, and Thailand also displaying Tiger-like characteristics of sustained economic growth and a fall in poverty.*

somewhat notorious 1993 treatise on the rise of East Asia.[3] "But these economies were also better able to allocate physical and human resources to highly productive investments and to acquire and master technology. In this sense there is nothing 'miraculous' about the East Asian economies' success: each has performed these essential functions of growth better than most economies." Between 1965 to 1990, the World Bank study said that all of East Asia grew faster than all the other regions of the world.

Three Laggards

Asia's economic resurgence would have been incomplete without the rise of China, Vietnam, and India. I call them the Three Laggards because they are recent arrivals to the Asian growth story, the 1990s, and have unquestionably dominated economic discourse ever since. While Japan and the East Asian Tigers surged ahead in previous decades, building success on integrating with the global economy, the laggards were literally asleep at the economic wheel. They were of course distracted with excesses of the Mao era (China), a savage multi-decade war with a superpower (Vietnam) and a successful experiment with nation-building which still delivered sub-par growth (India). In short, China, Vietnam and India were the poster child of economic failure. The late U.S. Ambassador to India John Kenneth Galbraith memorably described India as a "functioning anarchy" while other commentators were equally scathing about the dismal prospects for "red" China and Vietnam. Dystopia would prevail over utopia, we were told.

While these predictions did not materialise, the pendulum today has swung in the opposite direction with commentators rushing to proclaim that the future is Asia or that the Asian century is upon us. The central thesis of this book is that we are only halfway or two-thirds the way through a riveting drama before Asian success can be assured. Yes, prospects for a valiant Asia prevailing to emerge as the world's dominant economic and political power

---

[3] World Bank, *The East Asian Economic Miracle: Economic Growth and Public Policy* (Oxford University Press, 1993).

remain positive. However, the region has to overcome formidable foes — political and economic dysfunction, rent seeking, climate change, a changing global economy, growing geopolitical risks, income inequality and gender imbalance to name a few — before victory is assured. Complacency and linear predictions about economic growth are always risky. Later in this chapter we will focus on the perils of economic forecasting, an inexact

Yes, prospects for a valiant Asia prevailing to emerge as the world's dominant economic and political power remain positive.

science which has singularly failed to predict significant positive trends (the rise of the smartphone) or even tail-risks (the 2008 Global Financial Crisis). By focusing attention on developments in Asia during the last 25 years, I hope to sketch contours of the future during the next 25.

I first visited Shanghai in 1994, a sleepy backwater town compared with the dizzying, dazzling metropolis it has become today. Hong Kong was then the unquestioned business capital of Greater China, the safe place to transact business on the mainland because of its adherence to the rule of law. China itself was in a state of flux. Five years had elapsed after the bloody Tiananmen Square student protests that had made China an international pariah from which it was just emerging. It was less than two years after a recently retired Deng Xiaoping had made his now famous "Southern tour" to Guangzhou, Shenzhen, Zhuhai, exhorting citizens that "to get rich is glorious."[4] Deng's trip culminated in Shanghai, then as now the epicentre for economic reforms, and the 88-year-old leader used the city as a platform to rail against "leftist" forces in the Communist Party, led by stalwarts such as Chen Yun and Premier Li Peng, who were determined to reverse China's flirtation with capitalism.

Defending himself against accusations that he was abandoning Communist doctrine, Deng explained that the "very essence" of socialism was the

---

[4] What Deng actually said was *"Rang yi bu fen ren xian fu qi lai"* that translates to "Let some people get rich first".

liberation and development of productive systems. "We should be concerned about right-wing deviations, but most of all, we must be concerned about left-wing deviations."[5] Academic Suisheng Zhao[6] writes that Deng himself described the opposition to his reforms as "some people" having reservations and different opinions. "...[W]hen he established the SEZs, some people were opposed to them and said that it was building many systems within one country; when he tried to invigorate the economy, some people said they had to prevent capitalism and fight corruption; when he made it clear that economic construction was the central task, some people said this was a problem of direction and an abandonment of Marxism–Leninism."

I was a journalist based in Singapore at the time and accompanied a Japanese business delegation for the opening of a plastics extrusion factory. While American toy manufacturers dominated in southern China, savvy Japanese investors had set up shop in Shanghai. The head of a leading Japanese trading house or *sogo sosha* excitedly drew a map of eastern China and described Shanghai as representing the crossbow which would help Japanese firms penetrate the rest of the country. The factory visit was an eye-opener, not only because of Japan's technological sophistication but also the strides that China had to make in order to catch up. In contrast with today's Shanghai, English was not widely spoken, and our Singaporean interpreter to the delegation found his Chinese brethren to be unschooled in the ways of the world.

It was also an opportunity for me to wander on the Bund and marvel at the newly opened and soon to become iconic Oriental Pearl Tower. The new business centre of Pudong loomed in the distance like a mirage, with vigorous local debate on whether Puxi or the historic centre of Shanghai would yield prestige and influence to the arriviste across the river. Charmingly, in retrospect, I took a ride on the short 2.7-mile section of the newly opened

---

[5] This quote is taken from a collection of speeches which Deng gave after China's opening up and which he repeated during the course of 1994.

[6] Suisheng Zhao, "Deng Xiaoping's Southern Tour: Elite Politics in Post-Tiananmen China," *Asian Survey* 33, no.8 (August 1993).

Shanghai Metro, today the world's largest rapid transit system by route length. There was a simmering controversy over the new metro system, its huge construction costs and utility to ordinary Shanghainese because of rumoured escalation in fare prices. I visited the campus of the newly established China Europe International Business School (CEIBS), which is today one of Asia's top business schools. The European head at the time explained to me that the CEIBS' primary objective was to unlock Chinese student's potential to become entrepreneurs and world-class managers. In that mission it has succeeded by a large measure.

Yet Shanghai was not all glamour and sizzle. In side streets and the suburbs, the old dystopian China was very much evident. Open sewers, polluted rivers, and much of the population on bicycles, seemingly tentative about the benefits of economic reforms. On Nanjing Road, buried today under steel and concrete, it was still possible to savour the old Shanghai. Communist literature was ubiquitous in the bookstores, discourse with local officials were laced with time-worn references (*The Long March*), and the Peace Hotel on the Bund was a temple to the 1949 revolution. Here surly waiters in starched uniform plied guests with chilled Tsingtao beer and lukewarm dumplings. Tourists from Asia were relatively rare and I recall being asked strange questions on the street about where I was from. In the era before the selfie, the most popular tourist attraction on the Bund was to be photographed along with a grinning PLA soldier.

In short, Shanghai and China in 1994 were grappling with capitalism coupled with decidedly communist characteristics. That was a mere 26 years ago and the struggles underway at the time do not receive the attention they possibly deserve. The leftist forces held out the promise of a Communist, Marxist utopia, built on reversing the bold reforms of the past two-decades. The reformers, most notably Deng himself, who had witnessed the horrors and excesses of Maoist-era China wanted a new beginning after Tiananmen. It was on these radical choices that led China to become gloriously and seriously rich.

China was still a poor country in 1994. Its GDP at market exchange rates was a piffling $584 billion, percapita GDP was an even more

China was about to become the biggest game in Asia and eventually the world.

modest $473, and the population living in extreme poverty exceeded 200 million.[7] Yet to many foreign observers. China was about to become the biggest game in Asia and eventually the world. Sitting in his Hong Kong office, surrounded by busts of Chairman Mao, at the time quite possibly one of the world's largest private collections, investor Marc Faber told me in 1994 that as Shanghai and China advanced, Hongkong would become more and more "irrelevant to China," a prophecy that has materialised. He also predicted that as China and India advanced, the centre of gravity would also shift eastwards, he noted.

Viet Crisis

Vietnam, second in the Asian laggards gallery, was in a more parlous and pitiful state in 1994. It was hard to see how a united Vietnam would ever be able to get its act together. GDP was a tiny $16 billion and $220 on a per capita basis, even lower than poor neighbours like Cambodia and Laos. If China's post-1949 generation was consumed with the horrors of the Mao era, successive generations of Vietnamese were exposed to the horrors of war. Four years after the fall of Saigon in 1975, a victorious Vietnam was forced by China to wage a brief but bloody war. The apparent provocation was Vietnam's decision to support dissident Khmer Rouge forces led by Hun Sen to invade Cambodia in 1978 and put an end to Pol Pot and the bloody genocide. If Japan and the Asian Tigers excelled in trade, Vietnam's comparative advantage it seemed was in waging war.

---

[7] I have used World Bank data here, with people's income of US$1.25 a day as the measure of being above or below the poverty line. This is an inexact measure because different benchmarks yield different results.

Buoyed by its success in prevailing over French, American, and now Chinese forces, Vietnam's political leadership spent much of the early eighties basking in their military successes. The Vietnamese delegation to the 1976 summit of the now defunct Non-Aligned Movement (NAM) was treated with joy and trepidation by fellow Asian nations, fearful of a rising regional power in their neighbourhood. A journalist friend told me a story, perhaps apocryphal, which described the buoyant militaristic mood in the country in the 1980s. There was a single weekly international commercial flight from Bangkok into Ho Chi Minh city (formerly Saigon). As the international flight prepared to leave, it was routinely held up on the tarmac for a show of force — the aging fleet of the Vietnam Air Force took off from the runaway to demonstrate to foreigners that the country was still a power to be reckoned with. This was pure theatre, but a bigger drama was unfolding on the streets.

The impact of successive wars was beginning to have an adverse impact on the economy and its most visible manifestation was hyperinflation. It is worth remembering that while Asian policymakers overall have had a peerless record in macroeconomic management, including during the Asian Financial Crisis, Vietnam has been an outlier in terms of dealing with hyperinflation, Latin-American style. Economist Quan Hoang Vuong[8] says that from national unification in 1975, Vietnam struggled for a decade in lifting agricultural and industrial production, unwittingly following the disastrous policies of Mao's China several decades earlier. Policymakers in Hanoi experimented with several flawed economic policies, culminating in a failed attempt to control monetary policy in 1985. "Upon the failure of the 1985 price-wage-currency adjustment scheme, a severe economic crisis followed, resulting in hyperinflation of 775% in 1986, scarcity of staples and consumer goods, impoverished living conditions, industrial stagnation, and mounting foreign debt." Vuong writes.

---

[8] Quan Huang Vuong, "Vietnam's Political Economy: A Discussion on the 1986-2016 Period", CEB Working Paper (Centre Emile Bernheim, May 2014).

The ensuing economic chaos forced the hand of the Communist Party of Vietnam (CPV). If China had its Deng Xiaoping, Vietnam's answer was Nguyen Van Linh, general secretary of the CPV at a critical time after the economic collapse of 1985-1986. Very much like China after the death of Mao, Vietnam's economic reformers under Linh fought a protracted political and ideological battle with CPV hard-liners keen to retain the primacy of Communist and Marxist ideology. Linh and his supporters won the battle and launched *doi moi* (or renovation) in 1986, as dramatic a change in economic direction as Deng's China reforms of 1978. Vuong notes that "the old fashioned, centrally planned economy was replaced with a socialist market mechanism, which promoted the concept of a multi-sectoral economy, open door policies towards international trade and investment, and recognised private property rights." There was an immediate, tangible improvement in Vietnam's economic fundamentals. For example, the new Law on Foreign Investment introduced in 1987 resulted in a surge in foreign direct investment, mainly from Asian sources (Japan, South Korea, Singapore, and Taiwan), which touched a phenomenal 10% of GDP by 1994. Vietnam's economic resurgence was also helped with the signing of the October 1991 Paris Peace Agreements, which marked the official end to the Cambodia–Vietnam war and were essential in bringing Indochina back to the trajectory of peace after four decades of conflict. Vietnam today has been granted "Tiger" status because of its rapid economic growth in recent years as well as its superb handling of the pandemic, that is in contrast with other ASEAN nations which have stumbled.

India Rises

India, third in our Asian laggards gallery, had a ringside seat to China and Vietnam's economic rise but was more hesitant to change direction. During her 1980-1984 tenure, cut short by her brutal assassination in October 1984, Prime Minister Indira Gandhi started the hesitant process of economic reforms, under the tutelage of a controversial programme supported by the

International Monetary Fund (IMF). The process was further accelerated under the leadership of her son Rajiv Gandhi, who was Prime Minister between 1984 and 1989. Like China and Vietnam, India's economic fault-lines were domestic and ideological. Suspicious of foreign investors and trade, the Indian economy was anaemic for much of the 1950-1980 period, expanding at an average of 3.5%, which economist Raj Krishna has memorably described as the "Hindu rate of growth." In 1977, the coalition government led by Mrs Gandhi's rivals had asked Coca-Cola and IBM to leave the country, which was presented as a nationalistic attempt to Make India Great Again.

I was a business journalist in India for much of the eighties. The economic and political narrative of that era is in sharp contrast with what is on view today. Much of my reporting was focused on the struggles of foreign and local business to navigate the excesses of the notorious license-permit *raj,* the bureaucratic dead-weight of economic policies aimed at checking the rise of the private sector. Since India's public sector was supposed to control the commanding heights[9] of the economy, a specific state objective, all of my conversations with business leaders were focused on securing licences and permits (and subtle and not-so-subtle efforts to subvert the law). There were specific capacity restrictions on exactly how much output a factory could produce, depriving Indian manufacturers of scale and global market share. There were exceptions to this of course, with a group of new and old oligarchs indulging in rent-seeking on a massive scale, a topic discussed later in this book.

Although the decade appeared to be a period of stagnation, change was definitely in the air. In 1984, Japanese car manufacturer Suzuki launched the Maruti car to much fanfare and adulation by the Indian consumer. The 800-c.c. rickety, claustrophobic Maruti Suzuki car represented a great leap forward in India's attitude towards foreign investors, albeit with the state

---

[9] A phrase which has its origins with central planners in the Soviet Union, emulated by China and India.

still controlling the majority of shares in the joint venture. Suzuki today has majority ownership and is India's largest automobile manufacturer. Also, in the same decade Pepsi was also allowed to set up a joint venture with the regulator's insistence that the American cola manufacturer had to "Indianize" the brand. Thus, Pepsi Cola briefly became Lehar Pepsi (or wave) and foreign companies had to wait until 1991 before they could use their own internationally recognised brands.

In the popular narrative, India unleashed bold economic reforms only in 1991, following a severe balance of payments crisis which forced the central bank to ship its gold holdings to London to stay current on international transactions. However, economist Arvind Panagariya, who served under Prime Minister Narendra Modi has written a fascinating paper on India's economic journey since the 1980s.[10] He notes that there is a contrarian view which argues that the growth rate in India had accelerated in the 1980s, around the same time as China, making it impossible to credit serious reforms with the improved performance of the country. "If those sceptics were right, it would be a major blow to liberal trade and market-friendly policies not only with respect of India but to developing countries around the world," he writes. "But a closer look reveals that the story is more complex than the sceptics would have us believe." Panagariya adds that three specific points emerge from a detailed analysis of trends. First, growth during the 1980s was patchy, with the last three years of the decade contributing a phenomenal 7.6 % growth. Second, without those three years, India's growth in the 1980s would look, at best, marginally better than that of the previous decades. Finally, growth was stimulated partially by expansionary policies that involved accumulation of large external debt that ended in an economic crisis. "In the end it was the 1991 market reforms and subsequent liberalizing policy changes that helped sustain growth," says Panagariya.

---

[10] Arvind Panagariya, "The Triumph of India's Market Reforms. The Record of the 1980s and 1990s", *Policy Analysis* (Cato Institute) no. 554 (November 2005).

Like China's Deng and Vietnam's Linh, India had its own economic reformers at a critical time for the country. Prime Minister P.V. Narasimha Rao, tragically forgotten in today's India, had taken over the helm after the assassination of Congress leader Rajiv Gandhi while campaigning for the June 1991 national elections. PM Rao's finance minister Manmohan Singh was a well-known economist and central banker, but new to politics. The Congress Party won that election in a sympathy wave, but it was soon faced with the grim reality of dealing with an unprecedented economic crisis. India's foreign reserves were running low and the Rao-Singh duo were faced with making hard choices, the most important of them being accepting IMF conditions through a major economic adjustment programme. *New York Times* journalist Bernard Weinraub, who was India correspondent at the time, captured the country's ambivalence in accepting loans from the IMF. "Facing a grave economic crisis, the newly elected Indian government has begun urgent talks with the International Monetary Fund seeking emergency aid of several billion dollars," Weinraub wrote in 1991. "Yet the conditions for such assistance are stirring anxiety in this nation, which historically prides itself on self-reliance. At issue is not only the economy, but also India's sensitivity to Western involvement." As an illustration of India's grave economic situation, the country's foreign debt had trebled to $72 billion in less than a decade, but the central bank only had $1.1 billion in hard currency reserves. This explains the central bank's emergency sale of gold in London and the historic IMF programme.

The reforms unleashed by Prime Minister Rao and Finance Minister Singh were no less ambitious compared with China and Vietnam. A discussion paper published by the Finance Ministry in 1993 vividly captures the ambitions of the country's reform agenda "...to bring about rapid and sustained improvement in the quality of the people of India. Central to this goal is the rapid rise in incomes and productive employment." The paper said, "The only durable solution to the curse of poverty is sustained growth of incomes and employment. Such growth requires investment in farms, in roads, in irrigation, in industry, in power and above all, in people." With a flourish, the paper added that "within a generation," the countries of East Asia have transformed themselves. China, Indonesia, Korea, Thailand, and Malaysia "…today have living standards much above ours. What they have achieved, we must strive for." The licence-permit *raj* was gradually dismantled, the state was no longer placed on the commanding heights of the economy, and foreign and local investors were allowed to enter hitherto walled-off areas of the economy. This included aviation, financial services, automobiles, capital goods and retail.

Make no mistake, India was a minor player in the global economy in 1994. Its GDP was a modest $322 billion and GDP per capita was $362. Along with China and Vietnam, the troika barely made a dent in global commerce, services, manufacturing and economic output. Japan was the dominant economic force in the region, the only Asian member of the G7, closely followed by the Asian tigers. More than twenty-five years later, China and India are Asian giants and Vietnam is a tiger economy in the making. The inevitable question is what is wrong with this picture. All of Asia, with a few exceptions (North Korea comes to mind), appear to be on a fast escalator to economic success. Indeed, medium and long-term economic forecasts for the region, from public and private institutions, are uniformly positive. As a continent, Asia has been the single biggest beneficiary of globalisation, trade, and investment and this trend is unstoppable, so goes the mantra.

Perils of Forecasting

Let's start with consulting firm PWC which in the pre-pandemic era predicted that the world economy could more than double by 2050,[11] "assuming broadly growth-friendly policies and including no sustained long-term retreat into protectionism and no major global civilisation-threatening catastrophes," which Trumpism and Covid-19 clearly validate. "Emerging markets will

---

[11] "The Long View. How will the global economic order change by 2050?"(PWC, February 2017).

continue to be the growth engine of the global economy" according to the PWC report. "By 2050, the E7 economies (China, India, Indonesia, Brazil, Russia, Mexico, and Turkey) could have increased their share of world GDP from around 35 percent to 50 percent. China could be the largest economy in the world, accounting for around 20 percent of global GDP in 2050, with India in second place, and Indonesia in fourth place (based on GDP at purchasing power parity or PPP). PWC Chief Economist John Hawksworth acknowledges that we should not dismiss political shocks like Trump or Brexit to the extent "they point to deeper structural shifts, notably a populist backlash against globalisation, automation and the perceived impact of these trends in increasing income inequality and weakening social cohesion." This is a necessary caveat which was ignored in the media coverage, where the focus was on the eye-popping headline of China, India, and Indonesia dominating the global economy.

The Asian Development Bank (ADB), the premier regional development bank, is unsurprisingly equally bullish about Asia's prospects by 2050. "Asia is in the middle of a historic transformation. If it continues to follow its recent trajectory, by 2050 its per capita income could rise six-fold in purchasing power parity (PPP) terms to reach Europe's levels today."[12] The ADB report published in 2011 said, "It would make some 3 billion additional Asians affluent by current standards. By nearly doubling its share of global gross domestic product (GDP) to 52 percent by 2050, Asia would regain the dominant economic position it held 300 years ago, before the industrial revolution."

For a sense of Asia's dominance of the global economy during centuries past, we should turn to the late British economic historian Angus Maddison who has produced estimates of world GDP going all the way back to 1 AD. In 1000 AD, according to Maddison's calculation, China and India together

---

[12] "Asia 2050: Realizing the Asian Century" (ADB, August 2011).

contributed 50.5 percent of world GDP.[13] By 1600, that share had gone up to 51.4 percent, with China accounting for 29 percent and India 22.4 percent of world GDP. A hundred years later, China's GDP had fallen but India's went up to 24.4 per cent. However, both China and India started their steep economic descent in the 1800s, ceding ground to the growing dominance of Europe, and later more dramatically to America through the first half of the 20th century. India's share of global GDP, at an estimated 7.5 percent in 2017 has never recovered to double digits while China's share has more recently increased to a robust 17 percent. Predicting prospects for the global economy in 2030, Maddison himself was circumspect about what he described as "futurology." "As there has been such a striking divergence in the pace and pattern of growth in different regions of the world in the past 30 years, it is worth considering the changes which seem likely in the next quarter century," he said in a 2008 paper.[14] "Futurology is a more speculative business than history. Hard evidence is lacking, and we have to project trends from the past which seem plausible but may well be reversed by unforeseeable events."

Economists not only perform poorly in making long-range forecasts. IMF economist Prakash Loungani and his colleagues have done extensive research on the ability of the economics profession to forecast recessions in 63 countries, using data from 1992-2014. These are short-term forecasts, which provide some perspective on the profession's overall ability to project economic growth forward, say to 2030 or 2050, as the ADB and PWC have done. Loungani's[15] key conclusion: "The main finding is that, while forecasters are generally aware that recession years will be different from other years, they miss the magnitude of the recession by a wide margin until

---

[13] From an article in India's *MINT* newspaper, 25 August 2010. Maddison computed GDP in 1990 dollars and in purchasing power parity (PPP) terms.

[14] Angus Maddison, "The West and the Rest in the World Economy: 1000-2030", *World Economics* 9, no. 4 (October-December 2008).

[15] Zidong An, Joao Tovar Jalles and Prakash Loungani, "How Well Do Economists Forecast Recessions? IMF Working Paper, 5 March 2018.

the year is almost over. Forecasts during non-recession years are revised slowly; in recession years, the pace of revision picks up but not sufficiently to avoid large forecast errors." Loungani's second finding is that forecasts of the private sector and official sector are virtually identical; thus, both are equally good (or bad) at missing recessions.

Why isn't the performance of economic forecasters better? Loungani considers this is primarily because of excessive caution on the part of the economists. "Forecasts ought to be revised early and often so as to absorb new information properly," the paper notes, "But the evidence presented suggests that forecasters take very long to reflect information in their forecasts." Finally, and more relevant to the issue at hand, the IMF researchers found that economists have made more errors in forecasting growth and in projecting recessions in a group of emerging market nations (China, India, Korea, Mexico, Brazil, Russia, and Turkey) compared with that of the G7, where data is more reliable. The fact that economists often get short-term business cycle forecasts wrong should be factored in when considering the same profession's rather rosy and bullish projections about Asia's growth well into the future.

The Case of Argentina

Asia's bullish futurologists could also learn a lesson or two from Argentina, quite possibly the most spectacular example of a once rich and vibrant nation which lost its way in the 20th century. Sitting in Buenos Aires in the early 1900s, it would have been easy for an analyst to predict that Argentina's run of economic good luck would continue indefinitely. During the boom years, restaurants in Buenos Aires were the most expensive in the world and the city was a haven for luxury goods, not different from today's Asia. Since this was the pre-aviation era, bookstores in shipping terminals were probably groaning under metaphorical titles of "Argentina Rising" or "The Future is Argentinian." As *The Economist* noted in 2014, a hundred years ago Argentina was the future of the global economy. In the 43 years leading up to 1914, GDP had grown at an annual average of 6 percent, the fastest recorded in the world at the time. "The country was a magnet for European immigrants, who flocked to find work on the fertile pampas, where crops and cattle were propelling Argentina's expansion. In 1914, half of Buenos Aires's population was foreign born." The country ranked among the ten richest in the world, after the likes of Australia, Britain, and the United States, but ahead of France, Germany, and Italy. Its income per head was 92 percent of the average of 16 rich economies, compared with around 40 percent today.

Economic historians have offered a long list of reasons for Argentina's precipitous decline in the last century — the two world wars which disrupted Argentina's status as an agricultural superpower, domestic political conflict which culminated in reckless economic policies, and changing trends in the global economy. In *The Economist* article, historian Rafael di Tella offered three deep-rooted reasons for the country's decline. First, Argentina may have been rich 100 years ago, but it was not "modern." That made adjustment hard when the external shocks hit. The second theory stresses the role of trade policy, which turned sour after World War I. Third, when it needed to change, Argentina lacked the institutions to sustain economic success. Populist leaders like Juan Peron introduced policies which undermined long-term growth and increased the role of the state.

Asia's future is not pre-destined to go the way of Argentina, although the current blowback against trade and globalisation has eerie parallels to the 1920s and 1930s, decades which were characterised by closed markets and beggar-thy-neighbour economic policies which started the Latin American country's long decline. Asia's recent success in the post-World War II era has proven to be more durable, resilient, and long standing compared with that of Argentina.

However, today's Asia does represent a mix of utopia and dystopia, which I call *dysutopia*. As I hope to illustrate in this book, Asia's easy, dizzy phase of economic growth has come to an end. A more difficult task awaits the region's astute policymakers. The world around them has changed, even before the pandemic, because of the emergence of a new superpower on their doorstep. Policy challenges which I will discuss in depth include: skewed demographics with rapidly aging and youthful societies; political systems which have not kept in pace with the dramatic changes in the economy; rising public aspirations and rising inequality that will test the government's ability to deliver; an export and consumption-dependent economic model whose time may have passed due to structural changes to the global economy, arising from the rise of artificial intelligence and automation; and widespread environmental destruction which places Asia at the epicentre of global climate change.

Which brings me back to my friend Ravi. I briefed him on the book project and had asked him for permission on whether I could cite his own experience of living with high praise, high expectations, and the attendant impact on his career. He gracefully agreed, noting that he was a permanent student until his early forties, chalking up one impressive degree after another, over fears that he would stumble in what he describes as "real life." Now in his late fifties, Ravi has not strayed far away from academia, by his own admission building a middling career. His key message is that he was numbed by praise in his youth and was insufficiently challenged by peers and teachers during these formative years.

It is a stretch to compare the career trajectory of my friend with that of an entire continent. However, there are parallels between Asia's phenomenal rise since the end of World War II, the attendant high praise it has received for past success, and the more challenging times which lie ahead. There will be winners and losers in this new era. The convenient "Asia" label to explain the region's many achievements will no longer suffice. There will be a utopian Asia with high and equal incomes, strong social mobility, gender parity, and a clean environment which will co-exist with a dystopian Asia of dysfunctional politics, fractured societies, high income inequality, and social unrest. Covid-19 has placed unflattering attention on the latter. To paraphrase Kipling, will the fate of the two Asia's be never the twain shall meet? Before we discuss this in detail, let's turn to the Asia of today and examine where the region is excelling.

Chapter 2

Asiaphoria and Peak Asia?

Has Asia's remarkable economic performance peaked or is
there some more room to grow?

Economists disagree about almost everything. However, the general consensus amongst practitioners of the dismal science in Singapore is that during times of economic distress, you should head to the nearest container port to figure out how many container gantry cranes have their booms up or down. When I worked for the Singapore central bank, I had a privileged view of the Tanjong Pagar terminal from my 28th floor office. During the SARS epidemic and the Iraq war, circa 2003, it was normal to see a large number of container gantry cranes at the terminal with their booms up, signifying that the berth was empty. By this crude exercise, it was quite easy to calculate the number of container ships at terminals across Singapore and make a guestimate about the direction of regional trade. During Asia's great commodities super-cycle, which started its long climb up around the time of the Iraq war and ended in 2013, the booms in Singapore ports were mainly down as they were busy stuffing commodities destined to China and exports of finished goods headed to markets all over the world. Those good days have surely come to an end as Asia grapples with a twin crisis brought about by the pandemic and the U.S.–China trade war, that threatens to undermine the region's business model.

The question is are we at Peak Asia, where the booms will remain up for a prolonged period, as the region run outs of economic steam because its primary growth drivers — trade and investment — are facing a secular decline just at a time of rising societal expectations? Related to this is the forecaster's fallacy about extrapolating future growth rates based on present performance, as we discussed in the previous chapter. Here we learn a new word, "Asiaphoria," coined by economists Larry Summers and Lant Pritchard[1] who looked at historical data on growth rates and "conclude that with economic growth, as with investment returns, past performance is no guarantee of future performance." More on this later. In examining whether Asian growth and hyper-performance have indeed peaked, it is useful to look at where the region stands today in terms of economic might, some historical context, and whether the dizzy pace of growth can be sustained. For illustrative purposes, I will also explore the manic investment in infrastructure to see if some of the rush is justified.

> *The question is are we at Peak Asia, where the booms will remain up for a prolonged period, as the region run outs of economic steam because its primary growth drivers — trade and investment — are facing a secular decline just at a time of rising societal expectations?*

It is undeniable that Asia has achieved remarkable economic success over the past five decades, as the IMF noted in its Regional Economic Outlook for Asia-Pacific in October 2018. "Hundreds of millions of people have been lifted out of poverty, and successive waves of economies have made the transition to middle-income and even advanced-economy status," the IMF said. "And whereas the region used to be almost entirely dependent on foreign know-how, several of its economies are now on the cutting edge of technological advance." Even more striking, the IMF added, is that Asia's rise

---

[1] Lant Pritchard and Larry Summers, "Asiaphoria Meets Regression to the Mean", NBER Working Paper no. 20573, October 2014.

has happened within just a couple of generations, "the product of a winning mix of integration with the global economy via trade and foreign direct investment, high savings rates, large investments in human and physical capital, and sound macroeconomic policies."

Jin Liqun, President of the Asian Infrastructure Investment Bank, is equally eloquent about the region's promise and potential. "After Asia's economic growth far out-paced the global average for nearly three decades, Asia's economy has become a global heavyweight," he said at the institution's annual meeting in Mumbai in June 2018. "Asian developing countries now account for 60 percent of global growth, while roughly two-thirds of global trade is part of value chains passing through Asia." Jin added that Asian growth is just a means to an end. "The ultimate objective is to improve people's lives, enable individuals to reach their potential and enjoy prosperity and security. It is the dream of all of us Asians to live a middle-class lifestyle with good education and healthcare, a clean environment, and consumer comforts," he added. To fulfil the AIIB chief's dream, Asia needs to do a significantly better job to deliver for its citizens.

There is no contest, in my view, with Asia's incredible ability to adapt to new technologies and to scale it up, a good quality to have at a time of great technological disruption. Whenever I flew into Asia during the pre-Covid era from London or Washington D.C., I felt like I had already arrived in the future, echoing science fiction writer William Gibson's view that the "future is already here — it's just not evenly distributed." In China, all of my interlocutors are on WeChat, now banned in America, and my repeated

There is no contest, in my view, with Asia's incredible ability to adapt to new technologies and to scale it up, a good quality to have at a time of great technological disruption.

attempts to reach them via traditional email turns out to be a futile exercise. I get a WeChat account myself, with the help of a colleague, and spend an enormous amount of time trying to navigate its dazzling features. In India,

I can switch my cellphone to a local SIM card in less than 15 minutes as the store clerk uses his smartphone to conduct efficient due diligence, a process which could be interminable in Europe or America. In Jakarta, the preferred ride-hailing app is not Uber (which exited Southeast Asia recently) but a successful local upstart called Gojek that uses motorcycles to ferry passengers through the city's congested streets, a home-grown innovation which is adaptable across the region.

Asia's increased connectivity is being fed by two inter-linked factors — an explosive growth in access to the Internet and in smartphone usage. And it has room to grow. According to statistics about Internet usage in Asia as at 30 June 2020,[2] the region had over 2.36 billion Internet users, a 55 percent penetration rate compared with the rest of the world which is slightly higher on average. What is amazing about the data is the trend-line over the last two decades. In 2000, China had a less-than-modest 22 million Internet users, today that number stands at over 854 million. Indonesia had 2 million Internet users in 2000 which has since expanded to 171 million. The rise in Internet usage has been fuelled in part by growth in broadband connectivity across the region and due to the phenomenal increase in smartphone usage, where the user statistics are equally impressive. China alone has become such a critical market for Apple's flagship iPhone (and indeed for any number of global consumer and capital goods manufacturers) that a slowdown in sales during the last quarter of 2018 lead to a major sell-off in the American company's shares. The rise of tech has created a new class of entrepreneurs across the region, nimble compared with their *ancien regime* peers and more willing to disrupt.

Best Time in History

For the moment, policymakers will argue that all is well in Asia. To paraphrase Deng Xiaoping, to be rich now is indeed glorious. Asia is still

---

[2] Internet World Statistics — usage and population statistics provided by internetworldstats.com

seeing high rates of economic growth compared with peers in Africa, Middle East, and Latin America. Historians and politicians often ask the rhetorical question of which is the best time in history to be born. According to President Barack Obama: "If you had to choose a moment in history to be born, and you did not know ahead of time who you would be — you didn't know whether you were going to be born into a wealthy family or a poor family, what country you'd be born in, whether you were going to be a man or a woman — if you had to choose blindly what moment you'd want to be born, you'd choose now." The former President added that for young people in America "this is the best time in human history to be born, for you are more likely than ever before to be literate, to be healthy, and to be free to pursue your dreams." The former President's focus may have been the America of his eight-year term, but it is arguable if his infectious optimism about the present remains relevant, given the country's lurch toward nationalism and nativism under President Trump. Even in Asia, as we will discuss in Chapter 5, there is an inter-generational divide as a younger generation feels that economic opportunity, and the upward mobility of their parent's generation is out of grasp for many of them.

> *For the moment, policymakers will argue that all is well in Asia. To paraphrase Deng Xiaoping, to be rich now is indeed glorious. Asia is still seeing high rates of economic growth compared with peers in Africa, Middle East, and Latin America.*

Reflecting on Obama's infectious optimism about the merits of living in the here and now, manifested by the region's greater connectivity, I can't help but think of where the region is coming from, going by my own experience of growing up in a poor country in the 1960s and 1970s, which by the former President's yardstick were *certainly not the best era to be born into.* Over the years, I have asked friends of my generation across the region for their own recollections of growing up poor in a poor Asia. There are, as can be expected, striking similarities and differences. A Chinese friend, now a prominent academic, recalls being only 12-years old in 1968 and trapped in the madness of Mao's Cultural Revolution. He was too young to be sent away to the provinces for hard labour, as his brother was, but was part of the student committee tasked with identifying "reactionaries, revisionists, and capitalist roaders" in the cohort of teachers at the school. Although food shortages had abated somewhat, the academic recalls that he and his peers were brainwashed into believing that revolutionary fervour was more nutritious compared with material well-being.

A Korean diplomat, also of the same age group, recalls the bone-chilling winters in Seoul of the early 1960s. There were limited heating options and the family bundled up together in front of a single coal-fired oven to stay warm. South Korea had emerged from its conflict with the North and was at the early stages of a remarkable economic resurgence. Yet quality jobs were hard to find. The diplomat's father worked in a clerical job at the giant U.S. army base at Yongsan, at the time the most lucrative posting for any Korean as it provided steady income and access to hard-to-find American foodstuffs. To this day the diplomat, who rose to international prominence and influence, has an aversion to milk powder, the only viable substitute to milk during his childhood, an expensive product in Seoul at the time.

In contrast with my Chinese and Korean friends, I grew up in more temperate, more tropical climes in Southern India. The summers were extremely hot of course but it was more manageable compared with what my friends in Beijing and Seoul had to put up with during the winter. Yet things were also worse because India, unlike Korea, had plunged into an economic abyss from which it would take several decades to recover. Food shortages were rampant, everyone was issued with a ration card, and I recall standing with my mother routinely for hours outside a provision store to secure rice and other supplies. It was quite common to see packaging of foreign donor agencies on items that were stocked at the store, a powerful demonstration of India's aid dependency at the time. Indian parents of the post-independence era, unlike their forbears who had valiantly fought to free

> *Much of India's post-1991 economic uplift can be directly attributed to the struggle of parents in the 1960s and 1970s to ensure that their children were well-educated and well-positioned to capitalise on the country's rising economic tide. The question is whether today's generation of parents, who arguably have greater resources at their disposal, have favourable economic tailwinds to prepare their children to face the brave new world.*

the country from British colonial rule, faced the daily struggle for economic freedoms. One item which was fortunately not in short supply during that era was education and my parents, along with millions of others across the country and indeed the region, invested wisely by sending their children to school and subsequently to an expensive college education. Much of India's post-1991 economic uplift can be directly attributed to the struggle of parents in the 1960s and 1970s to ensure that their children were well-educated and well-positioned to capitalise on the country's rising economic tide. The question is whether today's generation of parents, who arguably have greater resources at their disposal, have favourable economic tailwinds to prepare their children to face the brave new world.

Western Presumptions

Asia's achievements are all the more remarkable because of shoddy Western presumptions during an earlier era about supposed climatic, cultural and geographical barriers which would forever impede the continent's progress. Writers Daron Acemoglu and James A. Robinson argue in their book[3] that the "geography hypothesis" was long accepted as the primary reason for the relative affluence of the West compared with the persistent poverty in the global South.

---

[3] Daron Acemoglu and James Robinson, *Why Nations Fall: The Origins of Power, Prosperity, and Poverty.* (Currency Books, 2012).

As early as the eighteenth century, the great French philosopher Montesquieu "noted the geographic concentration of prosperity and poverty" and proposed an explanation of it. "He argued that people in tropical climates tended to be lazy and to lack inquisitiveness. As a consequence, they didn't work hard and were not innovative, and this was the reason why they were poor," Acemoglu and Robinson write. They dismiss the geography and climate argument, which still has a few adherents in the academic community, and note that history illustrates that there is no simple or enduring connection between climate, or geography or economic success. They also dismiss the culture hypothesis, linking economic prosperity with cultural "differences" between an enlightened West and a less progressive rest of the world. "China, despite many imperfections in its economic and political system, has been the most rapidly growing nation of the past three decades. Chinese poverty until Mao Zedong's death had nothing to do with Chinese culture; it was due to the disastrous way Mao organised the economy and conducted policies," they write, noting that China has rebounded "from a process of economic transformation" unleashed by reforms implemented by Deng Xiaoping and his allies.

As early as the eighteenth century, the great French philosopher Montesquieu "noted the geographic concentration of prosperity and poverty" and proposed an explanation of it.

In contrast, Singapore's founding father, the late Lee Kuan Yew, was a strong believer that East Asian culture, particularly pillars of Confucian philosophy, better explained why the region was performing better than peers in the rest of the world. "Getting the fundamentals right would help, but these societies will not succeed in the same way as East Asia did because certain driving forces will be absent," Lee said in an 1994 interview with *Foreign Affairs*. "If you have a culture that doesn't place much value in learning and scholarship and hard work and thrift and deferment of present enjoyment for future gain, the going will be much slower," he said. The elder Lee would have also pushed back against the historical figures cited in the Acemoglu and Robinson book in their assertion that tropical climate can explain Asia's relative economic weakness compared with the affluent West, with one caveat. The elder Lee was famous for attributing the comforts of the air-conditioner, for example, in helping a horribly humid Singapore in raising economic productivity and well-being.

In short, depending on whom you believe, the rise of China and the rest of Asia has little to do with geography, and a lot or little to do with climate or culture. The region's success during the last five decades can essentially be boiled down to three factors — a progressive leadership with an economic vision, a benign global environment for trade and investment, and the blood, sweat, and toil of hundreds of millions of ordinary Asians determined to improve their lot. My thesis is that the first two can no longer be taken for granted.

> *In short, depending on whom you believe, the rise of China and the rest of Asia has little to do with geography, and a lot or little to do with climate or culture.*

Contribution to Global GDP

To return to the present and to better understand the peak, we should examine Asia's contribution to global GDP. The IMF estimates that Asia contributed more than two-thirds to global GDP growth in 2019, a contribution likely to decline this year and next due to the Covid-induced global slowdown. The 2019 number was not a one-off as the region had become the engine of the global economy and more than picked up the slack after the economies of America and Europe imploded after the GFC. It is useful to disaggregate these numbers a bit to look at exactly which countries are providing Asia with its growth impulse. On one side we have the developed economies of Japan, and the four Asian Tigers Korea, Taiwan, Hong Kong, and Singapore.

These are mature economies by any yardstick and the era of hyper-growth rates are firmly behind them. Indeed, it was in the decade before the 1973 oil shock that Japan last expanded at a China-like growth pace, with GDP expanding at an average 9.3 percent. In the period after the 1973 oil shock, Japan's GDP expanded at a more sedate pace averaging 3.6 percent. Japan's struggles most recently have been in managing a rapidly aging society, a rising domestic debt pile (a phenomenal 240 percent of GDP), and the Bank of Japan's efforts to stoke inflation through a massive programme of quantitative easing. Governor Haruhiko Kuroda's valiant attempt to boost inflation above 2 percent, via QE and by slyly manipulating consumer and business attitudes, has been all-consuming with limited success.

The struggles of the Tiger economies, while not as dramatic in scale as that of Japan, have also focused on ageing populations, inequality, fiscal rather than monetary policy, and attempts to boost productivity growth.

> *The struggles of the Tiger economies, while not as dramatic in scale as that of Japan, have also focused on ageing populations, inequality, fiscal rather than monetary policy, and attempts to boost productivity growth.*

"When you have been rich for so long, a little bit of a slowdown is not going to hurt," dryly remarked a Southeast Asian central banker when I recently asked him about Singapore's economic prospects. The central banker noted that as an advanced economy, Singapore (and indeed its fellow Tiger economies and Japan) had the wherewithal and the resources to tide over current uncertainties including Covid-19, trade tensions and reversing globalisation. "Policymakers in developing Asia do not have this luxury," he said. "We are constantly struggling to keep our economies on track and the treadmill is getting steeper and faster."

To be sure, emerging Asia[4] has not been a laggard and has indeed been a primary contributor to global growth as I noted before. Credit Suisse Research Institute[5] said recently that emerging Asia's progressively dominant contribution to growth and overall economic output has been an evolving feature of the global economy for the last three decades. "Over the last 30 years, Asia (excluding Japan) has added approximately $19 trillion (in nominal terms) to annual global GDP, rising to a 36 percent share of global output in 2018, from 14 percent in 1988," the report said. "Yet the means by which this activity is created is being transformed, primarily motivated by an intensifying focus on sustainability." Since the GFC, emerging Asia's contribution to global growth, in real terms, has stabilised close to 42 percent — plus or minus eight percentage points — almost twice the 22 percent contribution (with significantly greater volatility) that Asia averaged in the 25 years leading up to 2008. There has been a shift in the region's growth composition with a rise in Asian exports matched by imports of consumables, with the region today representing a significant source of global demand for a diverse range of capital goods, commodities and consumer products.

> *Automobile sales have literally exploded across the region — contributing to horrific traffic gridlock and pollution. Combined as a region, Asia today represents the single biggest source for global car sales.*

Automobile sales have literally exploded across the region — contributing to horrific traffic gridlock and pollution. Combined as a region, Asia today

---

[4] Emerging Asia is usually meant to be Asia excluding Japan. However, I am using the Credit Suisse formulation of emerging Asia 12 economies which includes Bangladesh, China, India, Indonesia, Malaysia, Pakistan, the Philippines, South Korea, Sri Lanka, Taiwan, Thailand, and Vietnam.

[5] "Asia in Transition", Credit Suisse Research Institute, November 2018.

represents the single biggest source for global car sales. In 2019, Asia as a whole accounted for a monumental 36 million car and LCV sales with China alone besting America[6] to emerge as the world's largest source of demand. For anyone who visited China or India in the 1980s and 1990s, the most remarkable feature used to be how scarce were cars on the street. During my first visit to Shanghai, the Volkswagen Santana was the only mode for transport, with sales limited to government and for taxi hire. Most of the population got on by on rickety public transport, foot and pedal. In India, the Maruti 800 had made its debut in the early 1980s and buying a car was still considered a luxury item. To anyone visiting these two countries today, or indeed any Asian capital, the first thing which hits you is the ubiquity of four and two-wheelers on the streets. What explains this shift?

The Asian consumption story is built on two factors — the rise of the region's middle and lower middle class, small by the standards of Europe and America, and the accompanying change in attitudes toward consumption. During the noisy debate in the 1990s on the merits of Asian v. Western values, Asian leaders emphasised that the region's success was built on traditional values which placed a premium on thrift rather than conspicuous consumption. This was indeed true during Asia's initial growth spurt, where countries enjoyed current account surpluses, slow growth in consumer lending, and negligible demand for what was regarded as "luxury" goods. More recently, Asian consumers have been behaving exactly like their counterparts in the developed world. Singapore and Korea have the highest rates of consumer debt to GDP in Asia today and consumers in developing Asia, China notably, are fast learners about the virtues of buying on credit and consumerism. Adding fuel to this fire is the mythology being built around Asian invincibility and the belief that opportunities will abound well into the future.

---

[6] For the statistically minded, market intelligence firm Statista estimates that China car sales topped 21.44 million units in 2019 compared with 17.04 million units for America. Other Asian leaders include Japan (4.3 million), India (2.92 million), and Korea (1.53 million).

Growth Obsession

This Asia's obsession with growth illustrates a bigger problem of reliance on economic growth statistics, so much so that qualitative factors like social mobility often receive short shrift. Nowhere is this more evident than in the handwringing which accompanies the release of China's GDP data. Partly fuelled by official intent and partly by market expectations, a slowdown in China's annual GDP growth rate to below 6 percent is regarded as a catastrophe. Premier Li Keqiang's decision not to set an official growth target for 2020, mainly due to Covid-19, will hopefully reset expectations. Financial markets have come to expect Tiger-like growth rates from China for the foreseeable future, with little regard to the manic and unsustainable increase in investment and environmental damage which it entails. China-watchers also have a problem in understanding the weight of the country's contribution to global GDP. It is estimated that if China continues to grow at the annual pace of 6 percent, it will be adding an economy the size of Australia every two years or so.

> *This Asia's obsession with growth illustrates a bigger problem of reliance on economic growth statistics, so much so that qualitative factors like social mobility often receive short shrift.*

> *These are staggering numbers, which offer some perspective as to why a China economic slowdown is not unusual and could actually prove to be healthy, both for itself and the global economy.*

These are staggering numbers, which offer some perspective as to why a China economic slowdown is not unusual and could actually prove to be healthy, both for itself and the global economy. In contrast, Bangladesh very much needs to maintain pre-2008 China-like growth rates of above 6 percent because of its rapidly growing population (165 million) and the attendant rising expectations of a volatile electorate. The rise of emerging Asia, with China's slowdown providing a strong contrast to Bangladesh's accelerated growth trajectory (GDP growth of 8.1 percent in 2019 was higher than that of India) is a kaleidoscope view of the Asian success story. Can this be sustained?

To return to Summers and Pritchett and their "Asiaphoria" hypothesis, they make three salient points which are worth considering as we examine if growth in Asia has peaked. First, they make the statistical point about *regression toward the mean*, that in the economic context means that abnormally rapid growth is "rarely persistent," i.e. it will not be sustained, even though economic forecasters continue to extrapolate from recent growth. Developing Asia has grown rapidly in the last five decades due to a "perfect storm" of favourable macro political and economic factors. This cannot last forever. The second point from Summers and Pritchard is that in developing countries as a whole, the growth process is marked by "sharp discontinuities," with very large accelerations and decelerations in growth being quite common. This is validated most recently in India, where self-inflicted policy errors have resulted in a sharp slowdown in growth, and in Indonesia, where the government has struggled to push growth above 5 percent since the Asian Financial Crisis. The third point from the economists is about the future trajectory of growth. They point out that from 1967 to 1980, Brazil's economy grew at 5.2 percent per year. "While many people might have identified macroeconomic and structural imbalances putting that growth at a risk of a recession or cyclical slowdown, no one in 1980 was predicting that for the next 22 years — from 1980 to 2002 — per capita growth would be zero."

I can see the collective rolling of the eyes at the mention of Brazil because many Asians feel that the region has little to learn from the Latin American experience. For the record, Brazil's per capita GDP[7] in 2018 was slightly

---

[7] World Bank data: Brazil's per capita GDP was $8,920 in 2018, compared with China's $9,770 and India's $2,338.

lower than China's and significantly higher than that of India. Brazil's recent record of political dysfunction, corruption, and economic malaise has some parallels with Asia. The country has not been able to escape the middle-income trap, the malady faced by many fast-growing nations who are unable to breakthrough to advanced economy status because of a complex set of structural, political, and social factors. It is for this reason that Charles de Gaulle is reported to have once said that "Brazil is the country of the future and will always be."

Middle-Income Trap

In Asia, only Japan and the Tigers have managed to achieve developed country status in the last seven decades. China, Malaysia, and Thailand are hoping to be admitted to in the next two decades with India, Indonesia, and other low-income nations further behind in the queue. There is no magical formula that can push China and others to the top shelf of advanced nations. In Korea prior to the 1997 financial crisis, there was much angst that the country

> *In Asia, only Japan and the Tigers have managed to achieve developed country status in the last seven decades.*

would never achieve high-income status and would have to settle for the OECD definition of becoming a "superior developing nation." To make matters worse, the Asian crisis intervened and seemingly destroyed Korea's hopes forever. On hindsight it was the astute management of that crisis that enabled Korea to vault to the ranks of developed nations. "Growth in high-income countries differs qualitatively from that of middle-income countries, and hence requires different factor endowments, industrial structures, and policies," explains the Asian Development Bank[8] in an interesting book which has sparked debate in the region. ADB authors stress that middle-income countries often get stuck in the transition from growth strategies

---

[8] Bihong Huang, Peter Morgan, & Nooyuki Yoshino, eds. , *Avoiding the Middle-Income Trap in Asia: The Role of Trade, Manufacturing, and Finance* (Asian Development Bank, 2018).

that are effective at low-income levels to growth strategies that are effective at high-income levels.

This might seem simplistic until you begin to consider the important role played by total factor productivity[9] (TFP for short) in accelerating a country's transition into high-income status. ADB researchers emphasise that there are limits to capital accumulation, noting that high investments have a decreasing marginal return over a period of time, and reiterate the important role played by education, research and innovation, and structural reforms. Here is an illustrative example. The growth drivers for Bangladesh or Cambodia are in garment exports, which is a low-wage, low-value-add product which the two countries churn out to meet rising global demand for fast fashion. Until exporters in Bangladesh and Cambodia master the product design, global marketing, finance, and innovation aspects of the garment trade, which requires a higher level of knowledge accumulation and sophistication, the two countries will remain low-cost suppliers unable to make the transition to higher value exports. This in essence is the challenge faced by developing Asia as it recalibrates the composition of growth to more productive areas. China is certainly positioning itself to make this transition by investing in frontier technology as part of its "Made in China 2025" plan, which in part was responsible for fuelling U.S.–China trade tensions and the efforts to limit the reach of Huawei and Tik Tok.

China's fingerprints are evident in the region's frenetic investment in infrastructure as well. In the scenarios explored in this chapter, many Asian nations have the possibility of making the transition to advanced economy status, provided they pursue sound economic and social policies. Investment in quality infrastructure is regarded as the binding force which will make this transition possible, or perhaps inevitable. My cautionary

---

[9] A simple definition of TFP would be that it is a measure of productivity where the growth in real output is in excess of the growth in inputs such as labour and capital.

question is whether developing Asia is rushing toward peak infrastructure, building too much at a high cost with questionable benefits, notwithstanding claims made by many economists that the region is suffering from a serious infrastructure gap. Developing Asia's infrastructure needs are staggering — the AIIB estimates that investment in infrastructure "must rise" to $2 trillion a year, or

> *My cautionary question is whether developing Asia is rushing toward peak infrastructure, building too much at a high cost with questionable benefits, notwithstanding claims made by many economists that the region is suffering from a serious infrastructure gap.*

roughly triple of what it has been in the past. I am circumspect about these numbers and have fundamental questions on whether Asian policymakers are making the right choices in building infrastructure.

Mumbai Metro

I was reminded of this when I visited family in the central Mumbai suburb of Dadar last year where I encountered the vicissitudes of a major infrastructure project. The street where my Uber driver had supposedly dropped me off had disappeared from sight. The main road itself had been carved up into two, divided by a deep hole. The muffled noise, aggravating the usual Mumbai din came from what I discovered later to be giant tunnel-boring machines. I was gazing into the heart of the $3.3 billion Mumbai Metro Line 3 project.

"More than 8000 workers and a fleet of 360-foot long boring machines are working 24 hours a day — even through monsoon rains — to finish the 27-station, 21-mile subway through some of the world's most densely populated neighbourhoods, around the edge of one of Asia's biggest slums, below an airport and under temples and colonial buildings to end at a green edge of forests where leopards still roam," reported Corinne Abrams of *The Wall Street Journal.*[10] "The train is cutting a path through the country's religious traditions, legal system and every layer of its society, with challenges at each stop." In a disputatious society such as India, grass-roots democracy is far better organised to deal with or to obstruct disruptive change. Foreign and local investors in India will testify to many an ambitious infrastructure or

> *Foreign and local investors in India will testify to many an ambitious infrastructure or manufacturing venture which have been torpedoed by grass-roots protests.*

manufacturing venture which have been torpedoed by grass-roots protests. Yet this Mumbai metro project, along with many others in India's sprawling metropolis, have moved forward with the tacit blessings of the local populace and bolstered by the usual social and environmental assessments validated by the World Bank. What is happening here?

The metro projects have been particularly difficult for Mumbai residents, or Mumbaikars as they are referred to, because of the sheer scope of the disruption — parts of the neighbourhood along the metro trail in densely populated south and central Mumbai are inaccessible or simply difficult to traverse during the duration of the project. Daily routines had to be reorganised and residents had to figure out ways to cope with the dust and noise. Yet as Abrams reports, despite the many difficulties the project encountered (including negotiating land access rights with a diverse group of difficult stakeholders), the project is proceeding and is scheduled to open by the end of 2021. The puzzle for me is the apparent acquiescence of local residents to the project, despite the heartache and disruption. Very few questions are also being raised about the costs of the project. An obvious answer is that Mumbai's existing transport options are either too slow or too deadly. The daily commute by road from the distant suburbs to the city

---

[10] Corinne Abrams, "'You Have to Actually Cut Open Mumbai's Belly' — Inside One of the World's Most Audacious Transit Projects", *The Wall Street Journal*, 6 January 2019.

centre could take over two to three hours, eating into work schedules and time away from home. The only other option, a train journey via Mumbai's existing over-ground suburban network could be lethal and suffocating. "Close to eight people die a day on the network, according to rail officials. In the first 11 months of 2018, 650 passengers died falling from trains alone, and even more killed crossing the tracks, rail officials said," Abrams reports. I was a regular commuter on Mumbai's suburban trains during the eighties, when the trains were less congested. Yet I remember approaching the daily commute with trepidation — aggravating my claustrophobia and fear of being crushed in the melee.

Mumbai's shiny new metro project promises to be radically different. The trains will be air-conditioned, a productive leap forward in hot and humid Mumbai, and it is on the promise of a safer, secure, and a more comfortable daily commute which may have persuaded many Mumbaikars that the pains of the construction phase are worth bearing. Or even perhaps a philosophical recognition on their part that future windfall gains from this particular project far outweigh the current inconvenience. "The negative environmental impacts stemming out of the proposed project can be mitigated with a simple set of measures, dealing with careful planning and designing of the metro alignment and structures. Adequate provision of environmental clauses in work contracts and efficient contract management will eliminate or reduce significantly all possible problems," reads a detailed 404-page environmental impact assessment of the project, which complies with standards set by Japan's International Cooperation Agency (JICA) and the World Bank.

Rush for Infrastructure

All over developing Asia, people are making similar calculations about sacrificing current pain over future gains in infrastructure. It appears to be a race between Japan, China, and Korea in securing metro construction contracts and in supplying the actual trains to run the system. The first phase of Jakarta's mass rapid transit (MRT) system, spanning 10 miles along

All over developing Asia, people are making similar calculations about sacrificing current pain over future gains in infrastructure. It appears to be a race between Japan, China, and Korea in securing metro construction contracts and in supplying the actual trains to run the system.

the Indonesian capital's north-south corridor has just opened, to be supplemented in the second phase now under construction. Like the Mumbai metro project, Jakarta's MRT is financed by JICA and the trains come from a Japanese rail manufacturer. Not to be left behind, China Railway Corporation, reputedly the world's largest railway operator, is building the 142 km Jakarta–Bandung high-speed train line. When commissioned, the train line will cut the journey time from more than three hours currently to less than 40 minutes, a dramatic sign of progress. And Korea's Hyundai is supplying the trains for Jakarta's recently opened Light Rail Transit (LRT), which will be connected to the MRT and alleviate some of the Indonesian capital's notorious traffic jams.

In previous decades, the race to build rail networks in Asia would have surely involved American or European firms. In a sign of Asia's growing confidence and dare I say self-sufficiency, Asian infrastructure will increasingly be built by home-grown Asian firms with the North Asian giants of Japan, Korea, and China in the lead.

China is of course the unchallenged leader of them all, both in terms of building world-class infrastructure in a short period of time and now possessing the technological and financial prowess to export this model to the region, indeed the world. China, however, should also serve as a cautionary tale about infrastructure excess which other countries should learn from. Since Shanghai metro's modest beginnings in the early 1990s, the system has evolved to become the world's largest by route length with 16 lines, 413 stations, system length of 420 miles, and an annual ridership of over

3.5 billion. The system continues to expand with over 75 miles of metro under construction. In contrast, London's 157-year old tube system has 11 lines, 270 stations, system length of 250 miles, and annual ridership of 1.37 billion, less than a third of the new kid on the block. Expanding London's transport infrastructure, in contrast with that of China, has

China is of course the unchallenged leader of them all, both in terms of building world-class infrastructure in a short period of time and now possessing the technological and financial prowess to export this model to the region, indeed the world.

been mired in political controversy and runaway cost escalations. The $20 billion Crossrail project, described as Europe's largest infrastructure project, is running over $1 billion over budget and will add a modest 13 miles to the city's existing tube network.

China's economic rise in the last four decades can be plotted using several different metrics but infrastructure investment stands out for ambition, bravado and sheer *chutzpah*. Consulting firm McKinsey estimates that China's infrastructure stock as a percentage of GDP has been consistently above the world average. Japan is of course a standout nation in this regard with its total infrastructure stock at a stunning 179 percent of GDP at the end of 2012. This is mainly because of Japan's "lost decade" in the 1990s after the collapse of the bubble economy and extended well into the first decade of the new century. The country over-spent on infrastructure, building "bridges to nowhere" all over the country. However, China is catching up fast and has in fact now overtaken America and Europe to become the world's largest investor in infrastructure. "Infrastructure development remains a top priority for China's government, which has long recognised that a modern economy runs on reliable roads and rails, electricity, and telecommunications," the *McKinsey Quarterly* said in 2013.[11] "From the late 1990s to 2005, 100 million

---

[11] Yougang Chen et al., "Chinese Infrastructure: The Big Picture", *McKinsey Quarterly*, 1 June 2013.

Chinese benefitted from power and telecommunication upgrades. Between 2001 and 2004, investment in rural roads grew by a massive 51 percent annually."

There is of course an element of hubris to China's kinetic investments in infrastructure. Until the Global Financial Crisis (GFC) of 2008, China's infrastructure development was regarded as prudent and in support of the country's growth trajectory. This prudence was thrown out of the window with the GFC. With the economies of Europe and America in meltdown and the global economy contracting at a pace not seen since the 1930s, China came to the rescue with an ambitious $600 billion fiscal stimulus designed to boost growth at home and abroad. As a percentage of GDP (an estimated 3.1 percent in 2009 and 2.7 percent in 2010), China's stimulus trailed behind that of Russia and Saudi Arabia. However, it had a significantly bigger impact on the global economy because much of the spending was on infrastructure, setting in motion a super-commodities cycle as China, for example, started importing huge quantities of iron ore to feed its gluttonous appetite for steel. Two of the biggest beneficiaries in the region were Australia and Indonesia. For Indonesia, the China boom came at a propitious time. In the early 2000s, Indonesia was still reeling from the after-effects of the Asian Financial Crisis and political revolution. There was a credible question on whether the country could find a viable growth model and Chinese demand for commodities came as a godsend.

There is of course an element of hubris to China's kinetic investments in infrastructure.

China Hubris

In 2008, it was the second time in less than a decade that China had come to the rescue of the global economy. In 1997-1998, Beijing tactically chose not to devalue its currency during the height of the Asian Financial Crisis, earning the respect and goodwill of its neighbours. It was a clear sign of

China's growing confidence about its abilities to influence regional and global politics. While China's decision not to devalue the renminbi in 1998 had a benign domestic and external impact, the 2008 stimulus came with a steep economic price. Much of the stimulus money as we know was deployed toward infrastructure investment, with Beijing and local provincial leaders veritably building bridges to nowhere all around the country.

Investment in property was the most notable manifestation of China's largesse. A senior World Bank official told me a few years ago about a road journey he undertook between Shanghai and a

Investment in property was the most notable manifestation of China's largesse.

neighbouring province during the go-go investment years. Undertaking the journey by day, he was staggered by the sheer scale of investment in roads, office buildings, shopping malls and apartments along the route. It all looked very impressive until his return journey at night. Mile after mile of apartments and shopping malls were in pitch darkness, contradicting the long-held view of property developers of building it and they will come. In China quite simply the builders built too much, with the overhang in supply taking several years to digest.

In what should be a lesson for the rest of Asia, researchers at Oxford University's Said Business School[12] question two key assumptions about infrastructure projects in China. The first is that infrastructure investment creates economic value. The second is that China has a distinct advantage in infrastructure delivery. Both, they argue, are fallacies: "The evidence suggests that over half of the infrastructure investments in China made in the last three decades, the costs are larger than the benefits they generate, which means the projects destroy economic value instead of generating it," researcher Atif Ansar of the Oxford Said Business School notes. This is a

---

[12] Atif Ansar et al., "Does Infrastructure Investment Lead to Economic Growth or Economic Fragility? Evidence from China", *Oxford Review of Economic Policy* 32, no. 3 (2016).

harsh critique of China's pell-mell race to build world-class infrastructure, which has created vulnerabilities to the environment and to economic stability. However, the critical question is whether China serves as a model for developing Asia in its race to build infrastructure? My answer is a qualified yes given the region's overwhelming need for roads, bridges, telecommunications, electricity, water, and other essentials. At the same time, developing Asia can learn from China's mistakes.

> *While China's objectives in extending financial support to developing Asia and Africa for BRI projects appear to be benign, it has come under sustained criticism for non-transparency and debt sustainability concerns.*

I would argue that there are three distinct China infrastructure models that the rest of Asia has the option to follow. First, there is infrastructure development led by China's 34 administrative divisions (23 of them provinces) with opaque investment structures, questionable analysis on cost-benefits, and massive governance failures, which has been the subject of President Xi Jinping's controversial anti-corruption drive since assuming office in 2012. A majority of these projects, one might argue, were not bankable to begin with and would simply not be built if commercial considerations were factored in. Second, there is China's global push via the Belt and Road Initiative (BRI), which is channelling an estimated $1-2 trillion[13] into infrastructure projects along the old Silk Road and maritime Asia. While China's objectives in extending financial support to developing Asia and Africa for BRI projects appear to be benign, it has come under sustained criticism for non-transparency and debt sustainability concerns.

---

[13] It is impossible to estimate precisely how much China has invested along the Belt and Road. Adding up publicly disclosed data on infrastructure projects, I have come up with an estimate of $1-2 trillion. This sum could of course be higher or significantly lower.

The third China infrastructure model is being delivered through new multilateral economic institutions which it helped create — the Asian Infrastructure Investment Bank (AIIB) and the New Development Bank (NDB). Jin Liqun, the seasoned Chinese technocrat at the helm of the AIIB has sought to build the institution along the lines of the World Bank — with greater transparency in project lending, supported by stakeholder engagement, and environmental and social impact analysis. Over time, China's global infrastructure footprint will hopefully follow the AIIB model and recipient countries conduct their cost and benefit analysis before rushing to build roads and bridges to nowhere. If developing Asia over-spends on physical infrastructure and under-spends on social infrastructure – in building schools and hospitals – this mismatch will undermine the region's growth prospects.

Where does Asia go from here? The zeitgeist, a word which I absolutely detest, has it that Asia's future is stable, predictable, and its upward momentum is unstoppable. To help with my contrarian take, I decided to go back in time and consult with the 13th century Florentine poet and statesman Dante Alighieri. We meet him in the next chapter.

Chapter 3

A Short Introduction to Dante

Dante Alighieri (1265-1321) was a great Florentine politician, poet, and philosopher who as far as we know never visited Asia.[1] We take some artistic liberties.

A logical question as you begin to read this chapter is the implied connection between one of Italy's greatest poets, circa 13th century, with the travails and tribulations of Asia, circa the second decade of the 21st century. We will get to this shortly. On a personal note, Dante has always been my favourite poet and political theorist. I was introduced to *Divine Comedy* in high school by a fabulous English teacher who saw many parallels between the hell, purgatory, and paradise which Dante describes in his masterwork with the contemporary India of the early 1970s. There is of course a great deal of theological references in *Divine Comedy*, which one cannot ignore, but Dante's own tumultuous political career and tussle with the Catholic Church, which led to exile from his beloved Florence, played a significant role in shaping his writings. In short, Dante would have probably approved of what I am about to do.

---

[1] Having said that there are multiple references to the River Ganges in Dante's Purgatory, a point made by Italian Prime Minister in a conversation with PM Modi in November 2020, inviting India to participate in Dante's 700th death anniversary celebrations in 2021.

The first connection which I drew between contemporary Asia and Dante's body of work came in Mumbai via a bumpy ride on a three-wheeler, or auto rickshaw as it is popularly known, in 2019. Traffic had ground to a halt, and I struck up a casual conversation with the driver, let's call him Pramod, an intense young man in his thirties. Like almost everyone in India's business capital, the driver was a migrant into Mumbai, hailing from a small town in the north Indian state of Uttar Pradesh, where his wife and daughter still lived. Our three-wheeler was uncomfortably sandwiched between a truck and a spanking new black Audi A3, driven no doubt by one of Mumbai's freshly minted millionaires (or wannabe millionaires stretching their credit and imagination). I asked Pramod if living in Mumbai gave him and his family the opportunity to move up the economic ladder. I paraphrased my question with a rhetorical point about India doing so well economically as evidenced by the number of luxury Audi cars on the street.

> *His response, in Hindi, was withering. "We live in the same city, same country sir. But you live in* swarg *and I live in* narq*," he said,* swarg *and* narq *being the Hindi words to describe heaven and hell.*

Instead of responding to my question, Pramod proceeded to ask me a series of questions about where I lived, what I did, and why I was taking the ride in his humble auto-rickshaw rather than be at the wheel of a fancy car myself. Placed on the defensive, I mumbled something about always preferring to ride in the three-wheeler as it was the best way to catch a glimpse of a changing Mumbai. His response, in Hindi, was withering. "We live in the same city, same country sir. But you live in *swarg* and I live in *narq*," he said, *swarg* and *narq* being the Hindi words to describe heaven and hell.

Pramod's story, which he went on to describe, has parallels across Asia, certainly in Jakarta, Hanoi, Bangkok, Manila, and a hundred other Asian towns today. He was an economic migrant into Mumbai, he said, out of necessity rather than choice. Although he had completed middle school and was relatively better educated in his small town compared with peers, there were no jobs. Across India's so-called cow belt, densely populated states to the north and centre of the country, this is a familiar problem faced by millions of young men and women. Indian economists call them "money order" economies, towns which are heavily dependent on remittances from those who have left for a better life. Forced to emigrate to Mumbai or Delhi, big cities with the most jobs and opportunities, young men like Pramod are caught in a vicious cycle. On one hand, he is certainly making more money from urban India's booming economy compared with the pitiful offerings at home. This provided a secure safety net for the family. On the other hand, Pramod described his living conditions as *narq* or hell. He stays with three other friends in a tiny shack in one of Mumbai's teeming slums without modern plumbing or running water. During the heavy monsoon season, which lasts from June through September each year, Pramod says he is never sure on any particular day if his shack will hold up or be completely flooded. "You say things are getting better," he told me at the end of our journey. "Maybe for you but not for people like me." Stunned by the conversation, I left the vehicle in silence.

Growing Inequality

Pramod's stinging rebuke, certainly of my naïve and happy vision of a shining India and Asia, was the genesis of this book. His comments certainly resonated with me because, ironically enough, of where I currently reside —

> *Pramod's stinging rebuke, certainly of my naïve and happy vision of a shining India and Asia, was the genesis of this book.*

Washington D.C., capital of a superpower currently being ripped apart by what can be best described as social, economic, and cultural jealousies. As a sucker for torture, I also lived in London during the tumultuous Brexit referendum. Brexit happened not merely because the UK was prepared to commit economic suicide, as it did, jeopardising trade and investment relations with its most important partner, the European Union. There were deep internal social, economic, and cultural fissures as well, fuelled by perceptions of a privileged elite reaping all of the rewards, out-of-control immigration, and loss of cultural identity which were cynically exploited by politicians. My proposition is that Asia used to be relatively insulated from these fissures, largely because steady economic growth delivered tangible improvements year after year to the lives of hundreds of millions of Asians. However, these gains, most certainly in recent years, have accrued to those at the top of the income ladder, depriving smart, young men like Pramod the opportunity for social mobility.

In his magisterial work *Capital in the Twenty-First Century*,[2] French economist Thomas Piketty writes that thanks to colonial administrators, income tax data has been available for India, Pakistan, and Indonesia since the early part of the 20th century. Piketty's core analysis on rising inequality in rich and poor countries is based partly on such data. His key observation on India, Indonesia and other countries included in his survey (Argentina, South Africa): "The most striking result is probably that the upper centile's share of national income in poor and emerging economies is roughly the same as in rich economies," he writes. Based on tax data, Piketty divides India and Indonesia's economic journey and the resultant equality/inequality into three phases. During the colonial era, the "most inegalitarian phases," especially 1910-1950, he says that the top centile took around 20 percent of the national income, around 18-20 percent in India and 22-25 percent in Indonesia. A more egalitarian phase ensued in newly independent India and Indonesia (1950-1980), where the top centile's share fell to between 6 and 12 percent in the two countries. This data has been contested by Indian economist Swaminathan Aiyar[3] who asserts that tax data from the colonial era is imprecise because it does not include the wealth and earnings of the

---

[2] Thomas Piketty, *Capital in the 21st Century* (Harvard University Press, 2014).

[3] Swaminathan Aiyar, "Why Thomas Piketty is wrong about inequality in India," *Financial Times*, September 2017.

country's cossetted princely class and low growth in the region in the 1950-1980 period kept hundreds of millions in poverty.

It has been downhill and uphill ever since, certainly for the poor in terms of their income trajectory. Starting in the 1980s to the present, the top centile's share rebounded, and today stands at about 15 percent of national income (12-13 percent in India and 16-18 percent in Indonesia). Curiously, Piketty argues that although inequality has widened in China as well, the data does not necessarily suggest that it is faring any worse than India and Indonesia. "Chinese inequality increased very rapidly following the liberalisation of the economy in the 1980s and accelerated growth in the period 1990-2000, but according to my estimates, the upper centile's share in 2000-2010 was 10-11 percent, less than India and Indonesia (12-14 percent, roughly the same as Britain and Canada) and much lower than in South Africa or Argentina (16-18 percent, approximately the same as the United States)." Aiyar takes issue with this analysis as well noting that while inequality has certainly risen in India, the post-1991 period has also seen a sharp reduction in the number of people living in poverty.

Human Development

Piketty's hard data and logical argument, that inequality in emerging Asia is rising but is perhaps not as bad (or at least not as yet) compared with that of the United States will not persuade Pramod and millions of his low-income brethren across the region. In urban Asia today, the most tangible reality is of the yawning divide between rich and poor. This manifests itself not only

Piketty's hard data and logical argument, that inequality in emerging Asia is rising but is perhaps not as bad (or at least not as yet) compared with that of the United States will not persuade Pramod and millions of his low-income brethren across the region.

in income divides, which are widening, but also in terms of equal access to education, health, and economic opportunity. In 2010, *Forbes* magazine's widely watched listing of the world's billionaires had 64 from China, which rose spectacularly to 372 in 2018, before rising further to 456 in 2020 (including Hong Kong and Macau).[4] The magazine said that regionally, the Asia-Pacific region boasted the most billionaires, with an eye-popping 778, followed by the United States with 614, and Europe with 511. By country, the U.S. still leads with the greatest number of billionaires, followed by China (456), Germany (107), India (102), and Russia (99).

This is best exemplified with the region's obsession with the World Bank's annual Doing Business report, which attracts huge media attention across the region, as countries are anxious to improve their ranking in order to attract foreign investment.

We will explore rent-seeking and the rise of the Asian oligarch in a subsequent chapter, but it does seem odd that lower and upper middle-income nations like China and India are leading the global league table of billionaires. While the billionaires' entrepreneurship skills must certainly be celebrated, there is something amiss with Asia's public policy framework which enables the rise of corporate billionaires but leaves behind a significant portion of population in terms of access to economic opportunity and basic services. This is best exemplified with the region's obsession with the World Bank's annual Doing Business report, which attracts huge media attention across the region, as countries are anxious to improve their ranking in order to attract foreign investment. Indian Prime Minister Narendra Modi was determined to improve his country's rankings in the DBI earlier in the tenure and even established an inter-ministerial team to help with the process. As a result, India's rankings did improve from 100 in 2017 to 77 in 2019. China was ranked 46, with

---

[4] *Forbes* magazine's "34th Annual List of Billionaires" was published on 7 April 2020.

Singapore, Korea, and Hong Kong amongst the top ten. Improving country rankings in an index aimed at increasing foreign investment is nothing to sniff at but it should be seen in the broader context of how India and developing Asia are faring in other indices tracking human development. In August 2020, the World Bank paused publication of the Doing Business reports altogether to conduct an internal review of "irregularities" in data (for a select group of countries) in the 2018 and 2020 reports.

The United Nation's Human Development Report and Index,[5] released annually by the United Nations Development Program (UNDP), receives scant attention and very little self-examination from policymakers. The 2019 report, for which Singapore Senior Minister Tharman Shanmugaratnam served as Co-Chair of the Advisory Board, cautions that the demonstrations sweeping the world today signal that, despite unprecedented progress against poverty, hunger, and disease, "many societies are not working as they should. The connecting thread, is inequality."

For the record, Hong Kong (4), Singapore (9), and Japan (19) featured amongst the top 20 in the 2019 report, with Brunei (43) and Malaysia (61), Sri Lanka (70), Thailand (77), China (85), and Mongolia (92) in the top 100. Asia's human development record, particularly in eliminating extreme poverty has few parallels in the post-1945 world. In sheer numbers, over 1.5 billion have been lifted out of poverty in a generation. Yet at the same time, the region should reflect on the fact that Latin America, a region notoriously prone to hyper political and economic crises does not fare too badly in the UN rankings. The top 100 feature Chile (42), Argentina (48), Uruguay (57), Barbados (56), Costa Rica (68), and Panama (67), followed by several other Caribbean isles. Asia has a lot of catching up to do as demonstrated by India's rank at 129, well behind the Philippines (106), Vietnam (118), and Indonesia (111) but ahead of Bangladesh, Pakistan, and Myanmar who are

---

[5] The Human Development Index looks at life expectancy, education, and percapita income indicators which are used to rank countries in four tiers of human development. See <Hdr.undp.org>.

further down the list. Asia's task of lifting people out of poverty has been an unprecedented success but the task remains unfinished. The region is increasingly divided between the haves, have-a-little, and have nots.

Social Mobility

Social mobility and an improvement in human development rankings is the fuel to build a more cohesive and less unstable Asia, which is beginning to attract the attention of the region's policymakers. Singapore Prime Minister Lee Hsien Loong warned in 2018 that the city-state's politics will "turn vicious, it's society will fracture,

> *Social mobility and an improvement in human development rankings is the fuel to build a more cohesive and less unstable Asia, which is beginning to attract the attention of the region's policymakers.*

and the country will wither if it allows widening income inequalities to create a rigid and stratified social system,"[6] he said. "The issues of mitigating income inequality, ensuring social mobility, and enhancing social integration are critical." To reverse what it regards as a deepening class divide, Singapore policymakers have intervened by raising social spending, targeted at low-income families. During the Covid-19 pandemic, Singapore stood out as one of the few Asian nations to raise fiscal spending by a phenomenal 10 percent of GDP. The rich city-state of Hong Kong has also faced rising social pressures because of rising inequality, manifested by growing social unrest. In 2018, Oxfam reported[7] alarmingly that poverty had worsened over the last 15 years, the richest now earn 44 times more than the poorest, and according to latest statistics, there are over 1.3 million people living in poverty (out of total population of around 6 million). Oxfam appealed to HK authorities to make "poverty alleviation and reducing inequality" a top

---

[6] From a report in *The Straits Times*, 6 February, 2018. Prime Minister Lee was responding in reply to a question raised in Parliament.

[7] Oxfam Hong Kong, "Hong Kong Inequality Report", September 2018.

policy priority, something which Carrie Lam should have heeded before social unrest spun out of control.

It is difficult to square prosperous Singapore and Hong Kong with worrying reports about stalled social mobility and rising poverty. The two city-states are among Asia's richest and sensible public policies in the past have consistently delivered egalitarian outcomes. However, a visit to a hawker centre in Singapore or the airport in Hong Kong shows a growing number of elderly still at work, a sign perhaps of fragile social safety nets. While Singapore and Hong Kong have the wherewithal to

> *It is difficult to square prosperous Singapore and Hong Kong with worrying reports about stalled social mobility and rising poverty.*

increase social spending, policymakers in middle and low-income Asia will struggle to deliver viable social programmes. "What we now face is the contradiction between unbalanced and inadequate development and the people's ever-growing needs for a better life," Chinese leader Xi Jinping warned in his marathon 205-minute speech to the Communist Party Congress in October 2017, marking the end of his first term in office. Xi's definition of improving people's lives included measures to reduce the country's devastating pollution, improving education and healthcare, and the justice system.

Enter Dante

Which in a long and circuitous way brings me back to Dante Alighieri and Florence. "At the end of the thirteenth century Florence was a city developing at a pace that was virtually off the scale of contemporary European urbanization," writes historian and Dante scholar Edward Peters.[8] "In immense size within the new walls, its recent population growth, scale

---

[8] Edward Peters, "The Shadowy, Violent Perimeter: Dante Enters Florentine Political Life", *Dante Studies* no. 113 (1995).

of consumption, industrial and financial enterprise, and its disparities of wealth and poverty provided both work and confusion for its government." For its time, the late middle ages, Florence was both fabulously wealthy and fabulously unequal, fabled for its vicious, venal politics, pitting the Catholic Church (notably the Pope) and various political factions. I am paraphrasing and abbreviating of course to make a singular point that while inequality is not a new phenomenon, it usually manifests itself in political and social conflict.

> *There are parallels between Florence's rich tapestry of political and social life in the late 1200s with contemporary Asia, which forms the core of this book.*

There are parallels between Florence's rich tapestry of political and social life in the late 1200s with contemporary Asia, which forms the core of this book. From what we know based on historical research by scholars, Dante was an outsider to politics. His political activities between 1295 and 1302 are sketchy to say the least and he was on the losing side of a bitter power struggle against the Pope. In short order, the future poet and philosopher was charged with extortion and offering resistance to the rule of Pope Boniface VIII and was eventually sentenced in absentia to be burned to death. Exiled from Florence, Dante made several failed attempts for a rapprochement with the Pope and the new political players. He would never return to Florence. "Can I not anywhere gaze upon the face of the sun and the stars? Can I not under any sky contemplate the most precious truths, without I first return to Florence, disgraced, nay dishonoured, in the eyes of my fellow citizens? Assuredly, bread will not fail me,"[9] he wrote defiantly.

On the run from his detractors and forced to live away from his beloved Florence, Dante turned to poetry and philosophy to heal his wounds and to

---

[9] Dante's letter to a Florentine friend,in Paget Toynbee, *Dante Alighieri: His Life and Works* (Dover Publications, 2005).

strike back against the Pope. The resultant work written in exile was *Divine Commedia*, or *Divine Comedy*, an epic poem which has aged rather well, holding a mirror to society's ills through successive centuries and generations in Europe and beyond. "It might not sound all that funny, but Dante called his epic poem a comedy because, unlike tragedies that begin on a high note and end tragically, comedies begin badly and end well," writes University of Sydney academic Frances Di Lauro.[10] "The poem indeed ends well, with the protagonist, also named Dante, reaching his desired destination — heaven — a place of beauty and calm, light and ultimate good. Conversely, the inferno is dark, morose, and inhabited by irredeemable monsters."

Abandon all hope, ye who enter here!

So, reads the inscription on the gates of the inferno, the first section of *Divine Comedy*, which in simplified terms Di Lauro describes as an imaginary journey through the three realms of afterlife: inferno (hell), purgatorio (purgatory), and of course paradiso (heaven). The Roman poet Virgil guides Dante through hell and purgatory while Beatrice, described as the "ideal woman," accompanies him through heaven. Dante drew on theological and philosophical sources in writing his master-work but what is often forgotten is the political context, his exile and bitterness with Florence's new leadership which obviously coloured his worldview and writing.

Of more relevance to us is Dante's vision of the underworld comprising nine circles of hell (or *narq* as Pramod would describe it) including limbo, lust, gluttony, greed, anger, heresy, violence, fraud, and treachery. Each of these circles, populated by real and mythical figures whom Dante obviously disliked, is over-laid with religious and theological allegory and the *Divine Comedy* has been read through the ages as a cautionary tract for those tempted to tread the path of evil. However, it is hard not to read Dante's work as a searing work of political philosophy for the ages. "Thus, to retrace

---

[10] "Guide to the Classics – Dante's Divine Comedy", in the blog The Conversation, October 2017.

the moral journey of the pilgrim through Hell, Purgatory, and Paradise, is to follow the journey of the citizen from a corrupt society, through the transition from selfishness to social responsibility, to his goal in the ideal society," writes historian Joan Ferrante,[11] adding that the moral level of Dante's allegory is also the political level.

When I started researching this book, I was struggling to build a framework to describe Asia's great promise, a significant portion of which has been realised and celebrated, but its many shortcomings and challenges, which perhaps receive less attention. How to reconcile shining Asia, the rosy vision of an Asia which can do no wrong which is sharply at odds with the on-the-ground perspective of Pramod and millions of his low-income brethren across the region? Has the Asian economic story been subjected to elite capture, where a privileged group of foreign and domestic voices drawn from business, politics, media, and the academic community are in effect dominating the narrative, drowning out other voices? The answer is a deafening yes.

So, with Pramod at the wheel of his auto rickshaw, I would like to take readers through a journey of Asia's own eight circles of hell, adapted for the age we live in and for the challenges that the region has to overcome to live up to its full potential of becoming the world's most dynamic and equal region.

I hasten to add that I am not pompously attempting to re-create Dante's masterpiece to describe 21st century Asia, this is not my objective and such a task is clearly beyond my limited poetic abilities. But reading *Inferno* as a political allegory does allow me to take some poetic licence, to adapt Dante's medieval conceit and concept to modern-day Asia. So, with Pramod at the wheel of his auto rickshaw, I would like to take readers through a journey of Asia's own eight circles of hell, adapted for

---

[11] Joan Ferrante, *The Political Vision of the Divine Comedy* (Columbia University Press, 1984).

the age we live in and for the challenges that the region has to overcome to live up to its full potential of becoming the world's most dynamic and equal region. To be sure, we will take liberties and short-cuts (what is poetic licence after all) and in my rendering, Asia's eight circles of hell are rather different in tone and imagery compared with Dante's nine. Each circle has a specific political, economic, and social theme and I have carefully stayed away from religious symbolism.

Let me start by asking three broad questions about Asia's future:

Is Asia prepared for massive deglobalisation and the end of high growth rates?

Is Asia prepared for massive technological disruption which will destroy jobs and livelihoods?

Is Asia's political system resilient or febrile to deal with societal pressures and challenges of the future, including protecting the environment?

Slowbalisation

Globalisation first. As *The Economist* noted recenty,[12] large and sustained increases in the cross-border flow of goods, money, ideas, and people have been the most important factor in world affairs for the past three decades. "They have reshaped relations between states both large and small, and have increasingly come to affect international politics, too. From iPhones to France's *gilet jaunes* (the yellow vested protestors who took the streets of Paris in early 2019), globalisation and its discontents have remade the world," the magazine said, adding that the pace of integration around the world has slowed (by many though not all measures), leading to what Dutch economist Adjiedj Bakas described as the new reality of "slowbalisation."

In this context, 1990 was an epochal year as China's economic growth accelerated and India and Russia joined the global economy by putting

---

[12] "Slowbalisation: The Future of Global Commerce", *The Economist*, 26 January 2019.

> *The data on the pace of global integration as a result of pro-globalisation economic policies are truly mind-boggling.*

its faith in trade, investment, and markets. The data on the pace of global integration as a result of pro-globalisation economic policies are truly mind-boggling. World trade rose from 39 percent of global GDP in 1990 to 58 percent at the end of 2018, as countries traded more with each other and global supply chains created a network of national suppliers who had a shared interest in faster integration. International assets and liabilities, fundamentally underpinned by trade finance and other cross-border financial transactions, rose dramatically from 128 percent of global GDP to a phenomenal 401 percent.

How did Asia perform during his epochal period for globalisation? To put it mildly, if globalisation were a Marvel movie, Asia would be best placed to play *all* of the super-heroes and heroines – Iron Man, Wonder Woman, The Hulk, with Captain America serving as the singular source of demand. Asia has been a huge beneficiary of open markets and free trade. The International Chamber of Commerce estimates that around 57 percent of global letters of credit, the key document to facilitate imports and exports, originate to or from Asia. How will the region perform when key measures of globalisation begin to slow or worse, start to decelerate from the heady expansion of the past few decades. Of the 12 measures of globalisation studied by *The Economist*, which include trade, intermediate imports, multinational

> *The International Chamber of Commerce estimates that around 57 percent of global letters of credit, the key document to facilitate imports and exports, originate to or from Asia.*

profits, FDI flows, stock of cross-border bank loans, gross capital flows, share of countries catching up, S&P 500 sales abroad, international parcel volume, permanent migrants to rich world, cross-border bandwidth, and international air travel — eight are in retreat or stagnating, of which seven lost steam as far back as 2008. Global trade itself fell from 61 percent of global GDP in 2008 to around 58 percent at the end of 2018. This is bound to hurt Asia since so much of its growth is tied up with global trade. Asia, ASEAN in particular, has sought to build trade resilience by signing two giant regional trade agreements — the Regional Comprehensive Economic Partnership (RCEP) which brings together ASEAN with China, Australia, Japan, Korea; the Comprehensive and Progressive Agreement for Trans-Pacific Partnership (CPTPP), which America under Trump backed out of and there is speculation on whether President Biden will seek to reengage. RCEP is a China-centred FTA while CPTPP used to be geared toward America until Trump pulled out.

The second major challenge for the region is the impact of technology on jobs and livelihoods. At first glance, this may appear to be an odd concern because of Asia's global dominance, along with that of America, of many aspects of technology. The region excels in hardware (China's Lenovo, Japan's Sony, Korea's Samsung), in software and services (India's giant technology companies like TCS, Infosys, and Wipro), e-commerce (thanks to the rise of Alibaba, Tencent, and national variants), and as an avid consumer of smart-phones, social media tools, and new gadgetry surrounding the Internet of Things (IoT). Allan Lau of McKinsey & Co[13] points out that in terms of technological adoption, there is "no one Asia." "One of the common myths is people think that developing Asia is behind in digital, and I think it's, in fact, the other way around," he said. The most interesting markets, he says, are not the likes of Japan or Korea but are going to be China, India, and Indonesia. "These are the markets that are really pushing the boundaries and innovating the most," he said.

While Asia is surging ahead in terms of going digital, there are uncomfortable questions of whether the digital leap-frogging will create a distinct set of

---

[13] "Digital innovation in Asia: What the world can learn", McKinsey Digital, 11 October 2016Podcast.

winners and losers. We will discuss in Chapter 5 the region's profound challenge in creating millions of jobs to sustain the arrival of new entrants, most of whom are not qualified to fill the jobs of the future — which will be in cutting- edge artificial intelligence, machine learning, and quantum computing.

Asia's third challenge is in its febrile politics, the topic of our next chapter. The model of governance is hopelessly out-of-date. To use a technological metaphor, Asian politics is still in the radio and telegraph era, where there is a clear hierarchy in how power is exercised. The most disturbing aspect of the rise of technology is that it can simultaneously empower and dis-intermediate vast sections of the population. The questions that I ask are Asian politicians fit-for-purpose in operating in an era where information is truly free but there are huge rewards and risks associated with slicing and dicing of this information? How will modern Asian politics deal with rising societal tensions and pressures which are bound to rise as the cold logic of automation begins to transform the workplace? To make matters worse, societal pressures will also rise from climate change or the lack of a credible response from Asian governments to severe flooding, raging forest fires, and catastrophic levels of pollution in the major urban centres.

Finally, I wish to clarify the geographic scope of this book. To be sure, I am less worried about Asia's advanced economies — Japan, Korea, Taiwan, Singapore, Brunei, and Hong Kong — that will be impacted by the headwinds outlined in this chapter but have the capacity to absorb the shock. I am rather more concerned with developing Asia — with billions of people straddling South, Southeast, and North Asia including China, India, Indonesia, Bangladesh, Sri Lanka, Nepal, Indo-China, Myanmar, Malaysia, Thailand, the Philippines, and often forgotten Mongolia. This massive sub-region is ground zero to our eight circles of hell, which we will visit consecutively starting with politics. We will be guided by the wise man from Florence and our very own Pramod.

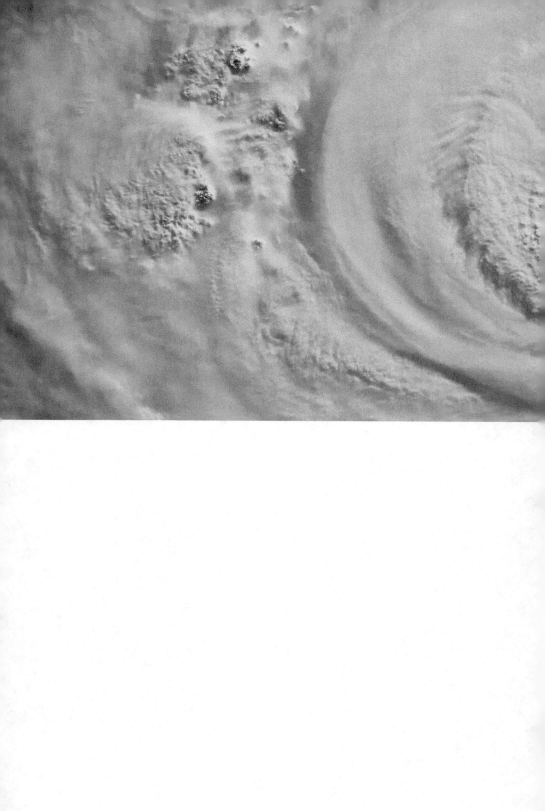

EIGHT CIRCLES
OF HELL

Chapter 4

Asia's Old Men

*Our first circle of hell is politics, where we examine the
preparedness of Asia's political class to disruptive change.*

obel Laureate Amartya Sen is renowned for his work on famines
and their political and economic impact on societies. "No famine
has ever taken place in the history of the world in a functioning
democracy," he famously wrote.[1] This is because democratic governments,
he added, "have to win elections and face public criticism, and have strong
incentive to undertake measures to avert famines and other catastrophes."

I reflected on this quote as Asia and the world deals with a pandemic
of biblical proportions in the form of Covid-19. The long-term political
impact is of course difficult to assess at this early stage. Through history
pandemics, natural disasters, and man-made phenomena like the Global
Financial Crisis have reshaped politics and society, and Covid-19 will make
its impact soon. For the moment, let's take a superficial look at which political
systems and leaders were more responsive and better prepared to deal with
the pandemic. The overall message is discouraging — democracies and

---

[1] Sen's analysis on famines was made several decades ago but I draw this quote from "Democracy in
Freedom", *The Anchor*, 1999.

dictatorships alike were equally unprepared to deal with the magnitude of the crisis wrought by Covid-19. Our prime exhibit for democracies in Asia shows winners (Korea, Taiwan, New Zealand) and major losers (India, the Philippines, Indonesia). One-party states did not perform better either, with the exception perhaps of Vietnam. China's vaunted command and control structure had fatal shortcomings as the virus seeped through Wuhan in December 2019. The lack of transparency bedevilled the initial response, and China eventually contained the pandemic by introducing one of the world's most rigid lockdowns. What initial political lessons should we therefore draw from Covid-19?

Political philosopher Francis Fukuyama, the famous proponent of the "end of history," writes[2] that on a global scale, it is already clear why some countries have done better than others in dealing with Covid-19. He notes that is *not* a matter of regime type — some democracies have performed well, but others have not, and the same is true of autocracies. "The factors responsible for successful pandemic responses have been state capacity, social trust, and leadership," according to Fukuyama. "Countries with all three — a competent state apparatus, a government that citizens trust and listen to, and effective leaders — have performed impressively." States with a high degree of polarisation, citizen's distrust, and political dysfunction, regardless of their income status, have floundered in their response.

> *Political philosopher Francis Fukuyama, the famous proponent of the "end of history", writes that on a global scale, it is already clear why some countries have done better than others in dealing with Covid-19.*

We should perhaps start by providing some perspective. Politics in Asia,

---

[2] Francis Fukuyama, "The Pandemic and Political Order. It Takes a State", *Foreign Affairs*, July/August 2020.

unlike their developed counterparts in the West, is a recent, post-colonial phenomenon and a work in progress. While Americans and Europeans have laboured over centuries to perfect their brand of democracy, newly independent Asian countries and their leaders have had to make choices in a hurry. These choices, be it communist dictatorships or democracies or a hybrid of both, inarguably worked well for Asia in the past. Politics did not get in the way of the Asian economic miracle and indeed was bolstered by pragmatic leaders. In the age of the pandemic and the far more disruptive era which lies ahead, Asian political systems may be less resilient and durable. Let me explain why.

Lao Charm

We start in Vientiane, one of Asia's sleepiest and charming capital cities, to gain a sense of politics frozen in time. Idling by the Mekong River, the capital city of Laos is a dazzling mixture of French charm, Laotian culture, and increasingly, Chinese dominance. It is also one of the least affected Covid-19 countries in Asia, which has more to do with its relative isolation rather than

> *One local wag told me that Laos in the 21st century had the best of all worlds — geographic (being located in dynamic Asia), food (sophisticated French-Laotian fusion cuisine), and historic (the Americans are long gone, thankfully!).*

superior management. I first visited Vientiane in 2004, when I was living in Washington D.C., then in the grip of hyper security following the 9/11 attacks. Visiting a Federal office building was an elaborate exercise which involved multiple checks on body and baggage. In contrast in Vientiane, I waltzed into the offices of the Finance Minister and Central Bank Governor without being stopped. Laotian officials have multiple reserves of charm, which spills over to impromptu dancing at official dinners. One local wag told me that Laos in the 21st century had the best of all worlds — geographic (being located in dynamic Asia), food (sophisticated French–Laotian fusion cuisine), and historic (the Americans are long gone, thankfully!).

The charm and humour are needed because landlocked Laos, which goes by its official name Lao PDR (People's Democratic Republic), is often over-looked in any discourse on Asia. In the west, Laos was well-known during an earlier generation because of American bombardment during the height of the Vietnam war. "From 1964 to 1973, the U.S. dropped more than two million tonnes of ordinance on Laos during 580,000 bombing missions-equal to a planeload of bombs every 8 minutes, 24-hours a day, for 9 years — making Laos the most heavily bombed country per-capita in history," notes the D.C.-based NGO Legacies of War. The bombings were part of the secret American war in support of the Royal Lao Government in its battle against the Communist-led Pathet Lao.

Laos not only survived the horrors of that war but appears to be thriving since it abandoned rigid communist economic doctrine in the late 1980s, very much along the lines of Vietnam's *doi moi*. Economic growth averaged more than 6 percent in the 1988-2008

> *Laos not only survived the horrors of that war but appears to be thriving since it abandoned rigid communist economic doctrine in the late 1980s*

period, and more recently growth has accelerated to the 7 percent range. Long placed at the bottom of Asia's economic ladder in terms of percapita GDP, Laos may well graduate out of the UN's definition of least-developed states in the next few years. Before this can happen, Laos needs to navigate itself out of a debt trap, fuelled by infrastructure projects funded by Chinese banks. How did Laos achieve high growth over the last few decades? Natural resources have certainly helped. The country has abundant reserves of copper and gold and logging on a massive scale has led to deforestation in recent years. Laos also has what energy-starved Southeast Asia desperately needs — cheap electricity driven by hydro-power dams along the Mekong River. In 2004, the talk in Laotian political circles was all about exploiting the hydro power bounty from the planned Nam Theun 2 project but to do it in a way that benefits local communities. I participated in an IMF-World Bank roundtable with members of the National Assembly (NA) and the conversation was lively, animated, and full of contention. One member even accused the government representative on the table of acting in bad faith by refusing to disclose sensitive information about resettlement of communities in the way of the dam project.

Watching members of the National Assembly express their views (and raising their voices) I felt like I was in a normal democratic country. In Taiwan and Korea, it is fairly normal for Members of Parliament to hurl abuses at each other and indulge in group violence. In India, Parliamentary walkouts are the usual vehicle of protest for opposition parties. The truth is Laos was at the time and remains one of the world's last remaining Marxist–Leninist communist regimes, blended with a healthy dose of Maoist thought. This is no democracy and power is centralised by the Lao People's Revolutionary Party (LPDR), the only recognised official party which rules with all of the trappings of a Communist state. The principal political governance platforms are a Politburo, comprised of the LDPR's senior-most leaders and a wider Central Committee. The LDPR holds a party congress every five years, bringing in members of the National Assembly who are all nominated to the post. The charming, assertive members of the NA whom I had encountered in 2004 were all part of this secretive body politic, prepared to engage and debate policy issues behind closed doors but who would brook no interference from the general public who wished to do the same.

In short, Lao PDR is a miniature version of the People's Republic of China, where the Communist Party of China (CPC) has held power without challenge since the 1949 revolution. The tiny land-locked nation mimics its giant northern neighbour in the way politics is organised, the economy is structured, and how the state uses surveillance and repression to root out any opposition to its rule or indeed independent thought. If you are any of the following, you are likely to do very well in Laos today — a senior Party official, head of a state-owned enterprise, or an entrepreneur with Party connections. Further down the food-chain, life gets tougher if you are a farm, factory, or construction labourer at the mercy of your employer. There are rudimentary labour and social protections, and such is paradise in a "people's democratic republic."

> *Further down the food-chain, life gets tougher if you are a farm, factory, or construction labourer at the mercy of your employer. There are rudimentary labour and social protections, and such is paradise in a "people's democratic republic."*

Democracy vs Dictatorship

At this stage, readers will no doubt groan about what possibly lies ahead in this chapter. I will also be expected to make an enthusiastic endorsement on the value of democracy, accountability, human rights, transparency, and the wisdom in letting a thousand competing ideas bloom. I will be expected to note China's tremendous economic and social progress, compared with democratic India and Indonesia, and argue vociferously about the merits of citizens exercising their franchise. Please be assured that I don't intend to go down this familiar path. While I happen to believe in democracy, my strongly held beliefs have been shaken in recent years by democracy's own failings in Asia in being responsive to people's concerns, and in delivering on good governance, and positive economic outcomes.

The creeping authoritarianism of Modi, Duterte, Sheikh Hasina in Bangladesh, and Thailand's Prayuth is symptomatic of the wrong-headed belief of political leaders who mistake an electoral mandate as a licence to consolidate power at all costs. There are striking similarities, for example, between Modi and Xi Jinping, in their mission to centralise and aggregate power rather than between Modi and Indonesia's Jokowi. Africa has its "big man" syndrome where political leaders remain in power for decades and snuff out the opposition. Asia's own Big Men are now following this model.

In short, my premise is that both Asian dictatorships and democracies have delivered tangible gains, evident in the Asian Miracle, but are failing in preparing their people for the future. There is also a technocratic deficit in Asia, the ability of the state to deliver efficient, competent

The creeping authoritarianism of Modi, Duterte, Sheikh Hasina in Bangladesh, and Thailand's Prayuth is symptomatic of the wrong-headed belief of political leaders who mistake an electoral mandate as a licence to consolidate power at all costs.

governance which was the driving force behind the Asian Miracle. During the Covid-19 pandemic, many Asian states have stumbled in handling the public health emergency with bumbling political leaders and bureaucrats mismanaging the crisis.

In that sense, the past few decades may well represent Asia's golden age. Operating under the U.S. security umbrella and focused on development, Asian nations had it easy compared with a more volatile Middle East, Africa, and Latin America. With the emergence of China as a putative superpower to challenge America's might, there will be a reordering in geopolitics, perhaps even conflict, which will transform the Asia we know.

It comes down to the central issue of whether 21st century Asia's disparate political systems, be they democracies, dictatorships, or monarchies, are well suited to deal with political, economic, technological and social disruption. To put it bluntly, is democracy working for Pramod and hundreds of millions of low-income families *currently* living in India, Indonesia, and other nominal democracies? They are certainly leading a better life compared with their parents but will economic opportunities for young people shrink as growth invariably slows, geopolitics disrupts stability, and technology eats away their jobs. What about the fate of those living under one-party rule like China, Vietnam, or Laos, whose boosters speak about superior technocratic management as the main reason why growth has accelerated and social indicators sharply improved? Overall, I wonder whether the region can sustain the pace of growth to meet the rising aspirations of a young, educated and well-informed populace. In the radio and telegraph era and before the rise of easy transport connectivity, it was quite possible for political leaders to manipulate the general populace into believing that life was getting better. In the smart-phone and social media era,

In the radio and television era and before the rise of easy transport connectivity, it was quite possible for political leaders to manipulate the general populace into believing that life was getting better.

such deception is no longer possible and even seemingly uneducated voters are capable of separating out substance from spin.

Before we get to these questions indepth, I want to rehash Chinese and Indian perspectives on their respective political systems and to illustrate how futile debating this issue is. Writing in the *South China Morning Post*, China scholar Chi Wang, President of the U.S.–China Policy Foundation,[3] noted that "China has no ideological basis for the development of a system that prizes personal freedom, nor any history with the rule of law." This somewhat puzzling construct comes with lots of caveats. Chi Wang acknowledges that however much Trump may be despised by a significant portion of the American public, they are at least able to track, analyse, and assess how it was that he came to power. In China, however, Xi's rise is as "big a question mark" to Chinese citizens as it is to foreign observers.

"After 70 years of rule in the People's Republic of China, authoritarianism has arguably only grown stronger, even as its people have become aware of alternative forms of government," he writes. "The current generation in China has the opportunity for more exposure to the outside world than

---

[3] Chi Wang,"China has no use for democracy. It needs a strong leader like Xi Jinping right now", *South China Morning Post*, 11 February 2019.

their parents, through the Internet, social media, and the lifting of many restrictions on trade, travel, and student exchanges." Chi Wang then raises the fundamental question of whether China could perhaps pursue a different political path, away from one-party rule and toward a pluralist democracy. His conclusion — it will not work because China lacks the "ideological framework" under which democracy could spontaneously develop or be fostered. "Confucianism is inherently undemocratic: it encourages obedience, not freedom or personal liberty," he writes adding that "understanding these realities" of leadership in China, it becomes apparent that regardless of how President Xi was selected, "he is the leader that China needs right now." Chi Wang's commentary flies in the face of neighbouring Confucian societies — Japan, Korea, and Taiwan — all thriving albeit imperfect democracies, with the latter two evolving from suffocating right-wing dictatorships to full-scale democracies *after* achieving high income growth.

During an earlier generation, Singapore founder Lee Kuan Yew[4] had also counselled patience on American and Western demands for greater democratic freedoms in China. "Can the habits and values of Chinese governance of over 4000 years be changed overnight by resolutions of the U.S. Congress," he asked, referring to U.S. sanctions proposed by Congress after the Tiananmen Square massacre. "I believe change will come to China. But it will be internally generated process of evolution. Indeed, the history of democracy in developed countries shows it to be a slow almost glacial process. They were so in the UK and the U.S. They reached full universal suffrage only after they had achieved a high level of economic growth with an educated population."

> *During an earlier generation, Singapore founder Lee Kuan Yew had also counselled patience on American and Western demands for greater democratic freedoms in China.*

---

[4] Lee Kuan Yew, speech at the Create 21 Asahi Forum, Tokyo, 20 November 1992.

Elections-Only Democracy

Political scientist Sumit Ganguly[5] argues that if you examine the panoply of former British colonies, the case of India is "exceptional" for its liberal and democratic institutions, and the power of ordinary people in exercising their voting rights.

Going back to the historic 1977 elections, which unseated Prime Minister Indira Gandhi and her Congress Party, Ganguly cites a story related by former *New York Times* reporter Steve Weisman. Two years earlier, Mrs. Gandhi had declared a state of emergency, India's first encounter with dictatorship, over an unfavourable court judgment on her previous electoral victory. After clamping down on press freedoms and detaining several hundred of her opponents, why did Mrs. Gandhi call for elections in 1977? "…because her sycophants told her that ' Madame, everybody loves you '" Ganguly quotes Weisman. "The poor turned out in droves, however, and put her out of her ear." This story, Ganguly writes, epitomises the power of the ballot — that the poor in India may have little else. "They are maltreated by the police. Often, they cannot approach the bench because they lack resources. Class privileges lead people to treat them as sub-human. But when they step into that booth, they recognise that they wield the power to throw out rascals and bring in new leadership. This is why Indian elections are so powerfully contested now, because you can no longer predict how the poor are going to vote." Indian voters are notorious for rejecting incumbent political parties, with

> *Indian voters are notorious for rejecting incumbent political parties, with a few notable exceptions as Modi's triumphant re-election in 2019 makes clear, and have an appetite for trying out new groupings and leaders with the expectation of better economic outcomes.*

---

[5] Sumit Ganguly, "The Story of Indian Democracy", FootNotes (Foreign Policy Research Institute), 16, no.5 (June 2011).

a few notable exceptions as Modi's triumphant re-election in 2019 makes clear, and have an appetite for trying out new groupings and leaders with the expectation of better economic outcomes.

Indian historian Ramachandra Guha, author of a biography of Gandhi, is also circumspect about the effectiveness of Indian democracy. Speaking in 2016,[6] Guha said that seventy years after Indian Independence, India was freer than when the British left the country's soil but perhaps much less free than what the framers of the Constitution hoped would be. "We have falsified the pundits who said we'll break up, but we still have much more work to do," he said, adding that as a nation-state, India was 80 percent successful but as a democracy, perhaps only 50 percent. "My worry is that we are not so much an electoral democracy as much as an elections-only democracy" he said "…. The deficiency of our democracy is manifest in the widespread corruption of our political class, deterioration of our public institutions, particularly our failure to provide quality education and health to our citizens." The quality of life has certainly improved in India for a certain segment of the population – urban, educated, and well-heeled – who will no doubt consider politics playing an enabling role in this improvement or despite it. However, as Guha notes, Indian politics can be venal and corrupt with the poor bearing the biggest burden of the state's inability to deliver effective governance.

So, there you have it, two sharply different visions of political systems as they function in two of the world's largest nations. One-party Communist rule in China is undemocratic but has delivered tangible economic and social benefits, particularly since 1979. Parliamentary democracy in India has been the binding force that has kept the country together but the country trails behind China on major socio-economic indicators. The two systems serve as a litmus test for countries in Asia on the efficacy of their own political systems. China-boosters say that the country's spectacular

---

[6] Ramachandra Guha, "We are more an elections-only democracy", The Hindu, 16 October 2016.

> *While the economic discourse in India is focused overwhelmingly on the material progress made by China and how to catch up, Beijing looks at India with a combination of bewilderment and annoyance.*

four-decade long economic track record proves that its system has delivered better governance and outcomes compared with democratic countries such as India. While the economic discourse in India is focused overwhelmingly on the material progress made by China and how to catch up, Beijing looks at India with a combination of bewilderment and annoyance. Bewilderment because Chinese policymakers or business folks who have visited India have come away feeling that there is no contest between the two countries. China has decisively won the race, in their view, and there is a hint of annoyance that the two nations are seen stacked against each other.

Hodgepodge of Systems

Leaving aside Japan and the Asian Tigers, developing Asia represents a hodgepodge of political systems and philosophies of governance. Aligned on China's side are North Korea, Vietnam, Cambodia, and Laos, in terms of one-party rule with broadly similar ideologies. It must be said that while Cambodia and Laos are dangerously veering in the direction or de facto have become Chinese satellite states, Vietnam has positioned itself in opposition to Beijing on a full range of issues, most notably the dispute in the South China Sea. North Korea is also an outlier because much of its Leninist-Marxist thinking has become subsumed in home-grown ideology, or idolatry, glorifying the Kim dynasty and juche, the philosophy of self-reliance. Yet there are sharp similarities in the way the state exercises complete control in China, North Korea, and the three Indo-China states. The tools of repression are similar — dissent is crushed, opposition parties and competing ideologies (Falun Gong in China, for example) are banned, and the rise of the smart phone and social media is providing the state with ever more intrusive ways of monitoring the lives of citizens. The Great Wall of China may be porous and crumbling in parts, but the Great Firewall of China is a near invincible cyber fortress. Any visitor to China will testify to the frustrations of living in a world where the primary global search engine is Microsoft's clunky Bing. There are rewards as well as in connecting with WeChat, Alibaba, and Baidu as they give us a glimpse of a world where China is the dominant standard-setter.

> *The Great Wall of China may be porous and crumbling in parts, but the Great Firewall of China is a near invincible cyber fortress.*

Moving away from one-party dictatorships, Asia has the "guided" democracies of Thailand and Myanmar, where the Army exercises absolute control over the levers of power, with little or nominal civilian control. The list of Asian democracies is formidable, yet each country has its own unique political characteristics and failings — India, Indonesia, Malaysia, the Philippines, Nepal, Bangladesh, Sri Lanka, and Mongolia. Thailand and Malaysia also happen to be constitutional monarchies, with Brunei on the other end of the spectrum representing the region's only absolute monarch.

We may quibble about the categorisation of many of the countries in the list above. For starters, Myanmar's Aung San Suu Kyi, recently deposed by the Army after securing an impressive election victory in November 2020, used to bristle at suggestions that she and her National League of Democracy (NLD) had nominal control over the country. However, the *Tatmadaw*, the country's all-powerful Armed Forces has once again taken over and the future path for democracy is highly uncertain. For outside observers, the NLD was never really in full charge of the country's destiny and indeed tacitly supported the persecution of the minority Rohingya community.

Myanmar is one of Asia's poorest nations with per capita GDP at 2018 prices at around $1,200 (Nepal is poorer at $1,000). So perhaps we could overlook or forgive the country's difficult political transition from full-scale military dictatorship to quasi civilian rule. The same principle, however, should not apply to a middle-income country like Thailand (2019 per capita GDP around $7,900) which has stumbled politically in the last two decades. Since the election of billionaire tycoon Thaksin Shinawatra and his Thai Rak Thai Party (TRT) in the 2000 elections, Thailand's political system has become hostage to two competing forces: First, Thaksin's election victory, following Thailand's economic meltdown during the 1997-1998 Asian Financial Crisis, represented a repudiation of the role and influence of Bangkok as the rural hinterland voted overwhelmingly in support of TRT's populist agenda. Second, Thaksin's populist rise was seen as a direct challenge to the role and influence of two of the country's great institutions — the monarchy and the Armed Forces.

To place things in a broader global context, Thaksin's electoral victory in 2000 was a Trump-like moment for Thailand. The billionaire telecom tycoon was disdainful of the ruling elite and sought to build a coalition of support with voters outside of the Bangkok metropolitan area, enticing them with subsidies and home-spun Make Thailand Great Again promises. TRT's grand political strategy was to build a permanent electoral majority from the Thai hinterland, which the Bangkok elite regarded as posing a fundamental challenge to their traditional leadership role. "Thaksin was committed to overcoming Thailand's economic problems by developing populist policies that gave some social protection

> *To place things in a broader global context, Thaksin's electoral victory in 2000 was a Trump-like moment for Thailand.*

to the lower classes," writes political scientist Grigoris Markou.[7] "Hence he introduced programs such as virtually free health care, fuel subsidies, and low-cost loans for farmers." My own introduction to Thaksinomics came in

---

[7] Grigoris Markou,"Thaksin, dictatorship and Thailand's new constitution", openDemocracy, 14 September 2016.

2001 when the TRT assumed power and one of the Prime Minister's advisors went on a rampage (at an official meeting with the IMF) against the Bank of Thailand (BoT), the country's respected central bank, for tightening monetary policy. The Thaksin advisor showed us a dubious chart setting out to prove that inflation was primarily a "Western construct" and price behaviour in Thailand was different from the global norm. Looking back, this has eerie parallels with Trump's harangue against the Federal Reserve Board Chairman Jerome Powell's stance on increasing interest rates. While Powell remains in place, thanks to Trump's departure, the BoT Governor at the time Chatumongol Sonakul was soon sacked.

At the same time Thaksin's populist economic policies had the positive impact of empowering the country's rural and small-town voters into the mainstream political process. Viewed in Trumpian and American terms, the populist struggle in Thailand is equivalent to voters in America's vast rural hinterland, the so-called overfly states or the rust belt, defeating entrenched coastal elites in the 2016 elections. The only difference is that in the case of Thailand, the elite has prevailed since the 2006 coup by ousting Thaksin and forced him into exile.

At the same time Thaksin's populist economic policies had the positive impact of empowering the country's rural and small-town voters into the mainstream political process.

There is no clear democratic path forward for Thailand, given that the new Constitution and electoral process introduced by the Army-backed government seeks to keep them in power permanently. Despite living away from Thailand for over a decade, Thaksin's political brand remains a powerful draw, signalling that rural and poor voters do feel disenfranchised by Bangkok-driven politics. As a populist leader, the billionaire tycoon has demonstrated an ability to connect with rural and poor voters in a way that the Bangkok elite is unable to compete with. However, Thailand's economy continued to chug along driven by tourism, auto exports, and

> *As a populist leader, the billionaire tycoon has demonstrated an ability to connect with rural and poor voters in a way that the Bangkok elite is unable to compete with.*

consumption until Covid-19 delivered an economic shock. An open question is whether Covid-19 will lead to structural, negative changes to the economy and impact Thailand's restive rural populace. A prolonged economic slowdown could impact rural and urban incomes. Urban Thailand is already getting restive — the student protests in Bangkok since the middle of 2020 have been astonishing in its durability and demands. The students are calling for reform of the political system as well as the monarchy, the latter being considered a taboo topic because of Thailand's enforcement of rigid *lese majeste* laws. During the long reign of King Bhumibol, the monarchy was held in high esteem by Thai citizens. His successor is facing a more difficult time in winning over hearts and minds, which will be essential in maintaining social stability. Should Thailand's rural populace also rise in protest like their urban brethren, the current political status quo will prove to be unsustainable.

Corruption Impact

It was precisely such an urban-rural coalition that was instrumental in ousting Malaysia's ruling UMNO from power for the very first time in the 2018 elections. The two principal opposition leaders who built this powerful coalition are as different as chalk and cheese, or perhaps not: the 95-year old Mahathir Mohammed, until recently the oldest head of government in the world, and his 73-year old former protégé-turned bitter rival-turned political partner Anwar Ibrahim. The Mahathir–Anwar love-hate-love relationship shows the toxic nature of democratic politics as well as its pragmatic side — the ability to bring together former rivals to oust a corrupt and unpopular leader, the former Prime Minister Najib Tun Razak and his ruling UMNO coalition. However, this experiment did not last long and political bickering between Mahathir and Anwar has resulted in their exit from government. The corruption of the Najib administration touched eye-popping levels with the 1MDB scandal. The Prime Minister was unable to account for how he and his associates stole billions of dollars and went on a shopping binge that unfortunately has several parallels in modern Southeast Asian history, the excesses of the Marcos and Suharto family come to mind.

The broader lesson here is that corruption, like inflation, is a tax on the poor and the most vulnerable segments of the population are least able to resist pressures from petty government bureaucrats and the police. The 2011 Arab Spring protests had their genesis in Tunisia where a street vendor set himself on fire because of petty harassment by local municipal officials. There are parallels with the daily trials and tribulations of low-income people all over developing Asia, be it in democracies or dictatorships. Our auto-rickshaw driver Pramod in Mumbai has to pay multiple facilitation fees to ensure the

The broader lesson here is that corruption, like inflation, is a tax on the poor and the most vulnerable segments of the population are least able to resist pressures from petty government bureaucrats and the police.

validity of his licence to operate. This is no different in China, where city enforcement officials routinely use violence and extortion to enforce local laws governing street trading. A March 2017 opinion poll by advocacy group Transparency International estimated that 900 million – or just over one in four – people living in 16 countries in Asia Pacific, including some of its biggest economies, are estimated to have paid a bribe.

It is not only petty corruption which stalls progress in developing Asia as the 2019 Corruption Perceptions Index (CPI) report, also by Transparency International shows. "A regional average of 45 on the index, after many consecutive years of an average score of 44, illustrates general stagnation across the Asia Pacific," TI said. "While often seen as an engine of the global economy, in terms of political integrity and governance, the region performs only marginally better than the global average." One reason offered by TI as to why the region was making little progress in its anti-corruption efforts is an "overall weakening" of democratic institutions and political rights. Here it takes to task both democracies as well as autocratic states. Coming to the theme of this book, if Asia truly aspires to remain the world's most dynamic and equitable regions, dealing with corruption should be a top priority of the political class. It has certainly been the case in China where President Xi Jinping and his Vice President Wang Qishan have led a controversial anti-corruption campaign against Party officials, although power consolidation does appear to be a primary motivation. It is precisely for this reason that TI emphasises the value of democratic systems. Ordinary Malaysians, who viewed UMNO with the same reverence as Thai do their monarchy, were sufficiently shocked to want to vote for the opposition in 2018, albeit to two former grandees from the ruling party itself. Not surprisingly, former Prime Minister Mahathir pursued a more populist economic course during this return to power, abolishing a sensible goods and services tax (GST) and threatening to cancel China-funded infrastructure projects which he fears will drive the country to debt distress.

Old and Powerful

Our political survey shows that Asian political systems, be they dictatorships or democracies, have some strengths and many weaknesses, or to paraphrase Leo Tolstoy, countries with happy political systems are all alike (Japan and some of the Asian Tigers perhaps), while every imperfect political system in developing Asia is imperfect in its own way. One serious problem is gerontocracy. Asia today is run by a group of seniors, a majority of whom were born during the radio and telegraph era of the 1940s and 1950s. They are ruling over a population who are skewing younger and younger — in India and Indonesia, those under the age of 30 constitute a significant chunk of the population. The United Nations[8] estimates that the Asia-Pacific region contains 60 percent of the world's youth population, or 750 million people aged 15 to 24 years. That there is a communication gap between ruler and ruled is not surprising. Visiting India or Indonesia is a chastening experience for those aged 50 or older. You are literally surrounded by twenty-somethings, demonstrating that countries with young populations have the potential to reap a demographic dividend, if public policy is deployed wisely, or mass social unrest is inevitable on the scale of the Arab spring.

Asia today is run by a group of seniors, a majority of whom were born during the radio and telegraph era of the 1940s and 1950s. They are ruling over a population who are skewing younger and younger

Here is a listing of the year of birth of current Asian heads of state and/or government. With four notable exceptions, they are all above the age of 60, a critical benchmark in figuring out how attuned they are to concerns of younger people:

India – Narendra Modi, 1950
China – Xi Jinping, 1953
Indonesia – Joko Widodo, 1961
Bangladesh – Sheikh Hasina Wajed, 1947
Sri Lanka – Gotabaya Rajapaksa, 1949
Maldives – Ibrahim Mohamed Solih, 1962
Nepal – Khadga Prasad Sharma Oli, 1952
Malaysia – Muhyiddin Muhammad Yassin, 1947
Thailand – General Prayuth Chan-o-cha, 1954
The Philippines – Rodrigo Duterte, 1945

---

[8] Economic and Social Commission for Asia and the Pacific (UNESCAP), "Regional Overview: Youth in Asia and the Pacific".

Brunei – Sultan Hassanal Bolkiah, 1946
Myanmar – Win Myint, 1951 (under arrest after February 2021 coup)
Vietnam – Nguyen Phu Trong, 1944
Cambodia – Hun Sen, 1952
Laos – Bounnhang Vorachith, 1938
Mongolia – Khaltmaagiin Battulga, 1963
North Korea – Kim Jong-un, 1984

If you include developed Asia, this list also does not skew young:

Japan – Yoshihide Suga, 1948
Taiwan – Tsai Ing-wen, 1956
Korea – Moon Jae-in, 1953
Singapore – Lee Hsien Loong, 1952

> *That the youngest leader in Asia today is the supreme leader of North Korea, who took over after the death of his father Kim Jong-il, demonstrates that there is something fundamentally wrong in the way the region manages inter-generational political transitions.*

That the youngest leader in Asia today is the supreme leader of North Korea, who took over after the death of his father Kim Jong-il, demonstrates that there is something fundamentally wrong in the way the region manages inter-generational political transitions. The problem is not only that Asian politicians are old and possibly out of touch with their electorate, but the political parties that they head themselves are showing their age. India's Congress Party was founded in 1885, China's Communist Party in 1921, Taiwan's Kuomintang in 1912, and Japan's LDP in 1955. For all the constant talk about leadership and party renewal, Asia's grand old parties have a vice-like grip on their nation's politics and it is extremely difficult for a new grouping or political challenger to make its mark. The number of new political parties or movements which have threatened Asian political oligarchs makes for a small list. Thailand's Thaksin clearly makes the mark, along with the more recent Future Forward Party.[9] Elsewhere in the region, examples include India's Common Man Party (AAP), Malaysia's Pakatan Harapan (PH), and smaller political parties in Indonesia. While Malaysia's PH was able to win the general election, it is hard to imagine it doing so without the leadership of political stalwarts like Mahathir and Anwar. There is also the pernicious Asian practice of dynastic succession — most visible in South and Southeast Asia — but also evident in China and Japan. Both Xi Jinping and Shinzo Abe are princelings, i.e. children of powerful leaders whose rise would not have been possible if not for their political pedigree.

Asian politicians could learn or two from the technology sector, where the region's younger generation is thriving and demonstrating able leadership. Jack Ma was only 31 years old when he founded Alibaba, Indonesia's Nadiem Makarim was 26 years old when he founded Gojek, and India's Binny Bansal was 25 years old when he started Flipkart, now owned by Walmart. All three companies have sky-high market valuations with Alibaba leading the pack with over $700 billion. While Silicon Valley and its Asian counterparts skew very young in terms of demographics, Asian politics skews very old. Xi Jinping could never have aspired to a senior leadership position while in his forties because the Chinese system rewards age and hierarchy. Each aspiring President is expected to serve two terms as Party Secretary in the provinces and wait his turn (it always appears to be a he) to be appointed to the State Council or the prized Politburo. India's Narendra Modi was heavily criticised early in this term for side-lining many

Asian politicians could learn or two from the technology sector, where the region's younger generation is thriving and demonstrating able leadership.

---

[9] The Future Forward Party was founded in 2018 by businessman Thanathorn Juangroongruangkit and has been targeted by the military-led regime.

of the elders in the ruling party hierarchy. Modi is no spring chicken, he is 70 years old, but he cannot be faulted for not offering a cabinet position to party stalwarts L.K. Advani (92) or Murli Manohar Joshi (86). While former Prime Minister Mahathir's political return, at age 93, was under extraordinary circumstances and possibly excused, it is obvious that politics is not a profession for the young in Asia.

When a younger person takes the helm, change is tangible. One of four leaders of the 1960s generation listed above includes Joko Widodo, who literally came from nowhere (Surakarta in Central Java) to become President of Indonesia. Jokowi's improbable rise within a decade from furniture-maker in 2005 to the Presidency in 2014 is both a reflection of Indonesia's vibrant post-1998 democracy, where virtual unknowns have a fair chance, and a young demographic eager for change. For someone who was only in his thirties when the Internet era was ushered in, Jokowi is skilfully able to meld home-spun philosophy with pop-culture references (The Avengers and Game of Thrones have featured in many of his speeches). In my book *Resurgent Indonesia:From Crisis to Confidence*[10] I wrote that Jokowi's election bid in 2014 was the most daring act of political entrepreneurship, certainly in Asia and perhaps the world. Using social media tools with aplomb and communicating with ordinary Indonesians in a style and context that they are comfortable with,

> *In his second term in office, unfortunately, Jokowi is behaving like his peers from the radio and telegraph era with several members of his family entering politics.*

Jokowi has transformed politics. He has also provided an incentive for young Indonesians to become more engaged in politics. "Jokowi's election lead to surge in interest in young educated professionals wanting to join government, a remarkable turn of events in a country where public sector jobs were previously regarded with disdain by the new generation," I write

---

[10] Vasuki Shastry, *Resurgent Indonesia: From Crisis to Confidence* (Straits Times Press, 2018).

in the book. "The young professionals, who are bursting with enthusiasm about their president and their country, work on modest salaries and display a determination to cut red tape and get things done. This bodes well for Indonesia." In his second term in office, unfortunately, Jokowi is behaving like his peers from the radio and telegraph era with several members of his family entering politics.

Youthful Protests

What is the price that countries pay for failing to engage with youth and for not bringing them into the mainstream? There are certainly global lessons. The Arab Spring of 2011, continued more recently with protests in Algeria and Sudan, stands out as an example of what happens when there is a demographic disconnect between the political order

> *What is the price that countries pay for failing to engage with youth and for not bringing them into the mainstream? There are certainly global lessons.*

and a large segment of the population who happen to be young. Asia is not immune from this divide as the developed part of the region demonstrates. In an op-ed published by the Brookings Institution in 2016,[11] the authors note that young people in Northeast Asia have become famous around the world for their creativity and consumer flair: K-pop and the Korean wave, fancy smart phones and IT entrepreneurism, high-end fashion, obsession with plastic surgery, and web-based social networks.

"Political activism and participation are not the first two words that pop into one's head when we think of young East Asians," according to the op-ed. "But in recent years, youth in Hong Kong, Japan, South Korea, and Taiwan are leading political movements and asserting their interests onto the

---

[11] Katherine H.S. Moon, Paul Park, and Maeve Whelan-Wuest, "Youth & Politics in East Asia", Op-ed, Brookings East Asia Commentary, 30 June 2016.

national political agenda. Although the specific issues of political concern differ, they are motivated by a common fear of economic decline for their generation, a rejection of political marginalization, and a moral awakening that their governments and the older generations are endangering their future, including democracy." The most spectacular manifestation of this trend of course is Hong Kong's Umbrella Movement and "Occupy Central" protests of 2014, and the more recent pre-Covid violent protests over the controversial extradition law, a movement which was masterminded by young, middle-class professionals and aimed at warning Beijing about the limits to encroaching on their freedoms. Not surprisingly, Beijing and the Hong Kong administration went after the protest leaders with a heavy hand, serving as a warning to others that there are limits to freedoms in one of the region's most prosperous enclaves. A broader lesson for Asia here is that given the demographic divide between the rulers and ruled, the risks are rising that impatient young people will agitate for change, particularly in the face of technological disruption.

The most intriguing story to come out of China in recent years has been the crackdown on a group of young students from privileged backgrounds who have been agitating for worker rights. The genesis of the group had innocuous beginnings on campus, as a "study" group focused on the teachings of Karl Marx, which should be unobjectionable in China where the German thinker is held in very high esteem. Indeed, to mark the 200th birth anniversary of Marx, China gifted the German city of Trier, where he was born, with a 14-foot bronze statue. President Xi has described Marx as the "greatest thinker of modern times" and that the German thinker "pointed out the direction, with scientific theory, toward an

> *The most intriguing story to come out of China in recent years has been the crackdown on a group of young students from privileged backgrounds who have been agitating for worker rights.*

ideal society with no oppression or exploitation." The high praise for Marx notwithstanding, Xi's administration had no hesitation in moving against a group of students who attempted to put Marxist theory into practice.

In a detailed article in the *Financial Times*,[12] journalist Yuan Yang meticulously lays out what happened to an undergraduate student called Luke (not his real name) and his fellow students who attempted to organise a union and agitate for better worker benefits at a welding equipment factory at Shenzhen. "On August 24, not long after his arrival, Luke's dormitory of activists was raided by police, and about 50 students were taken into custody," the article said. "The mass detention was one of the most contentious crackdowns on student protestors since the Tiananmen Square massacre of 1989." Yuan Yang notes the irony of the arrests of the workers and the students, which highlights a paradox at the heart of modern China. "While the country is controlled by a Communist party government that trumpets Marxist rhetoric, its economy has flourished since the 1980s partly thanks to the development of 'state capitalism' — a liberalisation that allowed private markets and mass consumption to thrive within strict parameters set by the state." In Yuan Yang's article, Rana Mitter, Professor of History and Politics of Modern China at Oxford University summed up the grievances felt against the system. "The objection of many on China's new left – not just students – is that China is a socialist country in name but capitalist in reality, and that inequality, pollution, and corruption are a consequence of this anomaly," he said.

For an under-graduate student like Luke, who was not even born when China's embarked on its great leap outward in 1979, his reference point is the grim realities of the here and now, not the piety and platitudes offered by China's leadership on the country's historic class struggle. Anyone with a millennial in the family, I certainly have one, will relate to the challenge that

---

[12] Yuan Yang, "Inside China's Crackdown on Young Marxists", *Financial Times Magazine*, 14 February 2019.

dealing with the new generation requires tools and tact radically different from the traditional skills of top-down parenting and supervision. Invoking past struggles of the nation and glorious battles to secure independence, as aging political leaders routinely do these days, simply does not resonate with twenty-and-thirty-year olds focused on dealing with anxieties of globalisation and technological disruption.

Digitalisation of Politics

So how can Asia deal with the generation gap between the ruler and ruled? This is not simply an issue of succession planning, i.e. the old preparing the ground for young leadership. With rapid technological advancement and disruption, the time is not far away when the region's gerontocratic leadership will simply fail to grasp the challenges of the moment. Financial analyst and academic Costa Vayenas writes[13] that digitisation is changing all aspects of how modern societies operate, including democracy. Costa notes that he set out to answer the central question as to whether democracy was immune to disintermediation. Was there a special reason why the job of lawmaker had not changed in the digital age. His conclusion is that disintermediation is beginning to happen in politics as well, not just in the developed West but globally.

> *With rapid technological advancement and disruption, the time is not far away when the region's gerontocratic leadership will simply fail to grasp the challenges of the moment.*

"While very little has changed in the machinery of the American representative system in the late 1700s, this arrangement is starting to unravel," he writes. "The technology by which people receive their information and make their

---

[13] Costa Vayenas, "How Technology is Disrupting Political Systems", Centre for Public Impact, 21 June 2017.

will known is being revolutionised. Technology now holds the capacity to transfer more power directly to the people, including the all-important question of how the state taxes and spends." Costa adds that the shift toward a more digital form of interaction between ruler and ruled is being driven by five major forces:

- Democracy is not static, and the advancement of technology and the ubiquitous smartphone is placing more power in the hands of people. Social media tools enable greater use of petitions and referendums. Power is getting decentralised.

- Governments themselves are forcing greater digital interaction by introducing e-governance initiatives.

- Technology and software advancements are making it easier for people to organise and express their views in the political sphere.

- A disparate group of NGOs and grass-root political activists, be it in democracies or dictatorships, are transforming on-the-ground politics and opening up new possibilities for citizens to participate even more in the democratic process.

- Finally, as more and more government services to the public migrate online, people will begin to notice that one interaction remains unchanged — the really important one of instructing the people's representatives.

How might these five forces translate into political change or disruption in Asia? To return to my auto-rickshaw ride in Mumbai with Pramod, young Asians today are empowered by technology and feel emboldened to express their views and/or agitate for change via social media channels. Pramod told me that he was on a WhatsApp group with fellow drivers who alerted each other on police activity and to stay away from congested streets. On a more impactful scale, Hong Kong protestors used the messaging app Telegram to organise the 2019 protests, which was highly effective in bringing the city-state to a halt.

Asian governments of all stripes are so concerned about the rise of social media tools that enable the general public to organise, agitate, and demonstrate at such short notice. Aging politicians and the bureaucracy have reacted to these challenges in a familiar way — shut down social media channels, organise an official army of trolls to tamp down dissent, and strengthen surveillance of the general public. China of course represents the most sophisticated example of a hyper-surveillance state where almost every public and increasingly private activity of citizens is monitored and analysed. The Chinese surveillance model itself has gone regional as an article in the *Nikkei Asian Review*[14] demonstrates. "Chinese surveillance and security start-up Yitu Technology has made its first foray into Malaysia, supplying wearable cameras with artificial intelligence powered facial recognition technology to a local law enforcement agency," the article said, adding that the deal marks the first use of wearable devices by the country's law enforcement agencies. Instructively, a spokesperson for the police unit told the magazine that it would "consider the introduction of streaming facial-recognition functions in real time in the near future."

> *Asian governments of all stripes are so concerned about the rise of social media tools that enable the general public to organise, agitate, and demonstrate at such short notice.*

In India, the Supreme Court recently intervened and declared privacy to be a fundamental right after the Indian Government's ham-handed attempt to use Aadhar, the biometric identification system, as a tool for state surveillance. Other countries, notably Singapore, have introduced legislation to combat

---

[14] C.K. Tan, "Malaysian police adopt Chinese AI surveillance technology", *Nikkei Asian Review*, 18 April 2018.

fake news but critics contend that in reality they are an attempt to curb free speech. To quote Dante: "One ought to be afraid of nothing other than things possessed of power to do us harm, but things innocuous need not be feared." Asian youth, like their counterparts elsewhere, have come of age in an era of anxiety and anger. While it is hard to generalise, their parents belonged to a lucky generation when jobs were abundant and the path to upward mobility more secure. Let us explore the economic destiny of this young generation — when the same-old politics of today collides with the cold techno-economic reality of tomorrow.

Chapter 5
Middle-Class Trap

Our second circle of hell is Asia's economic model, long durable but soon-to-be disrupted with unpredictable consequences for the region's middle and aspiring lower middle class.

To be a graduate in Asia used to be a ticket to economic opportunity. My friend Leonard[1] epitomises this very Asian success story over the last seven decades. Born in 1947, Leonard was 18-years old when Singapore separated from Malaysia in 1965 and became an independent nation. He was in the post-independence, pioneer group of graduates from the National University of Singapore (NUS), where he majored in economics. By Leonard's own admission, he was a mediocre student and winged his way through college with indifferent grades. However, helping Leonard early in his career was a special kind of rocket fuel — powered by Singapore's emergence from Third World to First and a global economy which handsomely rewarded Asia's openness to trade, investment, and free markets. "I was an ordinary person who happened to be at the right place and the right time," Leonard told me last year. "My generation in Singapore, who complain a lot, came of age during an extraordinary period of economic

---

[1] Not his real name. I have changed it at his request.

opportunity and social mobility." Leonard started his career in the lower managerial ranks of a local corporation, which has since gone global and catapulted him into the ranks of senior management. With the exception of taking an advanced management programme at one of America's Ivy League institutions, at the insistence he says of his CEO, Leonard's under-whelming undergraduate degree has taken him a long way. Something to be said about a rising tide lifting all boats.

Sitting at the Singapore Cricket Club, the mainstay watering hole of the establishment, Leonard pointed out that his children and grandchildren have not been so fortunate, with a son out-of-work after a corporate restructuring and grandson struggling to make a success of his start-up. "Our fortunes were built on steady, fast, and reliable economic growth," he said "Asians with a university education were in short supply when I entered the job market. We were the chosen ones. Today we have an over-supply of graduates and technology is about to take us down an unpredictable path."

> However, like property in major metros, Asia may be suffering from a glut in talent.

While Singapore and Hong Kong have set quotas and indeed a cap on the number of 17-to-18-year olds admitted to public universities, the rest of Asia is suffering from a glut in university graduates with fierce competition for the limited jobs on offer. In theory, an over-supply should be good news since the private sector needs a pool of qualified graduates and everyone will eventually be absorbed provided the economy keeps humming along. However, like property in major metros, Asia may be suffering from a glut in talent.

"Massification" of Higher Education

Academic Joshua Mok ka-ho[2] of Lingnan University in Hong Kong, who

---

[2] Mok Ka-ho, "Massification of higher education, graduate employment, and social mobility in the Greater China region", *British Journal of Sociology of Education* 37, no.1 (2016).

has extensively researched the "massification" of higher education notes that universities in East and Southeast Asia have experienced significant expansion in enrolment in the last few decades. According to Mok, enrolment in higher education in Asia has increased by over 50 percent in the last ten years and by a higher percentage in countries such as China, where the country produced over 8.7 million graduates in 2020 compared with one million in 2000. This has raised serious concerns over academic standards. Mok highlights strong empirical evidence suggesting that the massification of higher education to the masses and not just an elite has resulted in rising graduate unemployment and underemployment in East Asia.

Mok ka-ho cites worrying statistics in South Korea, there are an estimated three million "economically inactive" graduates; in Japan, approximately 38 percent of graduates were unemployed eight months after graduation in 2009, and graduate employment has not improved since then; in India, one in three graduates are unemployed; in China, although accurate data is hard to come by, Mok's research found that only 38 percent of graduates were issued contracts, a low indicator for quality jobs on offer. His broad conclusion is that the role of education in upward social mobility in Asia should be under scrutiny. "In a less globalised and more elite higher education system, a university degree may contribute to increased earnings and possibilities for a young graduate," he writes. "But the status quo has changed with the ever-intensifying globalisation of higher education and its expansion to more and more parts of society."

To put it bluntly, as Mok ka-ho does, a degree no longer assures employment, high earnings, and upward social mobility in Asia. The Asian Dream, like its older American counterpart, is in peril. When the Indian Railways advertised 90,000 open positions in 2018, it was soon inundated with over 2 million applications. "The railways recruitment effort

> *To put it bluntly, as Mok ka-ho does, a degree no longer assures employment, high earnings, and upward social mobility in Asia.*

is a potent symbol of India's employment conundrum," the UK's *Independent* newspaper reported.[3] "The country is one of the fastest-growing major economies in the world, but it is not generating enough jobs – let alone good jobs – for the increasingly educated young people entering the workforce." The newspaper added that by 2021, the number of people in India between the ages of 15 and 34 is expected to reach 480 million. "They have higher levels of literacy and are staying in school longer than any previous generation of Indians," the paper added. "The youth surge represents an opportunity for this country of 1.3 billion, economists say, but if only such young people can find productive work." The massification of higher education is by no means an Asian phenomenon. In 2010, an American academic Peter Turchin[4] had predicted that the next decade was "likely to be a period of growing instability in the United States and Europe," in part due to the "overproduction of young graduates with advanced degrees." Turchin has become an academic celebrity because his predictions turned out to be true due to rising nationalism and protests in America and Europe. Closer to home, the surge in student protests in Hongkong and Thailand are perhaps a manifestation of an excess supply of qualified graduates with limited job opportunities, which if replicated in the rest of Asia will surely lead to social and political instability.

The massive rush for young Asians to secure university degrees is due to three competing forces. First, rising incomes in the region over the past few decades have created an aspirational lower middle class who see education as a ticket to economic stability and prosperity. Second, the rate and pace of employment in Asian economies is beginning to slow, due to increased automation in the workplace, the dominant role of services, and the decline of manufacturing. Third and

> *The massive rush for young Asians to secure university degrees is due to three competing forces.*

---

[3] Article published in *The Independent*, 6 January 2019.

[4] From The Economist, October 24, 2020: "Graduates of the world, unite".

more worryingly, the Asian recipe of economic success built on openness to trade and investment is being challenged by leaders like Donald Trump, who want to bring jobs back home and disrupt two of the key tenets of globalisation — to build where labour is cheap and plentiful (i.e. Asia) and that trade is good for the global economy. Let's examine these three issues in turn, drawing from scholarly sources as well as voices from the ground.

Middle-Class Muddle

It is said of the impact of technology that evidence about rising productivity can be found everywhere but in the statistics. Similarly, evidence about the growth, size, and impact of developing Asia's middle class can be found everywhere but in the statistics. On the face of it, the rise of the middle class should be one of developing Asia's truly remarkable achievements. Over five decades, the confluence of stable economic policy, a favourable global environment, and strong economic outcomes in theory should have lifted all boats. The reality is depressingly different, although the Asian hype machine offers some fanciful estimates about the absolute size of the middle class. The World Economic Forum in a 2014 report[5] noted that the explosion of Asia's middle class is "stunning." "The size of this group currently stands at 500 million and will mushroom to 1.75 billion by 2020 — more than a threefold increase in just seven years. The world has never seen anything like this before: it's probably one of the biggest seismic shifts in history."

Digging deeper into the actual statistics of the middle class in developing Asia can be a frustrating exercise. The Asian Development Bank (ADB) has chosen an absolute measure, defining the middle class as those people with consumption

> *Digging deeper into the actual statistics of the middle class in developing Asia can be a frustrating exercise.*

expenditure of between $2-$20 per person per day. ADB further breaks this

---

[5] World Economic Forum, "Outlook for the Global Agenda 2014".

down into various sub-categories — a lower middle class with consumption of $2-$4 per day, a middle middle class with $4-$10 per day, and an upper middle with $10-$20 per day. This consumption measure is imperfect but is a helpful guide, particularly given the hype elsewhere. To qualify as "middle middle" class under ADB assumptions, a middle-class family of four in Shanghai should have consumption expenditure of around $1,200 per month or $14,400 annually, assuming the median consumption level of $10 per day. Given the spectacular rise in incomes in China in recent years, it is easy to postulate that the size of the urban middle middle class in the country to be around 200 million,[6] which is expected to rise to around 300 million by 2022. In contrast a family in Mumbai, India, with similar levels of consumption as defined by the ADB will have to spend around 90,000 rupees monthly in local currency. This is a princely sum since the family in India, as elsewhere in the region, will be expected to have a significantly higher annual income of $14,400 to qualify as middle middle class. By this measure, the absolute size of the Indian middle middle class, concentrated in urban centres, will be no more than 75 million, or even lower in a country of around 1.5 billion people. A similar analysis for Indonesia, population 260 million, is likely to yield a modest middle middle class size of around 20-30 million.

Extrapolating ADB data further, John West of the Asian Century Institute[7] notes that the lower middle class with a consumption level of $2-4 per person per day constitutes the predominant share of the middle class for most developing countries in Asia. "In China, Indonesia, and the Philippines, the lower middle class is more than half of the total middle class, and only a few percent of the population are in the upper middle-class group. In India, the lion's share of the middle class is in the lower middle-class group," West writes. In total, Asia's lower middle class is where the policy attention should be focused since this group is most vulnerable.

---

[6] McKinsey defines China's middle class as anyone earning $9,000-$34,000 a year, a significantly higher income yardstick compared with the ADB.

[7] For an analysis of ADB data , see John West, "Asia's Middle Class", Asian Century Institute, 26 March 2014.

What happens when economic growth slows in developing Asia and social mobility stalls? Asia's vast group of the aspirational lower middle class, who are educating themselves in greater numbers than ever before, are bound to feel disillusioned when higher education does not translate into quality jobs and income. Let's call this the middle-class trap, very much like the middle-income trap faced by nations with percapita GDP in the $1,000-$12,000 range who fail to

Asia's vast group of the aspirational lower middle class, who are educating themselves in greater numbers than ever before, are bound to feel disillusioned when higher education does not translate into quality jobs and income.

make it to advanced nation status due to structural and competitive reasons. Within Asia, the notable list of middle-income nations includes China, India, Indonesia, Malaysia, the Philippines, and Thailand. Their advancement to high income status depends on greater innovation and productivity, also the ticket for the lower middle class to rise.

Social Mobility

There is disturbing evidence of a slowing in social mobility, particularly in South Asia but also in poorer parts of Southeast Asia, according to a landmark 2018 World Bank report[8] which looked at the issue globally. "If you are born into a low-income family, what are the chances that you will rise higher regardless of your background?" the report's authors ask. "The ability to move up the income ladder, both in one's lifetime and with respect to one's parents, matters for fighting poverty, reducing inequality, and even for boosting growth. Yet mobility has stalled in recent years in large parts of the world, with the prospects of too many people across the world still too closely tied to their parent's social status rather than their own potential." The report found that Africa and South Asia, the regions with most of the world's

---

[8] The World Bank, "Fair Progress? Economic Mobility across Generations Around the World", 9 May 2018.

In the Philippines, faster growth over the past decade is still not stopping a brain-drain of talent as qualified Filipinos emigrate to other parts of the world to work in lower-level service positions.

poorest people, have the average lowest mobility. East Asia, in contrast, showed tremendous progress (helped in large part by the rise of Japan and the Asian Tigers) with parts of the region (Southeast Asia) displaying South Asian characteristics of stalled mobility. Strip away the middle class in Japan and the Asian Tigers, and the rest of East Asia begins to look a lot like South Asia. In the Philippines, faster growth over the past decade is still not stopping a brain-drain of talent as qualified Filipinos emigrate to other parts of the world to work in lower-level service positions. In Indonesia, only the wealthy appear to have access to high-quality education and jobs and a majority of the population is doomed to work overseas in labour-intensive jobs or at home in the service economy or in government.

Two measures of economic mobility which World Bank researchers deployed are worth highlighting. First, absolute, which measures the share of people who exceed their parent's standard of living or educational attainment. Second, relative, which measures the extent to which a person's position in the economic scale is independent from his or her parent's position. To illustrate the first measure, that absolute social mobility was probably easier during an earlier era in Asia, let me once again cite my own example of growing up in a lower-middle class family in India of the 1960s and 1970s. My parents were of limited means, my father worked for a newspaper and my mother was a music teacher. My parents did not have a college degree and India's fabled Hindu rate of growth limited opportunities to their generation and indeed a large segment of the population.

While food shortages were rampant when I was growing up, what was available was access to quality private education in my hometown of

Secunderabad managed by India's network of Catholic and Protestant churches. The fees were higher compared with state schools and my parents no doubt struggled financially to keep my sisters and me in school. However, the education on offer was top-notch and was my window to the world. My hometown also had a network of excellent public libraries and reading rooms, where I was introduced to the pleasures of reading the classics as well as contemporary accounts of what was happening in the world at large, courtesy *Time*, *Newsweek*, and *Life* magazines. Today thanks to the ubiquitous smartphone, everyone in theory is able to access worldly insight from their handheld devices. But greater access does not necessarily translate into greater opportunities.

There is a stark difference of course in the incidence of poverty in India when I was growing up, over 55 percent of the population was living in poor, penurious conditions, compared with around 15-20 percent today. For India's lower middle class, education has always been regarded as a guaranteed ticket to economic opportunity and social mobility. My generation of Indians was fortunate in reaping the rewards as we came of age just as the economy accelerated in the early 1990s, opening up significantly more options compared with my parents and their peers. It is questionable whether the lower middle-class generation of today and tomorrow in developing Asia will be able to access similar opportunities, given that significant structural change is underway to the nature of work and the global economy itself. The solution is in smarter government investment in education and health and in incentivising life-long learning of the

> *It is questionable whether the lower middle-class generation of today and tomorrow in developing Asia will be able to access similar opportunities, given that significant structural change is underway to the nature of work and the global economy itself.*

population. The incoming workforce should also be better prepared to deal with unpredictability of employment and to be nimble in picking up a range of skills.

New Globalisation

As we learnt in Chapters 1 and 2, Asia's remarkable success over the past seven decades has been built on globalisation, trade, and investment. It was a virtuous economic and social cycle starting with sound economic policies, openness to trade and the world at large, and consistently higher investments in infrastructure, education, and health. Asia did not originate the concept of the global supply chain but countries and companies in the region certainly perfected it, making it possible for complex electronic parts to be manufactured in various locations and the finished product assembled at a final location to ensure quality assurance. But what if Asia's familiar pillars of success begin to crumble? Consulting firm BCG[9] warned in a 2017 report by Arindam Bhattacharya et al. that the global economy is currently undergoing a historic reset — and this time it is particularly disorienting for business leaders. "The twin forces of rising economic nationalism and the rapid adoption of digital technologies are radically redefining globalisation as we have long known it," the report said. "The global economy is decentralising in many ways as a result of growing protectionism, a decade-long stagnation in the growth of world trade and foreign direct investment, and the weakening role of multilateral institutions that set the rules and provided governance for much of the post-war era."

> *Asia did not originate the concept of the global supply chain but countries and companies in the region certainly perfected it*

---

[9] Arindam Bhattacharya, Vaishali Rastogi, Michael Tan, and Hans-Paul Bürkner, "How Asia Can Win in the New Global Era", (Boston Consulting Group, September 2017).

On Asia, BCG analysts caution that this new globalisation presents steep challenges. "As some of the greatest beneficiaries of globalisation, Asian economies have most at stake under the evolving new framework. Manufacturing will remain an important contributor to growth in Asia, but export-led economic models are now under pressure in most of the region," the report said, highlighting that in China, exports as a percentage of GDP[10] have declined from 37 percent in 2006 to less than 20 percent in 2016. In Indonesia, exports have dropped from 31 percent of GDP to 19 percent, and are projected to fall further to 11 percent by 2030. Two reasons for this secular decline in exports include: first, global trade has been stalling since the 2008 Global Financial Crisis, directly impacting Asia. Second, Asia's enormous manufacturing cost advantages have shrunk as wage growth has outpaced productivity. Much has been made by analysts of the growth in intra-Asian trade and its capacity to replace the shrinking share of the West in Asia's overall trade with the world. Indeed, latest data from the ADB shows that the share of Asia's intraregional trade share – measured by value – rose to 57.3 percent in 2016, a record high, up from an average of 55.9 percent from 2010 to 2015.

The rise of Asia's intraregional trade should ease concerns about the region's economic durability should global trade tensions worsen, and the region's traditional export markets become inaccessible. The devil, however, is in the trade statistics. Asia's impressive intraregional trade data is overwhelmingly driven by two factors: China's growing role as an importer of Asian commodities and as an exporter of mass consumer goods to the rest of the region. More significantly, we should look at the interconnected nature of the region's global supply chains. Malaysia and Singapore's exports of electronic components to China may show buoyancy in intra-regional trade data. However, the destination for these components is China, for the

---

[10] I am quoting BCG here although other data sources will yield different percentages.

final assembly of the iPhone and Samsung Galaxy — which are sold in traditional global markets obsessed with getting the latest models of the smartphone. Asian academics who bang on about the region's ability to replace America as the source of global demand are over-estimating the ability of Asian consumers to consume just like the average American consumer does. The jury is also out on the efficacy of RCEP and the CPTPP to reconfigure regional trade and demand, with many sceptics noting that ASEAN already enjoyed access to China's markets under the China–ASEAN FTA and the CPTPP without America will be less impactful.

> *Asian academics who bang on about the region's ability to replace America as the source of global demand are over-estimating the ability of Asian consumers to consume just like the average American consumer does.*

Gou and Li

To understand the future of global supply chains and their impact on Asia, we should look at two business groups which have mastered them. Our Exhibit A is Terry Gou, Chairman of Taiwan's Hon Hai Precision Group, or Foxconn as it is popularly known, is the world's largest assembler of Apple devices and reported revenues of $178 billion in 2019. It is China's largest private employer and indeed employs over 1.2 million people globally. Our Exhibit B is Hong Kong's Li & Fung, an $18 billion supply-chain manager for some of the world's biggest apparel brands and e-commerce sites. Li & Fung's principal owners are the Fung brothers, Victor and William, whose phenomenal rise over the past few decades mirrors the rise of Hong Kong and Asia itself. Both Foxconn and Li and Fung are facing headwinds due to trade tensions, rising costs in Asia, and pressure from shareholders to build a new business model.

In a tiny nation with larger-than-life political and business figures, Terry Gou stands tallest in Taiwan. He is a brash billionaire, not unlike the soon-to-be former resident of the White House, and even made a tentative attempt to run for President of Taiwan last year. A visit to the Foxconn website yields little insight about the

> *In a tiny nation with larger-than-life political and business figures, Terry Gou stands tallest in Taiwan.*

founder and the group beyond the usual corporate homilies: "Founded in 1974, Foxconn Technology Group has achieved remarkable international milestones under the leadership of Group Chairman Terry Gou," the website says. "Guided by the key growth strategy that hinges on 'time to market', 'time to volume', and 'time to money', the Group has pioneered a holistic digital solution….."

By the usual standards of corporate propaganda, Foxconn may actually be under-stating the group's global impact. Here is how the *Financial Times*[11] described Gou in a profile just before he announced his Presidential plans. "Yet disruption is Mr. Gou's specialty," the FT said. "The son of a policeman from the Chinese province of Shanxi who fought for the Kuomintang army in the Chinese civil war, his is a true rags-to-riches tale. Since starting out making plastic knobs for television sets in 1974, he has tirelessly expanded into game consoles, personal computers and smartphones, squeezing out sometimes formidable incumbents in these sectors."

To put it simply, there would be no Apple and its spectacular line-up of blockbuster products without Gou and Foxconn's prowess in manufacturing. Terry Gou and the late Steve Jobs make for an odd couple: there are similarities in their temperaments (mercurial, stubborn) as well as sharp differences (Jobs was focused on innovation at all costs while Gou's forte is superb delivery at sharply reduced prices). The two firms had worked closely since the 1990s, but the partnership deepened in 2000 after Foxconn landed

---

[11] Kathrin Hillie, "Terry Gou: Taiwan's Disrupter in Chief", *Financial Times*, 19 April 2019.

an order to produce Apple iMacs to exacting standards set by Jobs. Gou rose to the challenge and very soon Foxconn became an indispensable and some might even suggest inseparable Apple supplier. "When it came to the iPhone, Foxconn not only handled production and met tight deadlines but also played a crucial role in realising Apple's aesthetic vision," reports the *Nikkei Asian Review*.[12] "The contract manufacturer was able to seamlessly combine aluminium parts with frictional heat, and used a technique called anodization to process the surface of the metal. It is no exaggeration to say the success of the iPhone depended on Foxconn, and Foxconn's growth hinged on the iPhone." The article added that Apple manages inventories of core parts at Foxconn's warehouses in real time, and Apple employees are on hand at the supplier's factories at all times. In some ways, the companies have practically integrated their operations, although relations according to news reports have cooled somewhat of late.

The broader story here is that Terry Gou's remarkable success story tracks Asia's own growth trajectory since the early 1970s.

The broader story here is that Terry Gou's remarkable success story tracks Asia's own growth trajectory since the early 1970s. There are monuments all over Asia for former Kings and Queens, independence heroes, and other luminaries big and small. There isn't one for the global supply chain or even the humble shipping container, which positioned Asia at the centre of the modern commerce and the global economy. Asia's out-sized contribution to global trade, or dependence as detractors have it, would not have been possible without the growth and development of supply chains in the region.

If Terry Gou's success was built in the frontier areas of technology, our Exhibit B, Hong Kong-based Li & Fung have distinguished themselves in bringing

---

[12] Yuichiro Kanematsu, "Foxconn, Apple, and the partnership that changed the tech sector", *Nikkei Asian Review*, 13 July 2017.

technological best practice to frontier markets in Asia. If Terry Gou is brash and very Trump-like in his approach, the Fung brothers are urbane, sophisticated, and epitomise a *very* Hong Kong success story. I have seen Victor Fung up close for several decades at Davos and other forums, expounding on the merits of globalisation, and he remains an able

> *If Terry Gou's specialty is assembling smartphones, the Fung brothers have built their niche in focusing on Asia's attractiveness as a low-cost producer of consumer goods.*

advocate for HK and Asia. The Li & Fung website does a far better job in setting the historical context of the firm's founding in 1906 and its role today. "Li & Fung was founded against a backdrop of great change in China. Fung Pak-liu, an English teacher, and Li To-ming, a merchant, established Li & Fung and it was one of the first companies financed solely by Chinese capital to export to the West." From these humble beginnings, Li & Fung today operates one of the most extensive global supply chain networks in the world. "With 17000 people in more than 230 offices and distribution centres across 40 different markets, we use our extensive global reach, depth of experience, market knowledge, and technology to help brands and retailers respond quickly to evolving consumer and production trends." At last count, the company had a network of 15,000 suppliers in Asia and elsewhere who supplied products to 8,000 customers globally. If Terry Gou's specialty is assembling smartphones, the Fung brothers have built their niche in focusing on Asia's attractiveness as a low-cost producer of consumer goods.

How does this work in practice? In managing complex supply chains, Li & Fung play the role which Hong Kong has ably done during the decades when China was closed for business as well as since. Li & Fung is the trusted intermediary and go-to corporation for global retailers such as Walmart as well as storied stand-alone brands in high fashion, apparel, furniture, toys, and other consumer products. They make developing Asia accessible to the world. Li & Fung assumes the responsibility of dealing with thousands of suppliers in developing Asia, with differing and conflicting standards, and essentially put together the final product for sale to the world. In the parlance *du jour*, Li & Fung was a business platform long before the rise of online retail behemoths such as Amazon. This is the good news.

However, in one of Asia's most difficult markets, Bangladesh, Li & Fung and others have struggled to maintain acceptable labour and health standards. In November 2012 and April 2013, Bangladesh witnessed two devastating work-place tragedies — a fire at the Tazreen garment factory which killed 111 people, and the collapse of the Rana Plaza factory building which killed over 1,000 workers. Li & Fung, which was sourcing goods from Tazreen, and the global brands it supplied faced intense scrutiny for failing to enforce tough health and safety standards on suppliers. These concerns escalated after the Rana Plaza factory collapse less than six months later. "The Rana Plaza tragedy focused the world's attention on Bangladesh's garment industry, which has made women their family bread-winners and been an enormous life-line for many people," Human Rights Watch[13] said in a report on the fifth anniversary of the tragedy. "But these gains have often come at an enormous cost to workers. At the time of the tragedy, few workers received fair wages, fair and decent working conditions, the right to unionise without retribution, and – as Rana Plaza showed us – to have safe working conditions." It must be said that Li & Fung, in its public pronouncements, is saying that is has made considerable progress in strengthening worker conditions and safety since the Tazreen tragedy.

> *In November 2012 and April 2013, Bangladesh witnessed two devastating work-place tragedies — a fire at the Tazreen garment factory which killed 111 people, and the collapse of the Rana Plaza factory building which killed over 1,000 workers.*

---

[13] Tejshree Thapa, "Remember Rana Plaza:Bangladesh's Garment Workers Still Need Better Protection", Human Rights Watch, 24 April 2018.

This is the ultimate dilemma for anyone wanting to do business in fast-growing countries in developing Asia. How to balance the positive contribution of firms such as Li & Fung with a push to strengthen

> *Governments in developing Asia have higher levels of tolerance to international sanctions compared with their fellow citizens.*

working conditions and overall financial outcomes for workers. "The clothing industry in Bangladesh is second only to China's in size and employs four million people, mainly women, in approximately 3500 factories," *The Guardian* reported in April 2015. "Ready-made garments account for nearly four-fifths of the country's exports and contribute more than 10 percent of GDP of the developing South Asian nation." Bangladesh's garment industry is a driver of economic growth and opportunity. Cambodia and Sri Lanka are equally dependent on garment exports and the European Union (EU) has used its "everything but arms" tariff-free access regime as a lever to strengthen human rights in developing countries. Cambodia's garment factories employ over 700,000 people and 2019 exports amounted to over $6 billion. Strip away the tariff-free access to Cambodian exports, as the EU has threatened to do, and the impact will be borne by workers rather than the Hun Sen regime. Governments in developing Asia have higher levels of tolerance to international sanctions compared with their fellow citizens.

Bangladesh has also emerged as the favoured location for ship-breaking, an industry renowned for poor safety standards. The pressure point here comes from international and local NGOs, who place pressure on international banks (to withdraw funding to firms engaged in ship-breaking) to help enforce tougher safety standards. The NGOs favoured approach, to force banks and foreign companies to withdraw financial and business support to erring local suppliers, ends up hurting the workers most. The state, which should be the standard-setter and regulator, is remarkably absent in developing Asia in either introducing sensible worker and social protections or in enforcing them.

Rising Wages

To return to the theme of this chapter, living standards have certainly been lifted by developing Asia's emergence as a low-cost manufacturing hub for products such as textiles and shipbreaking. In Bangladesh, this has seen the genuine rise of the lower middle class, benefitting from the country's high economic growth and easy-to-find jobs in mass manufacturing sectors. For those in the lower rungs of the social class, like the Indian auto-rickshaw driver Pramod, a job in a textile factory would be regarded as a steady progression from his current status, which he describes as being like hell.

Overall, the International Labour Organisation (ILO),[14] no cheerleader of the corporate sector, attributes the growth of Asian supply chains due to innovations in information and communications technology, reduced trade costs, harmonised standards and liberalised services under multilateral trade pacts, and investments in infrastructure and logistics. This may appear to be an anodyne list until one reads the section on employment, wages, and competitiveness. Adding the usual caveats that measuring global supply chain (GSC) employment in Asia is statistically difficult,

> *Overall, the International Labour Organisation (ILO), no cheerleader of the corporate sector, attributes the growth of Asian supply chains due to innovations in information and communications technology*

ILO researchers note that for a number of countries in the region, GSC employment was higher than for other major trade economies such as Mexico and the United States. "Between 2006 and 2013, Asia-Pacific experienced a wage growth rate of 6.3 percent, which was substantially higher than the global average of 2 percent over the same period," the ILO says. "However, the region remains cost competitive, and, as more advanced economies transition to higher value-added production stages, still offers

---

[14] "Global Supply Chains in Asia and the Pacific and the Arab States", ILO report, 8 November 2016.

opportunities for outsourcing and FDI in less developed countries. For instance, in the electronics industry, wage growth in China, Malaysia, and Thailand is prompting firms to seek more cost competitive suppliers in the region, particularly in Vietnam and Indonesia."

The first part of the ILO assessment, on wage growth in Asia, at a phenomenal 6.3 percent between 2006 and 2013, is worth examining. This is an impressive pace by global standards and demonstrates how above-average wage growth and social mobility was, until recently, feasible in Asia. Although there are serious allegations about worker abuse and poor governance, it is an incontestable fact that supply chains have been good for Asia. What happens when global supply chains begin to fracture, as appears to be happening in the case of China's Huawei, and national security considerations begin to trump sensible economics? Is Asia prepared for a world when manufacturing is re-shored or because of innovations in AI, robotics, machine learning, and 3-D printing or future-tech as we will refer to them from now on? The ILO observation about the region remaining cost competitive pre-supposes that the status quo — of Asia's dominance in low and high-end manufacturing — will hold after the era of high wage growth. Nothing could be further from the truth.

Let us first examine the fracturing in supply chains. The scenario which I am outlining is not academic and is drawn from current geopolitical developments, i.e. the new Cold War between America and China over technological primacy. The American position can be summarised as follows. It supported China's accession to the World Trade Organisation (WTO) in the early 2000s in the mistaken belief that Beijing would use rising incomes, trade and investment integration as a lever to become more like America and Europe, i.e. greater political freedoms at home and an acceptance of the trans-Atlantic world order created at the end of World War II. Instead China hawks in Washington D.C. assert that China's leadership has used the opening up under WTO to consolidate political power at home, which it most certainly has, and nurtured the creation of national champions in technology to challenge the primacy of the West. More to the point, America accuses China of stealing technology and attributes thievery to explain the country's dominance in areas such as AI and 5G networks. The Chinese position of course is unremarkably at odds with the American point of view. Beijing's narrative is focused on China's economic rise after centuries of humiliation in the hands of the West. The country's dramatic economic growth in the last four decades, the leadership says, should be attributed to the skill and hard work of ordinary Chinese, not the benevolence of the West in opening up markets or in granting WTO accession. As globalisation has retreated in the West, President Xi Jinping has also emerged as a champion of free trade and the rules-based international order. As this Cold War accelerates, the future for Asian supply chains does appear bleak and as does the fate of millions of low- and middle-class Asians who have benefitted from it.

> *More to the point, America accuses China of stealing technology and attributes thievery to explain the country's dominance in areas such as AI and 5G networks.*

Here are two scenarios under which Asian supply chains could fracture. They are two sides of the same coin. First, American pressure on U.S. firms to sharply reduce technological exposure to China is already underway, via scaling back on supply chains, partnership agreements, and equity stakes. For example, the Trump administration's decision to insist on a forced sale of Tik Tok's American operations is a game-changer in mixing business with messy geopolitics. The supply chain model built on China as the final assembly point will increasingly be replaced by countries like Vietnam, regarded without irony as a close ally of the U.S. Indeed, there has been a recent surge in Vietnam's

> *The supply chain model built on China as the final assembly point will increasingly be replaced by countries like Vietnam, regarded without irony as a close ally of the U.S.*

trade surplus with the U.S., the proximate reason for America's anger towards China.

Brad Setser of the Council on Foreign Relations (CFR) said in a 2019 paper[15] that Vietnam can argue that its growing trade surplus with America was, in some sense, made in America. "The recent jump in its surplus (and the surplus of many other East Asian economies) is almost certainly the consequence of Trump's tariffs on China." He noted the contradiction that Vietnam is increasingly the final assembly point in the Asian electronics supply chain. "That, in a sense, does make Vietnam the new China," he writes. "The U.S. will naturally run a large bilateral deficit with the final point in the Asian supply chain, even if the bulk of the manufacturing value-added comes from elsewhere." The upshot of this is that America (and China as we will explore soon) is inserting toxic politics into Asia's supply chain, undermining one of the region's great economic success stories. For the sake of argument, should there be a deterioration in America's relations with Vietnam in the future, Washington D.C. could designate another country as the favoured location for final assembly, upending long-term plans of business and throwing thousands of people out of work. This is central planning masquerading as geopolitics and it is odd for America, the world's strongest advocate for free enterprise to be meddling in business decisions. This is not to minimise genuine national security considerations, but the trade tensions have taken a menacing, and some would say irreversible turn. America's new President is unlikely to change China trade policy much due to strong public support at home.

On the flip side, China is unlikely to behave any differently from America as it attempts to build its own sphere of influence in Asia via a parallel supply chain. Singapore Foreign Minister Vivian Balakrishnan told a Washington

---

[15] Brad W. Setser, "Vietnam Looks To Be Winning Trump's Trade War", Council on Foreign Relations, 27 May 2019.

D.C. audience[16] in May 2019 that Asian countries should not be forced to make choices in supporting China or the U.S. "And one point is that for us in the middle, and especially for smaller countries, we do not wish to be forced into making invidious choices," he said bluntly. Huawei, for example, is building an alternative operating system since new handsets can no longer be loaded with Google's Android. The operating system on a smartphone, as we well know, not only ensures the smooth functioning of the device but is underpinned by an entire ecosystem of apps, e-commerce options, and a payments backbone.

China today accounts for over 64 percent of e-commerce transactions across Asia — due to the phenomenal rise of the BAT companies (Baidu, Alibaba, Tencent) and their incredible hold over Chinese, and increasingly Asian users. If President Xi Jinping is committed to preserving the rules-based international order (which we explore later in the book), it should be a strong advocate for depoliticising Asian supply chains. In the real Cold War waged between the U.S. and the former USSR in the five decades after the end of World War II , the battle was waged for nuclear and territorial supremacy. It

> *China today accounts for over 64 percent of e-commerce transactions across Asia – due to the phenomenal rise of the BAT companies (Baidu, Alibaba, Tencent) and their incredible hold over Chinese, and increasingly Asian users.*

was hard to imagine then, for example, for American companies sourcing components from behind the Iron Curtain, so deep was the mutual hostility and suspicions. The America–China economic partnership, in contrast, has been built on four decades of mutually beneficial trade and investment bonds, with companies like Apple and Foxconn becoming deeply embedded in each other. Disentangling from this partnership will involve real pain and

---

[16] Vivian Balakrishnan, "Seeking Opportunities Amidst Disruption – A View from Singapore", CSIS Banyan Tree Leadership Forum, 15 May 2019.

the first casualty may well be the supply chain, jeopardising jobs and social stability across the region.

Rise of Future-Tech

Technological dystopians will shrug aside these concerns by pointing out that Asia's economic model is likely to face a much bigger shock from the rise of future-tech, which is the disruption to jobs from the rise of automation, robotics, and AI. The jury, I must say, is out on this topic and there are deep divisions within the technology and policy community on the actual impact. Let's divide this group into the idealists, who believe that the rise of future-tech holds tremendous promise for Asia and the downsides (mainly from job losses) can be managed through smart public policy interventions. The doomsayers, on the other side, fear that Asia's intense over-dependence on the world as a source of demand makes it vulnerable to sudden, swift changes to the global economy. The first casualty will be blue- and white-collar workers, placing tremendous strain on governments to build an alternative economic model to sustain growth and create quality jobs. The problem is not only with the existing workforce but the millions who will enter the job market well into the future.

> *Technological dystopians will shrug aside these concerns by pointing out that Asia's economic model is likely to face a much bigger shock from the rise of future-tech*

The Asian Business Council (ABC)[17] estimates that 85 million Indians came of age between 2014 and 2020, implying that the country should be ready to absorb 10-12 million new entrants into the labour force each year. However, job creation has lagged demand with only 38 million new jobs expected to be created between 2011 and 2018, which explains the great rush for jobs

---

[17] Janet Pau and Ryan Brooks, "The Future of Jobs in Developing Asia", Asian Business Council Spring Forum, February 2014.

in the Indian Railways which was highlighted earlier in the chapter. This is not an India phenomenon alone. In China, the government faces the twin challenge of finding quality jobs for the millions of new graduates entering the market, one of the signature successes in tertiary education anywhere in the world, and simultaneously dealing with a rapidly ageing population. In the Philippines, the primary source of job growth in recent years has been in services, specifically in business process outsourcing (BPO), as anyone calling for help with bank or credit card accounts will testify.

The Philippines is a BPO superpower, assuming India's mantle, and although the industry has created over 400,000 jobs it is still a tiny fraction of what the country needs in terms of limiting emigration of Filipino talent. Indonesia with a population of 260 million also has an unremarkable track record in creating jobs. "Indonesia's potential remains locked in the informal sector," the ABC report noted. "More than three out of five of Indonesia's workers are trapped in low-skill, low productivity, and informal jobs. Informal work, including agriculture, still employs about 70 percent of the 109-million strong workforce. As the country's economy shifts from informal agriculture to manufacturing, these workers are ill-equipped to take up new jobs."

In an ideal world where future-tech disruption happens at a more leisurely pace, Asian policymakers would have the luxury of time in reconfiguring economic models to deal with fracturing of supply chains and a shift in trading patterns. However, change in future-tech is happening at warp speed while Asia's political class, with a few notable exceptions, are firmly rooted in the analogue era. Given the deep, structural change underway in the global economy, Asia needs a younger more innovative political class which is capable of recognising that disruptive change is coming and are able to prepare their people with more skills and education training. The task of

> *The task of finding quality jobs for hundreds of millions of Asians in the future will be easier if policy interventions happen today.*

finding quality jobs for hundreds of millions of Asians in the future will be easier if policy interventions happen today.

MIT professor Erik Brynjolfsson, who has written several books on future-tech and is one of the world's leading authorities on the topic, offers a nuanced analysis on the future of work and precisely how much of time we humans have to prepare for the onslaught from future-tech. In a paper[18] prepared for the American Economic Association, he says that it is time to shift the conversation around AI and machine learning from threats of job replacement to opportunities for job redesign. "Our findings suggest that a shift is needed in the debate about the effects of AI: away from the common focus on full automation of entire jobs and pervasive occupational replacement toward the redesign of jobs and reengineering of business practices," says Brynjolfsson, adding that "despite what Hollywood is saying," the world is far away from artificial general intelligence. At the same time, he says that the world does have access to "powerful narrow AI systems" which are capable of solving certain, specific problems at human or super-human levels typically using deep neural networks. Translation – future-tech has the capability *today* of taking over many routine human tasks in the workplace.

Kai-fu Lee, technologist par excellence and the architect of China's world-beating AI program also brushes aside concerns about machines replacing humans. "That's just inaccurate," he said in a conversation with Edge.org in March 2018. "As advanced as today's AI is, and as much as it is doing a phenomenal job beating humans in playing games, speech recognition, face recognition, autonomous vehicles, industrial robots, it is going to be limited in the following ways. Today's AI, which we call weak AI, is an optimiser, based on lots of data in one domain that they learn to do one thing extremely well." Lee then went on to dismiss dystopian concerns to say that today's AI is a "very vertical, single task robot." ".... You cannot teach it many things.

---

[18] Erik Brynjolfsson, Tom Mitchell, and Daniel Rock, "What Can Machines Learn, and What Does It Mean for Occupations and the Economy?" American Economic Association *Papers and Proceedings* vol.108 (May 2018).

You cannot teach it multi-domain. You cannot teach it to have common sense. You cannot give it emotions. It has no self-awareness, and therefore no desire or even understanding of how to love or dominate a human being."

All of this is very encouraging with one major caveat. Both Brynjolfsson and Lee have described today's AI as being "powerful, narrow" in scope, capable of solving certain, specific problems (Brynjolffson) and "a very, vertical single task robot," which can learn to do one thing extremely well (Lee). Without over-statement, developing Asia today has hundreds of millions of surplus labour, many of them with little formal education or training, who are very adept at performing routine, labour-intensive tasks. What will happen to their dreams and aspirations when the machines take over? Let's meet Asia's urban cowboys...and cowgirls.

Chapter 6

Urban Cowboys...and Cowgirls

Our third circle of hell is about the hundreds of millions of
Asia's teeming under-class – men and women – who have
moved to cities in search of better economic prospects.... with
horrifying results.

L et's start with the fact that there would be no Asian miracle without the contributions of migrant workers, our urban cowboys and cowgirls.[1] They are the region's hidden population in the formal and informal sectors, labouring away in the construction, manufacturing, and service industries. Taken together they are around 700-million strong and would be Asia's third largest nation in terms of population if grouped together. A bulk of these are of course internal migrants in large countries like India, China, and Indonesia. In recent decades due to Asia's economic boom, there has also been a surge in temporary migrants from poorer to richer parts of Asia. They labour away with minimal rights and protections, but Asia's dynamism would not be possible without their contributions. Providing a social safety net for these workers, building saving and investment options in the formal financial sector, and protection for their overall health and safety,

---

[1] To clarify, I define urban cowboys and cowgirls in the Asian context as men and women who leave their families to work in a different city or country.

> *As a truly global humanitarian tragedy, Covid-19 has conclusively proven that the world we live in — with rising income inequality, poor worker protections, and wafer-thin social safety nets — is unsustainable.*

will be forced on Asia if the region does not come together to address this fairly.

As a truly global humanitarian tragedy, Covid-19 has conclusively proven that the world we live in — with rising income inequality, poor worker protections, and wafer-thin social safety nets — is unsustainable. This tragedy has been magnified in Asia due to the sheer size of the region's underclass. For a region which prides itself on superior technocratic governance, the mishandling of Covid-19 in many countries is a singular public policy failure of this generation. We have seen heart-wrenching scenes from India, where millions of migrant workers have been forced to return to the rural hinterland because the lockdown has destroyed their livelihoods. This is the 21st century version of the Long March and India's own Partition of 1947. In developed Singapore, authorities struggled to deal with the second wave of infections in worker dormitories, which the government acknowledges could have been handled better. In Indonesia, President Jokowi had to formally block the traditional exodus of the urban workforce to their homes in rural Java and other parts of the country during the Ramadan break. The Philippines, which has a disproportionate share of its workforce living overseas, has bungled in repatriating overseas foreign workers after they lost their jobs. The process has been slow and complicated by the fact that that the population of foreign workers is over 2.3 million. In Bangladesh, textile factories were shuttered due to the pandemic and over a million workers lost their jobs, prompting the government to announce a massive stimulus package. Some factories have reopened and jobs restored but workers are still worried about Covid-19 risks due to reduced wages and cramped working conditions.[2]

---

[2] Lauren Frayer, "For Bangladesh's Struggling Garment Workers, Hunger Is A Bigger Worry Than The Pandemic", National Public Radio, 5 June 2020.

The IMF[3] estimates that informal workers in the Asia-Pacific region account for nearly 60 percent of non-farm employment, higher than in Latin America and Eastern Europe, and ranging from around 20 percent in Japan to over 80 percent in Myanmar. The informality of their work arrangements makes them vulnerable to economic and health shocks, as Covid-19 has demonstrated. "Time is everything," the IMF warns. "Effective policy responses must reach informal workers and their families quickly to prevent them from falling (deeper) into poverty and to protect their livelihoods." During the pandemic, many governments have stepped up social spending to deal with the health and the humanitarian tragedy. These spending surges, however, are likely to be temporary, and will not add to the stock of primary healthcare clinics and hospital beds which the region needs to invest in urgently. Healthcare insurance for the poor is also a recent phenomenon in Asia with India, China, and the Philippines taking baby steps to provide a semblance of universal health coverage.

It is the urban cowboys and cowgirls who bear the brunt of state inaction. Asia's treatment of its workers brings to mind the early stages of England's Industrial Revolution in the 18th century, immortalised in fiction by Charles Dickens. I exaggerate somewhat but the following description[4] of

It is the urban cowboys and cowgirls who bear the brunt of state inaction. Asia's treatment of its workers brings to mind the early stages of England's Industrial Revolution in the 18th century, immortalised in fiction by Charles Dickens.

working conditions in England's factories is not out of place in many parts of Asia today: "Simply the working conditions were terrible during the Industrial Revolution. As factories were being built, businesses were in need for workers. With a long line of people willing to work, employers

---

[3] Era Dabla-Norris and Chanyong Rhee, "A 'New Deal' for Informal Workers in Asia", IMFBlog 30 April 2020.

[4] "The First Industrial Revolution", <weebly.com>.

could set wages as low as they wanted because people were willing to work as long as they got paid. People worked fourteen to sixteen hours a day for six days a week. However, a majority were unskilled workers working at approximately 10 cents an hour." Women and children were ubiquitous in factories although they were paid significantly less compared with men. England moved decisively in the 1820s to introduce work-place protection, setting regular work hours and prohibiting the employment of children under nine years of age. But these measures were not enough. It was the horrors of the Industrial Revolution-era workplace in England, and the suffering of men and women that inspired a young German philosopher Karl Marx to write *Das Kapital* in 1867. Communism may have been discredited and have gone out of fashion in Asia, even in nominally Marxist-Leninist countries like China and Vietnam, but in its treatment of urban cowboys and cowgirls, Asia is dangerously sowing the seeds for future social unrest and discord.

China's Dispatch Workers

I was standing outside Beijing's Great Hall of the People — waiting in line to get into a G20 business meeting. It was a bitterly cold January morning in 2016 and I stepped away from the queue to take a photograph of Tiananmen Square. I did not see the man holding corrugated boxes, who got in my way and knocked me down. A Chinese colleague came to my rescue and peppered the poor man with abuse in Mandarin. He was profusely apologetic. The worker's dress, traditional trousers and tunic, sun-baked face (mottled with redness) betrayed his origins. He was clearly not a Beijinger. As we returned to the queue, my colleague shrugged his shoulders and muttered "dispatch worker," as though this explained everything. In densely urban Beijing and other major metros, China's army of dispatch workers toil away in anonymity, with little protection in the manufacturing and service sectors. They are urban cowboys — estimated to range between 40 to 100 million[5]

---

[5] Official Chinese statistics on dispatch labour were last released in 2011, when the government estimated their size to be around 37 million.

— and hired by recruiting agencies whose forte is to marshal cheap labour from China's hinterland. These dispatch workers carry out a hierarchy of tasks — ranging from menial labour to factory worker — that no Beijing or Shanghai sophisticate will touch.

Although Chinese authorities have clamped down against poor labour practices in recent years, the lot of dispatch workers has barely improved. They cluster together in congested accommodation on the fringes of China's major metros, an invisible army of toilers who receive few benefits or credit for their contributions to China's economy. In a scathing report in 2018, the New York-based China Labour Watch (CLW)[6] skewered Amazon and its supply chain provider Foxconn for poor labour practices. "From August 2017 to April 2018, China Labour Watch dispatched several investigators into Hengyang Foxconn, a factory that predominantly manufactures products for Amazon," the report said. "The investigation revealed

Although Chinese authorities have clamped down against poor labour practices in recent years, the lot of dispatch workers has barely improved.

that dispatch workers made up more than 40 percent of the workforce, a clear violation of the legally mandated 10 percent. Furthermore, the working conditions between dispatch workers and regular workers were markedly different despite working the same positions." The CLW study revealed sharp disparities in other areas as well — dispatch workers were laid-off during the factory's lean season, did not receive social insurance and other social protection benefits, and their pay only amounted to $2 per hour, which is significantly lower than the $5 per hour which regular workers were eligible for.

CLW noted that the treatment of dispatch workers remains a key issue not only at Amazon and Foxconn, but also in factories across China. Although

---

[6] China Labor Watch, "Amazon Profits from Secretly Oppressing Its Supplier's Workers: An Investigative Report on Hengyang Foxconn", 10 June 2018.

China has significantly tightened legislation to protect the rights of dispatch workers, this seldom works in practice because the workers are recruited by a dispatch company whose commitment to worker rights is at best questionable. "With the dispatch company being contractually obligated to the worker, this allows factories to shirk responsibility for worker rights abuses," CLW concluded. "Amazon has the ability to not only ensure its supplier factories respect the right of workers but also that there is equal pay for equal work. Amazon's profits have come at the expense of workers who labour in appalling working conditions and have no choice but to work excessive overtime hours to sustain a livelihood." Both Amazon and Foxconn reacted to the CLW report by reaffirming their commitment to improving working conditions for dispatch workers. "We are carrying out a full investigation of the areas raised by that report, and if found to be true, immediate actions will be taken to bring the operations into compliance with our Code of Conduct," a Foxconn spokesperson told Reuters.

> *CLW noted that the treatment of dispatch workers remains a key issue not only at Amazon and Foxconn, but also in factories across China. Although China has significantly tightened legislation to protect the rights*

This raises the question on how much control a major corporation like Amazon can exercise over its primary supplier operating in a remote corner of China? In my last job, I was responsible for what the private sector vaguely describes as sustainability — which is a mixture of corporate do-goodery (via philanthropy) and a commitment to adhere to internationally agreed environmental and social norms, policies, principles, and best practice. The social element of the work is squarely focused on protecting worker rights, health and safety standards, and other social protections. This is serious work carried out by corporate environmental and social experts, who are responsible for validating if a particular company is putting its high prose and rhetoric on social purpose to practice in the workplace. The uncomfortable truth in Asia, as I discovered in China and across the region, is that companies are often in breach of environmental and social rules. They prefer to see the rules shaded in grey, open to interpretation, rather than in simple black and white. Corporate propaganda machines also whitewash bad environmental and social practices by promoting pithy slogans about their social purpose and impact. In one of the most egregious examples, grassroots NGOs discovered that a palm oil company required domestic and foreign plantation workers to surrender their identity documents for the duration of the contract, raising uncomfortable questions on whether they were indeed indentured labour. Supply chains, as we discussed in the previous chapter, are horribly complex and in many respects too big for a single corporation to manage. This is compounded by the fact that in developing Asia, the state is notoriously asleep at the wheel when it comes to protecting basic rights of workers in the formal and informal sector.

> *Corporate propaganda machines also whitewash bad environmental and social practices by promoting pithy slogans about their social purpose and impact.*

Social Justice

In an impassioned speech[7] before the International Labour Organisation's annual general assembly in 2019, Director-General Guy Ryder called on the world to have the confidence, common purpose, the will, and the means to construct a future of work with social justice for all. "We will do so because labour conditions with injustice, hardship, and privation do imperil the peace and the harmony of the world....And we will do it together because poverty anywhere is a danger to prosperity everywhere, and we will do it because the

---

[7] Opening Remarks by Guy Ryder, ILO Director-General, at the 108th Session of the International Labour Conference, Geneva, 10 June 2019.

failure of any nation to adopt humane conditions of work obstructs other nations which wish to do so." Guy Ryder and the ILO have their heart in the right place in pushing countries to allow workers to organise, for providing basic social protections, and overall to ensure that everyone benefits from a growing economy.

However, this well-intended rhetoric meets harsh reality when you encounter thousands upon thousands of urban cowgirls at Hong Kong's Central or Singapore's Orchard Road on Sunday mornings. This is a weekly routine that has not changed in decades. On their only day off, foreign domestic workers (FDWs) from the Philippines, India, Sri Lanka, Nepal, Bangladesh, Myanmar, Indonesia and other poor parts of developing Asia congregate in central Hong Kong and Singapore to socialise, shop, and transfer money home at extortionate rates.

Although their contributions are unheralded, the FDWs contributions to Asia's economic success in recent decades should not be a subject of debate. The presence of a domestic helper at home has enabled millions of Asian women and men to enter the workforce, secure in the knowledge that they don't have to carry out routine household chores, care for elderly parents, and even childcare. The stabilising presence of FDWs, among many other factors, has resulted in a sharp spike in female labour participation in the East Asian economy, helping bridge the chronic gender divide in this conservative region. The Singapore Government estimates that female labour force participation in the city-state was around 61 percent in 2019, with concentration in the prime working ages of 25 to 54 years old. In Hong Kong, the overall labour force participation rate for women rose at a more sedate pace to 45 percent in 2018, but the percentage is significantly higher (72 percent) for females in the prime working age of

> *Although their contributions are unheralded, the FDWs contributions to Asia's economic success in recent decades should not be a subject of debate.*

25-54, according to data from the Legislative Council Secretariat.[8] By way of comparison, the average female participation rate in advanced OECD countries is well over 70 percent (India's by comparison is an abysmal 27 percent).

"Women's participation is critical to meet the demand for skilled labour in emerging markets. Investing in women's employment is a win-win for all, strengthening both companies and community and changing the face of the global economy," noted Usha Rao-Monari (then Director of the Internationl Finance Corporation's Sustainable Business Advisory) as quoted in the Global Payroll Association report. What she says is laudable and incontestable but there is a section of the female workforce in the region who barely receive international attention. As an illustration, the number of foreign domestic workers in Hong Kong was estimated to be 370,000 and around 250,000 in Singapore. You are of course likely to see a significantly higher number of DWs in other parts of developing Asia who labour away under more adverse conditions. As two of the region's wealthy enclaves, my focus on Hong Kong and Singapore is to drive home the point that as developed jurisdictions, they could be regional standard setters in terms of providing decent work for FDWs and better social protections.

> *As two of the region's wealthy enclaves, my focus on Hong Kong and Singapore is to drive home the point that as developed jurisdictions, they could be regional standard setters in terms of providing decent work for FDWs and better social protections.*

Maid Abuse

Local media reports are full of horror stories about maid abuse. In February 2018, the *South China Morning Post* interviewed several FDWs who

---

[8] Legislative Council Secretariat, "Opportunities and Challenges facing maternal workforce in Hong-Kong", *Research Brief* no.2 July 2019.

recounted horrific work conditions. "While the law provides for helpers to have a day of rest every week — of a full 24 hours — Marcelino said employers rarely honour the obligation. Sometimes, they impose a curfew requiring helpers to return before a certain time on Sunday, their usual rest day, or assign jobs for the morning before they head out, she said." FDWs spoke about food options being limited and of being on call around the clock to deal with demands made by employers.

Singapore does not fare any better as the home pages of *The Straits Times* and other local outlets are littered with stories about horrific abuse. The most recent example (March 2019)[9] was of a Singaporean couple, who were convicted two years ago for abusing their Indonesian maid, to be back in court once again, this time for abusing an FDW from Myanmar. The details of abuse subjected by the couple were unveiled during the trial. "During the trial, the court heard that their maid, 31-year old Myanmar national, was slapped and caned," Channel News Asia reported "She slept fewer than six hours a day and ate mostly rice on its own or with sugar. When she complained that she did not have enough to eat, she was forced to eat rice and sugar, poured down her mouth through a funnel." There are other horrific details of the abuse subjected by the couple, but I will spare readers. In December 2018, local media[10] reminded Singaporeans of Ministry of Manpower requirements that "employers have to provide FDWs with three meals a day and these have to be enough for a female engaged in moderate activity." The Ministry went on to specify that the meals should include "four slices of bread with spread for breakfast, and rice, cooked vegetables, a palm-sized amount of meat, and fruit for lunch and dinner." The government's writ runs large in Singapore, as is well known, and prescriptive policies on how FDWs should be treated is a sign that this issue is being taken seriously.

---

[9] Lydia Lam, "Couple convicted of maid abuse found guilty of abusing another domestic helper", Channel News Asia, 4 March 2019.

[10] Fann Sim, "Domestic Workers Must be Given Enough to Eat When Employers are Away: MOM, NGOs", Channel News Asia, 11 December 2018.

The broader point is that if developed Asia is unable to improve working conditions for foreign domestic workers, developing Asia is likely to become even more brazen in the way it treats urban cowboys and cowgirls. In their defence, both HK and Singapore authorities have asserted that they are clamping down against abuse of FDWs and require all domestic employers to provide basic medical and social protection. This may well be true but the average monthly salary of a domestic worker in Singapore is around S$400, with the employer

> *The broader point is that if developed Asia is unable to improve working conditions for foreign domestic workers, developing Asia is likely to become even more brazen in the way it treats urban cowboys and cowgirls.*

required to pay an official monthly levy of a similar amount. While their monthly salary is significantly higher than what they can make at home, this is still a subsistence wage for foreign domestic workers. A majority of them remit a major portion of earnings to support families at home and have little savings at the end of their tenure. In the context of the current pandemic, the World Bank estimates that remittances to East and South Asia, which were around $250 billion in 2019, will fall sharply in 2020.

As it happens, they also pay outrageously high remittance fees, as the World Bank's migration and remittances expert Dilip Ratha pointed out in a recent blog.[11] Reducing remittance costs to 3 percent by 2030 is a global target under the UN's Sustainable Development Goals (SDGs), Ratha says, with the global average cost of sending $200 remaining excessively high at around 7 percent. "The high costs involved in money transfers along many remittance corridors, particularly for poor workers who lack adequate access to banking services, reduce the benefits of migration, particularly for poor households in origin countries," Ratha said.

---

[11] Dilip Ratha, "Remittances on track to become the largest source of external financing in developing countries", World Bank Blogs, 8 April 2019.

While the temporary nature of their work status in a foreign country is understandable, it is still unconscionable that foreign domestic workers are not offered some level of social or savings options in a rising Asia. The region is home to world-leading financial centres — banks and fin-tech start-ups could be encouraged to come up with innovative savings and remittance products custom-designed for FDWs and to drive financial inclusion. Overall, remittances are an extremely valuable source of foreign exchange for many countries in developing Asia — with India, the Philippines, and Indonesia being the largest beneficiaries due to outward migration by their citizens. So, developed and developing Asia have a shared interest in protecting the rights of urban cowboys and cowgirls.

> *While the temporary nature of their work status in a foreign country is understandable, it is still unconscionable that foreign domestic workers are not offered some level of social or savings options in a rising Asia.*

The international community is beginning to pay attention with the Global Slavery Index[12] featuring several Asian nations as offenders for FDW abuse. Across developing Asia, the story gets murkier as the Global Slavery Index report makes clear. "On any given day in 2016, an estimated 24.9 million men, women, and children were living in modern slavery in Asia and across the Pacific. The region has the second highest prevalence of modern slavery in the world with 6.1 per 1000 people," the report said. Disaggregating the findings, the overall region had a high prevalence of forced labour (4.0 per 1,000 people) compared with other regions. The Asia and Pacific region also had the highest number of victims across all forms of modern slavery, accounting for 73 percent of victims of forced sexual exploitation, 68 percent

---

[12] The Global Slavery Index, Asia and the Pacific, 2018. Listed in the top ten are Cambodia, Mongolia Myanmar, Brunei, Lao PDR. The ranking is based on estimated prevalence of modern slavery practices per 1,000 of the population.

of those forced to work by state authorities, 64 percent of those in forced labour exploitation, and 42 percent of all those in forced marriages.

Surge in Migration

It is useful to move away from the raw statistics and understand why there has been a surge in migration across developing Asia and the attendant rise in exploitation and forced labour. This does not square with the region's global image of being economically dynamic, politically pragmatic, and somewhat progressive on social issues. Away from the glitz and glamour of Asia's major metropolitan centres, there are hundreds of millions of poor people living in shanty towns with limited rights and limited opportunities. What brought them here and how does this play out from a social, moral, and political perspective? This is Asia's moral crisis and will increasingly become a political and social one too if not addressed.

> *Away from the glitz and glamour of Asia's major metropolitan centres, there are hundreds of millions of poor people living in shanty towns with limited rights and limited opportunities.*

Mumbai's grand old Victoria Terminus (now Indianized to Chhatrapati Shivaji Terminus or CST) is ground zero to understanding rural migration patterns into India's most vibrant metropolis. During India's crippling drought of 1987, my editor sent me to CST to speak with arriving rural migrants via long-distance trains from eastern, northern, and central India. The cliché of the time was that Mumbai received over a thousand rural migrants a day and sure enough I encountered many of them during my reporting over three decades ago. Theirs was a familiar tale of rural distress and despair, with a move opening up possibilities for economic betterment. In a matter of minutes after our brief conversation, Mumbai's new residents left the cavernous terminus and were swallowed up by the city.

Two macro forces are driving the rush of migrants from rural Asia to the major metropolitan centres — relentless urbanisation and the diminishing share of agriculture in the modern economy. The UN's Economic and Social Commission for Asia and the Pacific[13] reports that the region until recently was predominantly rural, but from 2018 there will be more people living in urban areas than rural areas. "The region is home to more than 2.1 billion urban residents, or 60 percent of the world's urban population," the ESCAP report said. "Between 1980 and 2010, the region's cities grew by more than 1 billion, and 1 billion further will be added again by 2040. By 2050, two thirds of the region's population will live in cities.

> *Two macro forces are driving the rush of migrants from rural Asia to the major metropolitan centres — relentless urbanisation and the diminishing share of agriculture in the modern economy.*

There is no historical precedent for an urban transition on such a massive scale (italics mine)." The breakneck expansion of urbanisation in Asia is manifesting itself into mega-cities bursting at the seams. ESCAP notes that in 2014, 17 of the world's 28 mega-cities (i.e. cities with a population of over 10 million) were in the Asia and the Pacific. It is projected that by 2030, the region will have 22 mega-cities. Not surprisingly, China and India lead by numbers in the mega-city race but other metros in Asia are also expanding at a manic pace in terms of population and population density.

Urban Sprawl

Boosters offer three reasons why urbanisation, if managed properly, delivers superior economic, political, and social outcomes. First, greater mechanisation and higher productivity in agriculture has created a pool of surplus rural labour across Asia, who could be more effectively deployed

---

[13] ESCAP, "Urbanisation and sustainable development in Asia and the Pacific: Linkages and policy implications", 7 May 2017.

in the mega-cities. Second, mega-cities provide scale — the concentration of talent, capital, and labour in urban agglomerations benefits the country at large. Beijing, Shanghai, Jakarta, Manila, Mumbai, and New Delhi are drivers of growth in their respective countries. Finally, mega-cities are more egalitarian compared with rural areas as migrants are able to overcome rural prejudices about ethnicity, caste, clan, and religion. Over time, this leads to better and equal economic and social outcomes. All of these arguments are reasonable with one caveat — in developing Asia, the mega-cities are increasingly becoming uninhabitable. City planning cannot keep pace with the growth in population and urban development. There are exceptions of course, sophisticated urban planning

> *There are exceptions of course, sophisticated urban planning and world-class infrastructure are transforming Beijing and Shanghai into China's version of Tokyo or Seoul.*

and world-class infrastructure are transforming Beijing and Shanghai into China's version of Tokyo or Seoul. Prospects for other Asian mega-cities are more dismal. What is driving them to the ground?

Let me offer Exhibits A and B — Jakarta and the Southern Indian city of Chennai. The Indonesian capital which has an estimated population of over 10 million has a dirty secret — it is sinking at an alarming pace, 8 feet over the past decade in north Jakarta alone and at an average 1-15 cm a year. Since half of the capital's land area is below sea level, the annual rainy season brings unprecedented flooding and a major portion of central Jakarta is under water, cutting off the business, financial, and political districts from the rest of the city. Indonesian policymakers have decided to move the capital to East Kalimantan, a process which has started in earnest. Bangkok and Ho Chi Minh City's subsidence issues are far worse than Jakarta: The Thai capital is sinking at a pace of 2 cm annually, with some areas already dangerously below sea level, and Vietnam's business capital is facing rising costs to building construction. Yet Thai and Vietnam authorities are bravely pushing ahead with expansion plans, oblivious to the risks from a changing climate.

Exhibit B is Chennai, which has the reverse of Jakarta's problem — it is running out of water. One of India's largest cities is facing the prospect of not having running water for its 10 million citizens as the reservoirs and ground water sources have run dry. The water shortages will recede if the city receives its annual quota of rainfall, which is increasingly unpredictable as we will discuss in Chapter 8. *The Hindu* newspaper quoted an analyst from the World Resources Institute blaming the water crisis on mismanagement[14] rather than just meteorological reasons. "Reservoirs should be regularly desilted; we need to create more storage areas by making use of existing ponds and tanks and creeks. We need to manage the water channels that bring water into these — instead, we have built over them, allowed construction over them." For those who can afford it, Chennai's water shortage can be mitigated by purchasing water from private sources which is delivered home via a tanker. For urban cowboys and cowgirls, who live in the city's teeming shantytowns (or slums as they are referred to), potable water is out of reach, increasing the risks to public health.

> *It has become fashionable to romanticise Asia's shantytowns. There are so-called "poverty tours", for example, of Mumbai's sprawling Dharavi slum by virtue of it being one of Asia's largest.*

It has become fashionable to romanticise Asia's shantytowns. There are so-called "poverty tours," for example, of Mumbai's sprawling Dharavi slum by virtue of it being one of Asia's largest. I have been to Dharavi several times and marvel, like everyone else, at the energy, enthusiasm, and entrepreneurship on display in its tiny lanes and by-lanes. It becomes less romantic of course to those who live in it, our urban

---

[14] K. Lakshmi, "Chennai's Day Zero: It's not just meteorology but mismanagement that's made the city run dry", The Hindu, 28 June 2019.

cowboys and cowgirls who have to negotiate access to basic services, are subjected to regular harassment and extortion by local authorities. Running water and modern sanitation are a luxury. This is where Pramod lives. Although country circumstances naturally vary, the shantytowns of New Delhi, Manila, Jakarta, Ho Chi Minh city, and Yangon have common characteristics — they are an abject failure of urban planning.

Given that mega-city managers are unable to limit urban sprawl, it is probably more viable for developing Asia to rebalance growth away from the metros and build newer mini-cities, perhaps closer to rural areas with incentives provided to small and medium enterprises, with a focus on food processing and low-end manufacturing. Economists and urban planners regard such thinking as heretical. Until the pandemic, it was an article of faith that big cities and urban agglomerations are more efficient, and egalitarian compared with smaller towns. This pre-supposes that all cities benefit from sensible urban planning, a la Singapore, and are able to

There are huge regional economic disparities across developing Asia, which best explains the pace and path of migration away from rural areas.

absorb the rush in terms of population and urban growth. Major Asian metros already account for a sizeable portion of their country's population. Urbanisation appears unstoppable — in the case of Thailand, the urban population is over 50 percent, the Philippines (47 percent), Vietnam (35 percent), China (59 percent), Bangladesh (37 percent), India (34 percent) and Indonesia (55 percent). Covid-19 will hopefully lead to a rethink in our obsession with mega-cities.

There are huge regional economic disparities across developing Asia, which best explains the pace and path of migration away from rural areas. In China's decrepit rust-belt provinces of the northeast, a hollowing out is underway as the government attempts to move populations further south where growth and economic opportunities abound. North Indian cow-belt provinces have marginal economic growth and galloping expansion in populations, leading to inevitable emigration to New Delhi or Mumbai from cities and villages. Given the sheer pressure faced by Asian megacity planners, a regionally balanced economic growth strategy, which will include the creation of new cities or economic zones away from the metros, is perhaps inevitable.

Starting from scratch has its virtues because policymakers can learn from past mistakes. At the same time, this will also require a major rethink of agriculture, which most political leaders are loath to touch, because of the social and political ramifications of meddling with land and farm reforms.

Farmer Distress

In the absence of a major policy rethink, we have to live with the distressing aspect that rural migration is irreversible and continues apace even today, thanks to increased rural distress. Indian citizens, unlike their Chinese counterparts, have the constitutional protection to live and work anywhere in the country. For rural migrants in India and elsewhere, moving to the megacity is an attractive alternative because of diminishing returns from agriculture. Nawab Ali, a former Deputy Director General at the Indian Council of Agricultural Research (ICAR) has written a fascinating research paper[15] which details structural changes to Indian agriculture. Ali's key data points are: agriculture remains an integral part of the socio-economic fabric of rural India as it sustains over 70 percent of rural households and provides employment to over 60 percent of the population. This is in stark contrast with China and Indonesia, where only 35 percent and 31 percent of the population are involved with agriculture. India also has 140 million farmers, of which around 80 percent are defined as small and marginal. The average farmer income is only 30-40 percent of the percapita income

---

[15] Nawab Ali, "Checking Rural Migration through Enhancing Farmer's Income and Improving Their Living Conditions", *Indian Farming* 68, no.01 (January 2018).

levels of their urban counterparts. Nawab Ali notes that Indian agriculture's profound challenge is in meeting food and nutritional requirements of the ever-increasing Indian population "that too under multiple constraints like depleting water resources, diversion of human capital from agriculture, shrinking farm size, soil degradation, indiscriminate, and imbalanced use of chemical inputs, and overreaching effects of changing climate."

While India is self-sufficient in agriculture, like China and unlike Indonesia, small-holder farmers and farm labour are in deep distress, which has tragically manifested itself in the rising number of suicides. There is an entire industry out there examining the origins and causes which force Indian farmers to committing suicide. The numbers first. According to the National Crime Records Bureau,[16] the 12,000 farmer suicides in 2015 were centred around relatively prosperous states

> *While India is self-sufficient in agriculture, like China and unlike Indonesia, small-holder farmers and farm labour are in deep distress, which has tragically manifested itself in the rising number of suicides.*

in western, central, and southern India, which is unsurprising given that they also happen to be the country's primary food producing regions. The cause of farmer suicides was varied: around 38 percent for bankruptcy, 19.5 percent for unspecified farming-related issues, 11.7 percent due to "family problems," and the balance under a generic others category. However, in the popular media narrative, two competing reasons have been offered for the sharp rise in farmer suicides in recent years — rising debt from loans taken by farmers in the informal sector and the Indian farmer's dependence on the annual monsoon rains, which have been erratic in recent years, leading to droughts and distress.

---

[16] National Crime Records Bureau, "Accidental Deaths and Suicides in India 2015".

> *Carleton adds that despite lack of substantiation, public debate in India has centred around one possible cause of rapidly rising suicide rates — increased variability of agriculture income.*

In a controversial paper published in 2017,[17] researcher Tamma Carleton claims that it is high temperatures rather than high debt alone which is the primary cause of farmer suicides in India. Pairing national suicide data from the National Crime Records Bureau with information on agricultural crop yields, Carleton says that fluctuations in climate, particularly temperature, significantly influence suicide rates. To be precise, for temperatures above 20 degrees C, a 1 degree C increase in a single day's temperature causes ~70 suicides on average. Summer temperatures in India's rural hinterland are of course much higher. "The effect occurs only during India's agriculture growing season, when heat also lowers crop yields," she writes. "I find no evidence that acclimatization, rising incomes, or other unobserved drivers of adaptation are occurring. I estimate that warming over the last 30 years is responsible for 59,300 suicides in India, accounting for 6.8 percent of the total upward trend. These results deliver large-scale quantitative evidence linking climate and agriculture income to self-harm in a developing country." Carleton adds that despite lack of substantiation, public debate in India has centred around one possible cause of rapidly rising suicide rates — increased variability of agriculture income.

"However, the relationship between economic shocks and suicide is controversial, and, in India, the effect of income-damaging climate variation on suicide rates is unknown. Although the national government has recently announced a $1.3 billion climate-based crop insurance scheme motivated as suicide prevention policy, evidence to support such an intervention is lacking," she concludes. Bloomberg reporter Shamika Ravi[18] also challenged

---

[17] Tamma A. Carleton, "Crop-damaging temperatures increase suicide rates in India", Proceedings of the National Academy of Sciences, 31 July 2017.

[18] Shamika Ravi, "Debt Isn't Killing India's Farmers", Bloomberg, 24 December 2018.

the farmer suicide narrative in December 2018, months after several Indian states announced fiscally crippling loan waivers to farmers. Her main thesis is that there has been a spike in farmer suicides in relatively affluent parts of rural India and 90 percent of farmers committing self-harm in the western state of Maharashtra, for example, were landowners who owned more than two acres of land. She argues that what policymakers need to realise is that India has no "single" rural economy and there are several complex reasons for farmer distress, including psychological.

If Carleton's and Ravi's theses are correct, many of India's urban cowboys and cowgirls are climate refugees, forced to migrate to Mumbai and overseas because of a sharp and consistent increase in ground temperatures and psychological distress. China's dispatch workers, on the other hand, are the country's "floating mass" of rural and semi-urban migrants who are drawn to the major urban centres because of readily available jobs. In Indonesia, internal migration patterns are more complex. Within Java and Sumatra, migration happens for reasons not very different from China and India, i.e. from rural areas into Jakarta, Surabaya, and Medan. In Eastern Indonesia, the mining and forestry industry are a huge draw for migrants from other parts of the country. In resource-rich Kalimantan, former President Suharto experimented with his controversial "transmigration policy" in the 1970s and 1980s, where Indonesians from Java, Sumatra, and elsewhere were forcibly sent to rebalance the country's population distribution. I have encountered Javanese migrants at Samarinda who felt as adrift as though they had moved to a foreign country.

> *If Carleton and Ravi's theses are correct, many of India's urban cowboys and cowgirls are climate refugees, forced to migrate to Mumbai and overseas because of a sharp and consistent increase in ground temperatures and psychological distress.*

Social Dislocation

While country circumstances for migration are understandably varied, Asia's urban-centred economic boom is the unifying factor in attracting talent and despair. Emma Lazarus' famous sonnet which sits on the pedestal at New York's Statue of Liberty feels ever-more relevant for Asia.

> *"…Give me your tired, your poor.*
> *Your huddled masses yearning to breathe free,*
> *The wretched refuse of your teeming shore.*
> *Send these, the homeless, tempest-tossed to me,*
> *I lift my lamp beside the golden door."*[19]

There are striking similarities between the new migrant arrivals into Ellis Island in New York during the early part of the 20th century, evidenced today in grainy photographs and paintings, and more recent arrivals from the long-distance train at Platform 1 of Mumbai's Chhatrapati Shivaji Terminus or in Singapore's Changi Airport. The most startling difference is that today's migrants tend to travel alone, leaving behind families, and their rich web of social connections back home. This is social dislocation on a massive scale. In Asia's booming cities, millions of single men and women labour away in construction, services, and manufacturing sectors. They work long hours, are housed in dormitories, eat in communal canteens, and literally run amok on their single day off.

> *The most startling difference is that today's migrants tend to travel alone, leaving behind families, and their rich web of social connections back home.*

Unmoored from family and friends at home, Asia's army of foreign and domestic workers, male and female, are isolated and lonely. The impact on their psychological well-being and the dislocation that they face from their

---

[19] Emma Lazarus, "The New Colossus" (1883).

families is little documented. One of the more tragic cases was the suicide in 2014 of a 24-year old Xu Lizhi, a Chinese migrant labourer working at Shenzhen. The 24-year old migrant was also a poet[20] and penned the following verse titled "On My Death Bed" (translated from Mandarin by Libcom.org) just before his death.

> *I want to touch the sky, feel that blueness so light,*
> *But I can't do any of this, so I'm leaving this world,*
> *I was fine when I came, and fine when I left.*

It is hard to imagine a poor migrant worker being a poet in today's Asia, all glitz and glamour, so insensitive we have become to the invisible army of workers who toil away in silence. That they also have psychological or health problems should not be a surprise. The *South China Morning Post* article cites a 2014 research study by Cheng Yu, a professor of public health in a Guangzhou University on the mental health of migrant workers in the context of globalisation. "The study found that 58.5 percent of those surveyed suffered from depression, 17 percent from anxiety, and 4.6 percent had considered suicide. Cheng and his colleagues interviewed 807 workers in the Shenzhen area, more than half of them under 30, and had in-depth conversations with 60 of them." In short, the work by Chen Yu is rigorous and public health institutions in other parts of Asia should do more social surveys of migrant labour. It is hard for me to imagine being away for a protracted period from family, friends, and network of social connections to work in an alien nation under difficult circumstances. Asia's hard-own economic gains in recent decades and more

It is hard to imagine a poor migrant worker being a poet in today's Asia, all glitz and glamour, so insensitive we have become to the invisible army of workers who toil away in silence.

---

[20] Lijia Zhang, "The grim reality of China's migrant factory workers", *South China Morning Post*, 26 December 2014.

recent official pledges of inclusive growth will ring somewhat hollow if it does not take care of its urban cowboys and cowgirls.

What about technological disruption, discussed in the previous chapter, particularly with AI expert Kai-fu Lee's assertion that what we have are "single task, vertical robots" that are proficient in carrying out simple, repetitive tasks. It is glaringly obvious that once automation begins to take hold, labour-intensive industries such as textiles, construction, and basic services, where most of our urban cowboys and cowgirls are currently employed will face disruption, as employers will be ever-more tempted to invest in technology and reduce its current dependence on labour.

The threat should of course not be over-stated, but two examples should provide sobering clues about how technology is shaping the workplace. In Japan, faced with a shortage in caregivers to tend for the country's burgeoning elderly population, the government is encouraging the use of home-care robots. This task has traditionally been carried out by human home-care nurses, many of them women from the Philippines. "With Japan's ageing society facing a predicted shortfall of 370,000 care-givers by 2025, the government wants to increase community acceptance of technology that could help fill the gap in the nursing workforce," *The Guardian* reported in February 2018. "Developers have focused their efforts on producing simple robotic devices that help frail residents out of their bed and into a wheelchair, or that can ease senior citizens into bathtubs." Only 8 percent of Japan's nursing homes have currently deployed robotics in caregiving, a figure which is bound to rise significantly as societal acceptance begins to take hold.

Our second example is from the construction industry, where companies are experimenting with greater use of robotics, drones, unmanned bulldozers and dump trucks, with the sequence of tasks being simultaneously operated by a technically proficient person rather than by hundreds of workers. Asia's obsession with building new cities, real estate, and manufacturing sites has been on the back of millions of cheap labourers. Once automation gains critical mass, policymakers will have to wrestle with the prospect of mass unemployment of young urban cowboys and cowgirls. Who can blame Singapore authorities for example, from wanting greater automation in the city-state construction sites after the Covid-19 pandemic?

Technological disruption does not necessarily mean dystopian outcomes. Developing Asia, irrespective of political systems, will require a new social compact between governments and citizens. It is refreshing to see greater discussion on the provision of a universal basic income (UBI) and cash transfers due to the pandemic, although the fiscal costs are likely to be crippling. There is a need for greater investments in vocational training, and in preparing the young generation for a technology-intensive future that holds perils as well as potential. The private sector in the form of Asia's home-grown billionaires and entrepreneurs

> *Technological disruption does not necessarily mean dystopian outcomes. Developing Asia, irrespective of political systems, will require a new social compact between governments and citizens.*

have a huge role to play in this transition. They could partner with governments in skills development, in planning for the future of work, and devote their considerable resources to help urban cowboys and cowgirls. Regrettably, the primary obsession of Asia's billionaire class appears to be wealth accumulation at all costs. We will deal next with the rent extractors and other oligarchs.

Chapter 7

Rent Extractors and Other Oligarchs

Our fourth circle of hell is the power and influence of Asia's billionaire class and their negative impact on inequality, public policy, environmental and social protection, and corporate governance.

Credit should be given where credit is due. Asia's billionaire class (or ABCs for short) have contributed to and benefitted from the rise of Asia over the last seven decades. Some would say disproportionately benefitted but we will get to that shortly. Asia's economic miracle — from dirt-poor and aid-dependent to the glitzy, prosperous region on display today — manifests itself most dramatically with the swagger of the ABCs. A majority of them are male, itself reflective of the region's deeply patriarchal attitudes, and their calling card is designer suits, Bentley cars, private jets, helicopter rides atop congested cities, hyper-expensive birthday celebrations and weddings, and a publicity machine which airbrushes their reputation from any hint of negative news.

If America had its gilded age in the 1920s, most memorably captured by F. Scott Fitzgerald in *The Great Gatsby*, the ABCs are the 21st century version of that era, as seen in *Crazy Rich Asians*. The shadowy characters portrayed in the Fitzgerald classic would not be out of place in contemporary Asia. In Chapter 3, we had highlighted the fact that *Forbes* magazine's annual ranking of billionaires listed Asia with the largest number of billionaires (at 778), far above Europe and America. Between China and India alone, you have a stunning 558 billionaires. At Davos, ground-zero every January for plutocrats of all stripes, I have seen ABCs growl and grumble at the lack of "modern" conveniences in the Swiss resort town. Fed up with the poor hotels on offer, a South Asian tycoon told me in January 2017 that he had decided to buy a Swiss chalet and fit it with "Singapore-style" fittings and conveniences. Such are the travails that the ABCs have to go through a few days in a year at Davos, compared with the year-around troubles faced by our urban cowboys and cowgirls.

Another visible phenomenon, evident amongst Indian, Chinese, and Indonesian tycoons, are elaborate mansions and multi-day, multi-million-dollar birthday and wedding celebrations for kith and kin. The *piece de resistance* of ABC excess is surely Indian billionaire Mukesh Ambani's estimated $2 billion residence in south Mumbai. Designed by architects Perkins and Will, Antilia (as the residence is called) has 27 floors, 600 staff, a ballroom, three swimming pools, and houses the small Ambani clan of five. The building is also an eye-sore, soaring

> Another visible phenomenon, evident amongst Indian, Chinese, and Indonesian tycoons, are elaborate mansions and multi-day, multi-million-dollar birthday and wedding celebrations for kith and kin.

over south Bombay's more elegant buildings housing the city's *ancien regime*, seeming to challenge them by drawing vulgar attention to itself.[1] I used to cover the Ambani's and their Reliance empire in the 1980s and met with Mukesh's father, the inimitable Dhirubhai Ambani, several times. As a first-

---

[1] For fascinating insights into India's billionaire class, I would recommend James Crabtree's *The Billionaire Raj: A Journey through India's New Gilded Cage* (Tim Duggan Books, 2018) which explores their rise in detail.

generation tycoon, he was more certainly austere than his son, indicating that an earlier generation of business leaders in Asia were less interested in the lifestyle and trappings of being crazy rich. In his business, Mukesh Ambani has proven himself to be as astute as his father demonstrated by the rise of Jio Platforms as a mobile network, social media and e-commerce powerhouse, attracting investments from Facebook and Google. I make this point that it is possible to admire business acumen and simultaneously be horrified by lifestyle excesses.

To return to Dante's *Inferno*, what would best describe the behaviours of *some* of our ABCs, those in particular involved in extracting rents? My list includes greed, gluttony, and fraud. Strong words? Not if you consider the mounting evidence from the region that ABCs, in malign partnership with Asia's political class, are subverting public policy. There is lack of transparency and accountability in the awarding of major infrastructure projects, and the state is playing favourites by picking winners (and losers) in the business community. One should of course not malign all of our ABCs and there are several from the older and present generation who deserve praise for pursuing the straight

> *Many of Asia's newer billionaires have risen without family connections in businesses and in frontier areas like software, e-commerce, and payments.*

and narrow path. Many of Asia's newer billionaires have risen without family connections in businesses and in frontier areas like software, e-commerce, and payments. They are true disrupters by challenging legacy businesses, staying away from politics, and are able to push ahead without regulatory overreach. Unfortunately, this group is in a minority.

In the Philippines, President Rodrigo Duterte adopted a Putin-like approach[2] when he assumed office in 2016 by railing against local tycoons, particularly

---

[2] When he assumed office in 2000, Russian President Putin famously invited the country's oligarchs to a meeting where he offered to protect their interests in exchange for which the tycoons had to stay away from politics and unconditionally support him.

those with media interests. "The plan is to destroy the oligarchs embedded in the government," he said.[3] "I'll give you an example publicly: Ongpin, Roberto." His first target was tycoon Roberto Ongpin, who had to resign as Chair of his listed gambling company because of Presidential pressure. Rather than take a principled stand against all tycoons, analysts say that President Duterte has merely replaced Manila's business elite with scrubbier business associates from his home state of Mindanao.

The key difference differentiator of the Asian model of capitalism is that the state in Asia is judge, jury, business partner, and competitor. Defining and protecting the public interest becomes a challenge when the interests of the political class and the ABCs are aligned, often at the expense of the rest of the population. At a time of de-globalisation, stalled social mobility, and rising inequality in developing Asia, there is every reason to worry about the ABCs growing tentacles and the role of the state as an enabler.

Western Capitalism

I am not in any way placing Western capitalism on a pedestal that has been discredited since the Global Financial Crisis (GFC)and is going through its own pressures and challenges. The crisis in the West has its origins in the acceleration of globalisation in the early 1990s, which led to a sharp reduction in manufacturing employment, and what some analysts describe as the "financialisation" of the global economy (which lead to the GFC of 2008). The target of anti-capitalists in the West are not just

> *I am not in any way placing Western capitalism on a pedestal that has been discredited since the Global Financial Crisis (GFC)and is going through its own pressures and challenges.*

---

[3] Aurora Almendral, "Crony Capital: How Duterte embraced the oligarchs", *Nikkei Asia Weekly*, 4 December 2019.

billionaires but the entire ecosystem of capitalism with bankers, lawyers, accountants, and technologists receiving special mention.

In the UK, the Archbishop of Canterbury, representing England's Anglican Church, told the *Financial Times*[4] that the country is facing a "crisis of capitalism," citing excessive executive pay and unrepentant bankers as symptoms of a system that was teetering on the precipice. "Things could go very seriously wrong," the Archbishop said. "It can turn very, very strongly against business. So, you can get a snap back of the elastic, which is not good for business or society, because it's a revenge regulation." Archbishop Welby's biggest concern is that finance, the flagship sector of the UK economy which had caused the GFC, leading to expensive bank-bailouts by the state and an economic decline, was not reforming fast enough. Having spent the better part of the decade working in London's financial sector, I certainly recognise the source of public anger about self-entitled bankers and the fact that by imposing austerity since 2010, a sharp cutback in spending by

> *One of my best memories of the Brexit campaign was visiting the JD Wetherspoon chain of pubs, run by a pro-Brexit businessman, who repurposed beer mats with pithy slogans against the elite.*

successive Conservative governments had caused real damage to the fabric of society. Critics are right in pointing out the wilful contradiction in the UK authorities justification of bailing out several UK banks at the height of the financial crisis in 2008 and simultaneously imposing severe cuts in social spending, just as economic conditions started to improve in 2010. For ordinary Britons, it reinforced the perception about the elite protecting the elite and they had their revenge with the Brexit vote in 2016. One of my best memories of the Brexit campaign was visiting the JD Wetherspoon chain

---

[4] George Parker, "UK facing 'crisis of capitalism', says Archbishop of Canterbury", *Financial Times*, 8 September 2018.

of pubs, run by a pro-Brexit businessman, who repurposed beer mats with pithy slogans against the elite. One of the mats had a series of challenging questions for Christine Lagarde, the then Managing Director of the IMF, who had come out in support of the UK Government's position of remaining in the European Union. As the business community and several billionaires weighed in with similar calls, politician Michael Gove spoke for many voters by declaring that people are "fed up" with experts.

Over in America, ground zero of the 2008 GFC, the backlash against capitalism has most visibly manifested itself in the rise of Donald Trump and his populist, nativist brand of politics. The American ideals of free trade, free enterprise, and capitalism are under attack because President Trump portrayed America's global engagement as a sign of weakness. While the wrath of the UK public has largely been directed at the political class and bankers, public anger in America is directed at a much wider group of coastal, globalised elites. The billionaire class has come under special scrutiny with one caveat. Ordinary Americans don't see a contradiction in supporting a billionaire like Trump to become President (who has staffed his cabinet with several multi-millionaires and billionaires) and agreeing with the President's straight-faced assessment that liberal elites and other billionaires don't have the country's best interests at heart.

American writer Anand Giridharadas has written a terrific, provocative book,[5] which has triggered sharp debate about the role and contributions of the billionaire class. While I don't agree with some of the assertions made by Giridharadas, his serious analysis is worth considering because it has implications for Asia. He starts with a fundamental challenge to the proposition that the seriously wealthy in our societies are a force for good. Here is a short summary of what he said in a recent podcast. "Why, Giridharadas asked, should the world's problems be solved by an unelected elite who dodge taxes and lobby governments to entrench their own power,

---

[5] Anand Giridharadas, *Winners Take All: The Elite Charade of Changing the World* (Knopf, 2018).

rather than by public institutions supported by the taxpayer? And what needs to be done to make our institutions more robust and democratic so that they can take on the gruelling task of truly changing the world."[6] This is the frequent assertion made by the author and he is being heard, much to the discomfort of America's billionaire class. In April 2019, Giridharadas took on billionaire Ray Dalio, the founder of hedge fund Bridgewater Associates, who had recently commented on the need for the rich to pay more taxes and how capitalism should be reformed, all sensible proposals I should add. Here are Giridharadas' quotes[7] in full at a public event: "What Ray Dalio needs to understand, which members of his class so often struggle to understand, is that the reason his class has too much money is because it also has too much power. Power in Washington. Power in an under-taxed, under-regulated economy. Power exerted through big philanthropy. Power lubricated by a cultural narrative that deifies wealth and marginalises democratic solutions."

America's mainstream business media have attempted to portray Giridharadas as an extremist who is calling for the dismantling of the capitalist system in favour of communism and socialism. The author is calling for no such thing, as will become evident for anyone who has bothered to read the book. He vividly describes the symbiotic relationship between big business and the political class, which is often at the expense of the general public. Where I agree with Giridharadas is his assertion that the billionaire class, our ABCs included, have become too powerful and are subverting public policy. Where I disagree with him is the broad-brush nature of his attacks on the billionaire class: not all billionaires are evil, as

> *America's mainstream business media have attempted to portray Giridharadas as an extremist who is calling for the dismantling of the capitalist system in favour of communism and socialism.*

---

[6] Summary of Intelligence Squared podcast with Anand Giridharadas.

[7] *Business Insider*, 8 April 2019.

I noted before, and by extension to entrepreneurship which every country needs in large numbers. "You want businesses to want to innovate and have the ability to become monopolies," said Makan Delrahim Assistant Attorney General in the U.S. Department of Justice's powerful anti-trust division in 2018. "Being big should never be bad under anti-trust law or policy. Being big behaving badly should be bad." Yet the line dividing brute monopoly power and bad behaviour is becoming ever more blurred in America today.

My own observations about American capitalism, having witnessed it first-hand, is both the rapacious, monopolistic nature of big business as well its more competitive side. The competitive side first. There are huge swathes of American business that are hyper-competitive and animal spirits prevail — automobiles, small business, retail, technology hardware come to mind. There are tangible benefits to the consumer from greater competition — in terms of product innovation and pricing. Unlike developing Asia, America has strong institutions — the SEC, Department of Justice and the Federal Reserve, an independent judiciary — and checks and balances which, at least in theory, regulate and limit the power and reach of big corporations. However, the last major anti-trust action taken by the U.S. authorities against Big Business was Microsoft all the way back in 1999. Since that landmark ruling, U.S. business monopolies have only grown in size and influence, regardless of whether a Republican or a Democrat is in the White House. The competitive nature of American business is being particularly undermined by the dramatic increase in business funding of political candidates, via political action committees, who operate in the shadows and the insidious influence of corporate lobbying.

> *My own observations about American capitalism, having witnessed it first-hand, is both the rapacious, monopolistic nature of big business as well its more competitive side.*

Rent-Seeking in America

The rent-seeking side of American business, not surprisingly, dominates the landscape. In my suburban neighbourhood in Maryland, there used to be multiple coffee chain choices over a decade ago. Today there is mainly one — Starbucks, adding to the list of industries in America where customer choice is extremely limited. The price of a regular latte in a Starbucks in Washington D.C. is at least 50 percent higher compared with a similar brew in London, where rents are even more expensive but intense competition amongst coffee chains keeps retail prices under check.

It is not at all surprising that Starbucks founder Howard Schultz, buoyed by his company's dominance of the coffee market, made a failed attempt to run for the Presidency in 2019. The reception he received was universally hostile and he hastily backed away. Starbucks is not the only culprit. Similarly, American consumers pay some of the highest broadband rates in the world — in my neighbourhood the choice is down to two giant providers whose service is indifferent and rates extortionate.

> *The price of a regular latte in a Starbucks in Washington D.C. is at least 50 percent higher compared with a similar brew in London, where rents are even more expensive but intense competition amongst coffee chains keeps retail prices under check.*

The American airline industry, deregulated with fanfare in 1976, has become a tussle between three oligopolies, Delta, American and United, with several nimbler airlines like Southwest thriving on purely domestic routes. Compared with sleeker Asian and Gulf rivals, who upgrade their fleet at regular intervals and are fiercely competitive on long-haul routes, American airlines have little incentive to modernise or to focus on customer satisfaction. They still ply their ancient Boeing 757 and 767 aircraft and air fares are prohibitively expensive.

> *Given these examples, why shouldn't ordinary Americans turn against big business and question the merits of globalisation. The decline of competition appears to be endemic in America.*

My final, favourite example about American monopolies comes from electricity provider Pepco, which is responsible for generating and distributing power in the Maryland and Washington D.C. area. Pepco is quite possibly the worst utility in the developed world with its signature inability to deal with power outages, a frequent occurrence in the D.C. area because ancient electricity cables are above ground and prone to frequent outages due to summer and winter storms. *Business Insider* rated Pepco in 2012 as the "most hated company in America" and a 2010 *Washington Post* series found: "In reliability studies, the company ranks near the bottom in keeping the power on and bringing it back once it goes out."[8] Given these examples, why shouldn't ordinary Americans turn against big business and question the merits of globalisation. The decline of competition appears to be endemic in America.

Rana Foroohar, a columnist at the *Financial Times*, traces the economic ills of American capitalism to financialisation: "It's a term for the trend by which Wall Street and its ways of thinking have come to reign supreme in America, permeating not just Wall Street but all American business,"[9] she writes. "It includes everything from the growth in size and scope of finance and financial activity in our economy to rise of debt-fuelled speculation over productive lending, to the ascendancy of shareholder value as a model for corporate governance, to the proliferation of selfish thinking in both our private and public sectors, to the increasing political power of financiers and the chief executives they enrich." Harsh words indeed and Rana Foroohar is

---

[8] I have drawn the quotes from an article in *The Atlantic* monthly, July 2012.

[9] Rana Foroohar has written an interesting book titled *Makers and Takers: The Rise of Finance and the Fall of American Business* (Crown Business, 2016). This quote is taken from an excerpt of the book which appeared in *The Guardian* on 21 May 2016.

hardly a fire-breathing, leftist radical. She is a liberal and is clearly outraged with the status quo, arguing that we need to rewrite the rules of capitalism and create a more inclusive, sustainable society.

Chaebolisation of Asia

Which brings us back to ABCs and the nature of capitalism in Asia, which is also not functioning for the greater good of society. Is there a defining Asian model which could perhaps explain the region's phenomenal success these past few decades and the distortions? Asia has a hybrid model of capitalism where the state has not fully vacated business and business has not fully weaned itself off its dependence on the state. Both the state and the private sector feed-off each other, often to the detriment of the general public. There is the pure state-lead capitalism in nominally Communist countries like China and Vietnam where state-owned enterprises and banks dominate and co-exist with a nascent private sector. In China today, the private sector's share of GDP has risen phenomenally and is larger than the state sector. However, purely private firms such as Baidu, Alibaba and Tencent exist (BAT in the terminology) on the benevolence of the state and cannot defy the dictates of the government, like their counterparts in Silicon Valley often do. In democratic countries like India and Indonesia, state-owned sector enterprises dominate in specific sectors (finance, civil aviation) allowing the private sector to thrive in other segments of the economy. Singapore and Hong Kong offer striking contrasts in their approach toward the private sector. Hong Kong is pure *laissez-faire* with foreign and local firms dominating the economy. Singapore, on the other hand, has a vast number of government-linked companies (GLCs), not fully public or private, which in the eyes of the critics provide little space for smaller private sector rivals to flourish.

Asian capitalists often look to Korea for inspiration, where a uniquely Korean model has evolved and has remained unchallenged.

In short, Asian capitalism has many different strands and is fundamentally different from the more developed American model. Asian capitalists often look to Korea for inspiration, where a uniquely Korean model has evolved and has remained unchallenged.

The rise and rise of the Korean *chaebol* provides a fascinating case study in understanding the methods, temperament, and strategy of ABCs today. This is because if there is one group of tycoons who are held in awe and high esteem across Asia, it is most certainly the *chaebol*. Japanese firms, including Sony and the mighty *sogo sosha* are also well-regarded but their methods of accumulating power and influence are seen as being specifically *Japanese*, i.e. not easily replicated elsewhere. On the other hand, the Korean *chaebol* are regarded as the masters of the universe, with a small group of privileged, well-heeled tycoons who have consistently stayed on top for the last six decades regardless of the political grouping in power. Asian capitalism is increasingly being *chaebolised*.

"The story of South Korea's transformation from economic minnow to the world's fifth largest exporter owes much to its sprawling family-run conglomerates," Bloomberg reporter Peter Pae[10] writes. "Known as *chaebol*, these long-time pillars of the nation's 'miracle economy' include the likes of LG, Hyundai, SK, Lotte and – largest of them all – Samsung." Pae notes that the *chaebol's* out-sized influence and cosy relationship with government, highlighted by an influence-peddling scandal that cost the country's President (Park Geun-hye, who resigned in disgrace in 2017) and top Samsung executives their jobs, have cast an intense spotlight on the conglomerates at the same time as many are navigating generational transitions. In November 2018, over 150,000 workers representing Korea's powerful trade unions went on strike in what they described as Seoul's lack of progress in reforming the *chaebol*. "For the workers — represented by the powerful Korean Confederation of Trade Unions (KCTU) — (President)

---

[10] Peter Pae, "South Korea's Chaebol", Bloomberg QuickTake, updated 29 August 2019.

Moon has not done enough to wean the nation off its reliance on a handful of industrial conglomerates, such as Samsung and Hyundai," the *Financial Times* reported.[11] "The President, they argue, has also failed to reform the corporate governance of these groups, which is often characterised by murky cross-holdings and intragroup deals."

The Korean FairTrade Commission (FTC) reports that there are now 45 conglomerates in Korea that fit the definition of *chaebol*. The top ten *chaebol* own more than 27 percent of all business assets in the country, a phenomenal number given that Korea is an advanced OECD economy. Worse, the top five *chaebol* dominate over half of the market capitalisation of Korea's Kospi Index. This is incredible concentration of wealth in a few hands, which has triggered a backlash in Korea. "Ordinary South Koreans are also increasingly questioning the consolidation of wealth among a handful of families and the stifling effect they've had on small business and start-ups," according to the Bloomberg report. The Chairman of the FTC was also quoted as saying that people are "no longer prepared to turn a blind eye" to illegal and improper relationships between government and business.

> *The Korean FairTrade Commission (FTC) reports that there are now 45 conglomerates in Korea that fit the definition of* chaebol.

It is useful to look at the rise of one particular Korean conglomerate, Hyundai, to understand the *chaebolisation* of the Korean economy, and the lessons which can be drawn for the rest of Asia today. Today one company in the Hyundai stable alone, Hyundai Motors, is a colossus with 2019 revenues of $90 billion and is the world's third largest automobile producer after Japan's Toyota and Germany's Volkswagen. How did it get to pole position?

---

[11] Bryan Harris & Song Jung-a, "South Korea hit by strikes over lack of chaebol reform", *Financial Times*, 21 November 2018.

It is useful to look at the rise of one particular Korean conglomerate, Hyundai, to understand the chaebolisation of the Korean economy, and the lessons which can be drawn for the rest of Asia today.

A lot of the credit goes to Hyundai's late founder Chung Ju Yung, whose own hard-scrabble beginnings in the Korea of the 1920s and 1930s is the stuff of legend. After the brutal end to the Japanese occupation of Korea, Chung expanded his nascent automobile repair business into what is today Hyundai Construction. Diversification into shipbuilding, automobiles, and heavy and light industry followed, establishing Hyundai as one of Korea's indispensable business groups and Chung as a true business leader. In a hugely entertaining and insightful biography of the Hyundai founder, American journalist Don Kirk[12] writes that at his peak, Chung was a mercurial tycoon who brooked no interference or differences with his approach. "The mystique of the founder pervaded Korean business, Korean society," Kirk writes. "His minions zealously cultivated it through official, lavishly bound corporate histories and subsidised biographies as well as his own book of self-praise, *Ordeals but no Failures*, churned out in 1991 as he was about to plough into forming a political party and running for President." I was in freezing Seoul in early December 1992 as Hyundai's supremely self-confident founder went into Presidential battle with the establishment, this time represented against a mild-mannered Kim Yong-Sam, who eventually won. Kim was a non-entity in the race and pro-Hyundai sections of Korean media were resolute in declaring that only a *chaebol* King like Chung could lead Korea. Eventually the Hyundai tycoon did not prevail because the political establishment feared the loss of their own power and privileges. In the period since Chung's failed attempt, Korea has indeed elected a senior Hyundai official (Lee Myung-bak) as President although his post-Presidential retirement was interrupted by a corruption investigation.

---

[12] Donald Kirk, *Korean Dynasty: Hyundai and Chung Yu Jung* (Routledge, 1994).

While times have certainly changed in Asia today, some disturbing aspects still remain, particularly in the way we deify our ABCs. Chung was cut from the same cloth as Asia's post-colonial era business tycoons — be it Hong Kong's Li Ka Shing, India's Dhirubhai Ambani, or Indonesia's Liem Sioe Liong. They all came of age during the tumult of World War II and the messy business of the departure of colonial masters, although in Li's case it was the 1949 Communist revolution in China that forced him to leave Shanghai. There is a mythology surrounding the rise of each of these tycoons, which is not different from the rags-to-riches tales that pervade American corporate history. In Chung's case, Kirk writes that the popular perception is that he built his empire "with his bare hands," quoting an American academic as noting: "I have seen him on the assembly line roll up his sleeves. I

> *Chung was cut from the same cloth as Asia's post-colonial era business tycoons — be it Hong Kong's Li Ka Shing, India's Dhirubhai Ambani, or Indonesia's Liem Sioe Liong.*

have seen him digging out there with a shovel." This is not very different from the mythology being built around tech billionaire Elon Musk who is described by American business media as being so committed to electric car-maker Tesla that he often sleeps on the factory floor.

Active Government Support

What is forgotten is that the rise of Hyundai and fellow *chaebol* would not have been possible without active government support, in this case support from President Park Chung-hee who lead South Korea from 1961 until his brutal assassination in 1979. In a fascinating 2003 book published by the Peterson Institute for International Economics (PIIE),[13] the research

---

[13] See Edward M. Graham, *Reforming Korea's Industrial Conglomerates* (Columbia University Press), Chapter 2, *"The Miracle with a Dark Side: Korean Economic Development Under Park Chung-hee"* (PIIE, 2003).

highlights the active role played by the Park regime in nurturing and developing the Korean private sector. "In 1962, the Economic Planning Board (EPB) introduced the first of what was to become a series of five-year plans for Korea's development," the PIIE report notes. "State-owned banks were created to help implement the government's development plans, and laws were passed to force private banks effectively to become agents of their implementation. Over the next five years, the Korean government became, in the words of former EPB member and Deputy Prime Minister Sakong Il an "entrepreneur-manager." The PIIE report emphasised that as the Park years progressed, the Korean Government's role as "entrepreneur-manager" increasingly was manifested not so much in public enterprises, as important as these were, but rather in the government's direction of activities undertaken by the surging private sector. The Korean miracle was only possible due to active government intervention and support, combined with the hard work and audacity of the *chaebol* in pushing into areas (shipbuilding, cars) which were regarded as the preserve of developed nations.

> *It is the Korean Government's role as "entrepreneur-manager" that has had the most impact on businesses and public policy across Asia.*

It is the Korean Government's role as "entrepreneur-manager" that has had the most impact on businesses and public policy across Asia. From India to Indonesia, China to Malaysia, the government regards the domestic private sector as a handmaiden for economic growth and prosperity. However, there are serious conflicts of interest because when the private sector and government are on the *same side*, it is not always evident if the general public benefits. In this case, both the state and the private sector become rent seekers, a charming economics expression to describe the private sector's practice of manipulating public policy or economic conditions as a strategy for increasing profits. Developed and developing Asia is a rent-seeker's paradise as evident from two striking examples from the way land sales are regulated in Hong Kong and in much wider extraction of rents in developing Asia.

Hong Kong Property

Anyone who has visited Hong Kong is likely to marvel at the energy and creativity of the territory's property developers as they build tall towers of concrete and steel on ever more tiny slivers of land. Hong Kong boosters describe the DNA of the Chinese territory (or Special Administrative Region as it is formally referred to) as being the rule of law, property rights, and its primacy as a regional financial centre. This is all true, but it still falls short in explaining Hong Kong's *raison d'etre*. The blood racing through Hong Kong's veins is property development, trading in a commodity which is in extremely short supply — land. The agency which controls the purchase and sale

> *The blood racing through Hong Kong's veins is property development, trading in a commodity which is in extremely short supply — land.*

of land is the appropriately named Lands Department which is probably more influential in the territory than the Hong Kong Monetary Authority (HKMA), the *de facto* central bank.

In the 2018-2019 financial year alone, the *South China Morning Post* reported that the government raised around HK$133 billion (around US$17 billion) via land sales alone, a major contributor to operating revenues of around HK$436 billion. This has historically set in motion perverse incentives for the government because in order to keep revenues from land sales at sustainably high levels, it necessarily has to restrict the sale of land in any given year, driving up property prices and making them unaffordable to the general public. This policy has been attacked as the source of inequality in Hong Kong, including from Joseph Yam, the former chief of the HKMA and an advisor to the government. "From a macroeconomic point of view, Hong Kong does not need a massive financial surplus, and this will only drag economic development," Yam wrote in his blog in August 2018. "Besides, the income that the government makes from selling residential sites is a *de facto* tax paid by common citizens buying or renting flats at sky-high prices in the private market. This is against the government's housing policy." Yam is far too much of an establishment man to drive home the uncomfortable truth that Hong Kong's property market has become an unholy alliance between a government addicted to revenue from land auctions (for which it has to limit supply) and a small group of property developers who profit from rising prices as a result.

Hong Kong property developers feature prominently in the *Forbes* annual ranking of billionaires (no surprises here) while ordinary people in the territory are perpetually anxious about their housing status. According to data from research firm *Demographia*, Hong Kong has the world's least affordable housing market with a family earning the territory's median income having to save over 19 years without any additional expenditure in order to buy a flat.

> *Hong Kong property developers feature prominently in the Forbes annual ranking of billionaires (no surprises here) while ordinary people in the territory are perpetually anxious about their housing status.*

In a blistering analysis by *The New York Times*,[14] the newspaper reported that nearly one in five people live in poverty in the territory and the minimum wage is only $4.82 an hour, a pittance in advanced Hong Kong whose per capita GDP is in excess of $40,000. "We thought maybe if you get a better education, you can have a better income," a Hong Kong resident said. "But in Hongkong over the past two decades, people may be able to get a college education, but they are not making more money." This resident works 12 hours a day, six days a week as a security guard and makes around $5.75 an hour, at least double what a foreign domestic worker makes in the territory, but still a modest amount. Not surprisingly, the newspaper reported that the

---

[14] Alexandra Stevenson and Jin Wu, "Tiny Apartments and Punishing Working Hours: The Economic Roots of Hong Kong's Protests", by *The New York Times*, 22 July 2019.

resident joined the June 2019 protests, ostensibly against the passage of an extradition bill, but the root of his anger probably has more to do with rising inequality. "The numbers are striking. Hongkong's gap between the rich and the poor is at its widest in nearly half a century, and among the starkest in the world," the newspaper concluded. "It boasts the world's longest working hours and the highest rents. Wages have not kept up with rent, which has increased by nearly a quarter over the past six years. Housing prices have tripled over the past decade."

There is a seemingly simple public policy solution for Hong Kong authorities' stated commitment to unleash economic opportunity and equity — dismantle the iniquitous land auction system and make housing affordable to all citizens. Hong Kong residents are not asking for welfare benefits, only a fair system which will enable them to acquire residential accommodation at reasonable prices. Singapore, which also controls the sale of land, has a more equitable approach by providing affordable public housing ownership to all citizens. However, the dismantling of the Hong Kong land auction system will hurt property developers, many of whom are ABCs keen to protect their privileges. In a belated recognition of the economic challenges faced by Hong Kong residents due to the pandemic, the government has opened up the fiscal spigots by stepping up spending to support small business and the poor.

Loan Defaults

All over Asia, rent extraction has become the primary source of business for a small group of privileged tycoons who have the right connections with political leaders and senior officials of state-owned enterprises. Three examples highlight how the interests of the general public is being subverted by pliant government officials in cahoots with the ABCs. The first two examples are from India's giant state-owned banks which are in a perilous financial state because of a binge of lending over a decade ago — some to fund legitimate business expansion of the ABCs but a majority

All over Asia, rent extraction has become the primary source of business for a small group of privileged tycoons who have the right connections with political leaders and senior officials of state-owned enterprises.

of them for fraudulent purposes. The most notable example of this is 49-year old diamond tycoon Nirav Modi, diamantaire to celebrities in Bollywood and Hollywood, who went AWOL in early 2018 after defrauding state-owned Punjab National Bank (PNB) of $1.8 billion. Much to the embarrassment of the Indian Government and Prime Minister Modi (no relative of Nirav), the diamond tycoon appears in a group photograph taken at Davos in January 2018, along with PM Modi and other Indian business leaders, before he fled to London in apparent exile. The diamond tycoon has since been arrested and the Indian authorities have started the long process of extraditing him back to Mumbai, where he will face criminal proceedings. The state-owned PNB has faced little impact from this scandal, since it is owned by the government and will be bailed out for any shortages in capital or liquidity. The losses will be borne by taxpayers, many of them middle class, while senior management of state-owned banks continue with their bad behaviour.

The state-owned PNB has faced little impact from this scandal, since it is owned by the government and will be bailed out for any shortages in capital or liquidity.

The most egregious example from India of course is that of Chanda Kochhar, the former chief executive of ICICI Bank (partly owned by the state) who has been named in a fraud investigation conducted by the Central Bureau of Investigation (CBI) for "cheating and defrauding ICICI Bank." Ms Kochhar, who enjoyed an incredibly high profile as a woman CEO, was named by the CBI for colluding with her husband and a leading business tycoon in loans provided by ICICI Bank, which subsequently turned sour. To be sure,

Kochhar is innocent until proven otherwise as the case winds its way through India's serpentine legal system. However, the allegations have shocked India's establishment because Kochhar was regarded as a role model CEO who was attempting to bring about change to the banking system.

In Malaysia, the 1MDB scandal highlights what happens when it is the state that turns rogue and finds willing partners in the international financial sector to facilitate what must be the biggest money laundering operation in Southeast Asia in decades. The facts of the 1MDB scandal are well-known and I will not recycle[15] the circumstances of the scandal and the guilty verdict currently handed by Malaysian courts against former Prime Minister Najib and his associates. Suffice to say that the Malaysian Government in 2013 established the new sovereign wealth fund 1MDB to ostensibly fund domestic infrastructure but the money raised was recycled wilfully to a web of offshore vehicles. It was then illegally siphoned off to finance the acquisition of trophy properties all over the globe and even the Hollywood movie *The Wolf of Wall Street*. The 1MDB scandal is dramatically different from the examples cited above of the private sector colluding with the state for illegal gain. Here the state is the principal rogue actor and the international financial sector, led by august institutions such as Goldman Sachs, were the willing intermediaries to facilitate corrupt activities undertaken by former Prime Minister Najib. The fact that Goldman agreed to pay the Malaysian authorities $3.9 billion in cash and stolen assets in a settlement shows that global finance was a willing accessory to state plunder. In the end, perhaps shocked with the extent and scope of the thievery, Malaysian voters elected Najib's former mentor-turned-rival Mahathir Mohammed in 2018 to clean up the mess. Perversely, Mahathir resigned due to internecine rivalry within his party and the current Prime Minister Muhyiddin Yassin is once again on friendly terms with UMNO.

---

[15] For one of the best accounts of the scandal, see Tom Wright and Bradley Hope, *Billion Dollar Whale: The Man Who Fooled Wall Street, Hollywood, and the World* (Hachette Books, 2018).

Defamation Suits

Malaysia and IMDB was a high-profile example of justice being delivered by ordinary voters and brave journalists going the extra mile to investigate corruption. This is unfortunately the exception rather than the rule across Asia as ABCs and the political class are hyper-sensitive to criticism of any kind — from NGOs, opposition politicians, journalists, and even Twitter trolls. The ABCs are prodigious plaintiffs of defamation and libel, seeking protection in British colonial-era laws which have not been updated. The ABCs often seek damages in the hundreds of millions of dollars, claiming that a particular NGO report or newspaper article has caused them irreparable harm.

> *Malaysia and IMDB was a high-profile example of justice being delivered by ordinary voters and brave journalists going the extra mile to investigate corruption.*

> *However, the broader point here is while journalists and NGOs in Asia have a responsibility to publish reports based on objective facts, they are likely to be cowed if they felt that one of their ABC targets could sue for millions of dollars in damages.*

There also needs to be a parallel list to the annual *Forbes* listing of Asian billionaires of ABCs threatening or actually suing for defamation and libel each year, which no doubt will be equally interesting. One example is India's Adani Group, which has interests in mining, energy, and infrastructure. In June 2017, a reputed Indian online publication called *The Wire* published a damaging article about the Adani Group allegedly benefitting from concessional import duty on raw materials. The group filed three civil and three criminal defamation cases against *The Wire*, seeking damages in excess of $50 million, which if found guilty, could sink the publication. To be clear, I have not analysed the merits of the case and the Adani Group may well have been defamed by false claims made by *The Wire*. However, the broader point here is while journalists and NGOs in Asia have a responsibility to publish reports based on objective facts, they are likely to be cowed if they felt that one of their ABC targets could sue for millions of dollars in damages. As it happens, the Adani Group withdrew the civil and criminal defamation cases against *The Wire* around the time of India's election results in May 2019. But defamation cases have become a common practice amongst ABCs across the region, raising concerns about lack of accountability and transparency.

There is the August 2006 case when the Foxconn Group sued reporters of *China Business News* in Shenzhen for reporting on poor working conditions in the company's manufacturing facilities. A Chinese court had frozen the assets of the reporter and editor of CBN and Foxconn but eventually decided to withdraw the suit after intervention by Shenzhen authorities. A few years later when news surfaced about worker suicides at the Foxconn factory in China, Chairman Terry Gou magnanimously invited reporters to tour the facility to take a first-hand look. However, the *South China Morning Post* (SCMP) reported in 2015 that the 2006 case still had negative reverberations across Chinese media. "A public backlash eventually prompted Foxconn to drop the defamation case, but it effectively served to stifle media criticism of the company on the mainland. Afterwards, Shenzhen media began reporting positive stories on the firm's contributions to the local economy," Raymond Li of the *SCMP* reported.[16]

Why are the ABCs so sensitive and who do they draw their inspiration from? The first part of the question, on hypersensitivity, is perhaps understandable. ABCs are driven to success by a combination of sheer guile, business smarts, and being plugged into the home country's political class. This is a seriously competitive business as ABCs attempt to outsmart and bad mouth corporate rivals in their race for national and global dominance. Along the way and

---

[16] Raymond Li, "Foxconn seen as bullying the media", *South China Morning Post*, updated 8 May 2015.

particularly during the last two decades, the ABCs have accumulated serious wealth, influence, and prestige, thanks to Asia's dazzling growth rates as well as the development of stock markets, which have sent their share values soaring. Given shifting political winds, which could jeopardise their business fortunes, the ABCs regard any negative news article or NGO report as a fundamental attack against their interests. One of Duterte's closest business allies in the Philippines appears to be tycoon Ramon Ang, who acquired the fiercely independent *The Philippine Daily Inquirer* in 2017 after the President attacked the previous owners. "I'm not trying to scare you, but one day karma will catch up with you," the President said to the owners of the newspaper. Faced with a tax investigation and other threats, the owners of the PDN sold their stake to Ang, whom the President described as a "fast friend." More recently, the Duterte administration also forced a shutdown of the free-to-air TV channel ABS-CBN by refusing to renew its licence. The TV network was also a vocal critic of the President.

Intimidating journalists and/or buying their support is the secret sauce of ABCs. The head of communications of a leading Indian business house explained his strategy in engaging with journalists in his country. "There are three categories of journalists whom I deal with," he told me at one of Mumbai's exclusive bars. "Category 1 is the honest reporter who cannot be bought at any cost. He or she needs to be taken seriously. Category 2 is the corrupt reporter who could be persuaded with cash or kind to write favourable stuff. Category 3 is the most dangerous — he or she is the operator who works at the crossroads of politics and business, leveraging information about competitors, political affiliations." It is not at all surprising that the head of communications spends most of his time with Category 2 and 3 reporters, while damaging articles by Category 1 reporters will be dealt with via a real or threatened lawsuit.

> *Intimidating journalists and/or buying their support is the secret sauce of ABCs.*

Self-censorship also becomes the norm as appears to be happening in Korea, where online portal Naver took the preventive step last year of removing a number of "relevant search words" related to family members running conglomerates on its search engine last year. *The Korea Times* reported[17] that the Korea Internet Self-governance Organisation (KISO) took Naver to task for removing a total of 48,532 search words, which when searched and disseminated by users, could potentially impugn the reputation of owners of Korean chaebol and their families. "It was an excessive measure that did not go through proper procedures," KISO said, adding that Naver's defence that the decision was made on the firm's "self-judgement" was "not seen as a valid reason."

Corporate Governance

If media is being suppressed across Asia, what should be done to reverse the toxic tide of ABCs colluding with politics or *chaebolisation*, often to the detriment of ordinary people? A starting point is in reforming electoral and campaign finance laws which brings daylight into the murky process. It is simply impossible to compute business funding of political parties in Asia because much of it happens under the radar and in smoke-filled rooms

> *It is simply impossible to compute business funding of political parties in Asia because much of it happens under the radar and in smoke-filled rooms far away from prying media.*

far away from prying media. There is a pressure valve in the hands of voters, as happened in India in 2014 and Malaysia in 2018, to simply reject incumbent parties accused of massive corruption. However, not all Asian countries are democracies and crony capitalism mainly goes unchecked.

---

[17] Jun Ji-hye, "Naver deleted search words related to chaebol families", *The Korea Times*, 26 June 2018.

May I also offer four of the most boring words in the English lexicon for the ABCs and their companies to reform themselves — structural reforms and corporate governance. If the ABCs took a pledge to become more transparent in their political funding activities, and insist on transparent bidding and procurement practices, it could go some way in reducing collusion and anti-competitive practices. The state has a fundamental role in monitoring corporate behaviour through strong institutions like an independent central bank, securities regulator, and judicial system. On paper, Asian countries have made impressive strides in updating the business rulebook and in stricter governance requirements. Law firm Freshfields Bruckhaus Deringer said in a 2017 report[18] that Asia was paying more attention to unfair business practices like monopolies and cartels. "Undeniably, the centre of gravity of global competition law enforcement has shifted closer to Asia," says Alistair Mordaunt who runs the firm's anti-trust practice. "While there are still large variations across the region in terms of economic and political development, we are seeing Asian markets take a much more vigorous and sophisticated approach to competition law enforcement and companies should take notice."

This is definitely encouraging news because Asia needs strong, independent institutions and technocrats prepared to stand up to business and their own governments. Corporate governance standards in developed and developing Asia are much lower than in other developed markets, as noted in a 2016 survey by the Asian Corporate Governance Association on criteria such as regulations and enforcement. This despite the rapid growth in capital markets and the presence of domestic and foreign institutional investors. It is often difficult to distinguish corporate practices in family-owned businesses and state-owned enterprises across the region. Both suffer from a lack of transparency, opaque funding structures, and it is not always clear if the

---

[18] Freshfields Bruckhaus Deringer, "Anti-trust in Asia: The business impact of fast-evolving competition laws", 2018.

public interest is being served. China's giant state-owned banks have gone on successive lending binges over the past two decades, often at the dictates of the state and ostensibly to prop up economic growth. The outcomes, however, have proven to be extremely costly to Chinese citizens in terms of excess manufacturing capacity and a property and stockmarket bubble.

> *China's giant state-owned banks have gone on successive lending binges over the past two decades, often at the dictates of the state and ostensibly to prop up economic growth.*

A dramatic step forward would be for laws requiring the appointment of independent directors who would not be beholden to the family owner or the political leader. Nicholas Benes of Japan's Board Director Training Institute told the *Financial Times*[19] that things are changing in Japan, the most advanced nation in Asia. "The environment is vastly different from even four years ago. But there are firms which have not caught up to the 21st century in terms of corporate governance and attention to shareholder value," he said, "There is a divergence between companies which have independent directors and companies which don't want to have any outside directors at all." While I don't believe in trickle-down economics, I sincerely hope that this particular practice does trickle down to the rest of Asia.

As I end this chapter, a sceptic might wonder why I am creating such a fuss about Asia's billionaire class? They are wealth and job creators, who ought to be championed and celebrated. While I have no problem with ABCs becoming the toast of the town, they already are in many places, my fundamental disquiet is about how they wield power and influence. Rising inequality in Asia and stalled social mobility is not happening in isolation of the rise of the ABCs — it is in fact happening as a consequence. A business

---

[19] Tom Hankok, "Governance remains a risk for Asia-Pacific investors", *Financial Times*, 11 April 2018.

owner with political clout has little incentive to pay fair wages to employees and to adhere to environmental and social standards. As we will discover in the next chapter, Asia's environmental degradation is already exacerbating social and political tensions.

Chapter 8

The Death of Bali

Our fifth circle of hell is the environmental devastation across developing Asia, which is having a disproportionate impact on the poor.

The choices for ground zero for this chapter are not obvious — the tourist haven that is Bali, visited by over 12 million visitors in 2019, and the frozen wastelands of Mongolia, Asia's forgotten country. I have been visiting Bali since the early 1990s and am very familiar with its paddy fields and coastal terrain, both under pressure because of the adverse impact that tourism is having on the island. I have never visited Mongolia and have relied on riveting second-hand accounts, including from the country's former President, to sketch the scale of the impact from climate change. To be sure, I could have picked more obvious Asian locations to assess the region's environment damage — a predictable choice would be the foul air that people breathe in Beijing, Manila, Delhi, Jakarta, and other Asian metros. Or the massive deforestation underway in Southeast Asia's "lungs," the Indonesian-side of Borneo, because of the rampant development of palm oil plantations. We will examine these shortly, but Bali and Mongolia are good places to start, off the beaten track perhaps, to illustrate the hydra-headed nature of Asia's environmental challenges. Covid-19 should also worry us because pandemics will become more frequent due to habitat destruction, placing all of us in close contact with virus carriers like the humble bat.

Bali's singular challenge is in dealing with mass tourism. Quite simply, Bali's problem is one of plenty. The island is attracting too many tourists, and this is having intended positive and unintended negative environmental consequences. Bali is a dominant player with a single product to sell, very much like Saudi Arabia.[1] While oil seeps from the sands of remote eastern Saudi Arabia and is a traded commodity, Bali's selling points have been its once-spectacular terrain, the seemingly unlimited reserves of charm and grace of the Balinese (which unlike oil appears to be in infinite supply!), and the laid-back "island" vibe. All of these are under threat because of the unsustainable surge in foreign and domestic tourist arrivals. Official estimates suggest that around 6 million Indonesians visited the island in 2019, almost matching the number of foreign arrivals. Visitor arrivals for 2020 have cratered due to Covid-19, which should give Indonesian authorities and the tourism industry an opportunity to rethink Bali's dependence on a single, diminishing product line for survival.

> *Bali's singular challenge is in dealing with mass tourism. Quite simply, Bali's problem is one of plenty.*

For first-time visitors seeking to escape the heat and dust of other Asian metros, the Bali on view today must come as a shock. There are traffic snarls all over the island, like any other major metropolis, and once lush paddy fields are pock-marked with ugly hotels and villas. There was a time not so long ago that one could stay in a villa at Ubud and rise to the wonderful chatter of birds and insects. Today the persistent morning noise likely comes from the honk and clatter of traffic. My most recent visit to Bali, in October 2018 for the annual meetings of the IMF and the World Bank, was a stark reminder that the Bali of yore is perhaps lost forever.

---

[1] With due apologies to the Kingdom of Saudi Arabia for multiple references comparing its dependence on oil with Bangladesh (textiles) and now Bali.

The immediate casualty of Bali's unchecked development is in water availability as researchers from the Bali Water Protection Program (BWP)[2] have warned. "Bali's natural fresh water aquifers are at record lows of less than 20 percent and researchers warn the island will be in a state of ecological crisis before 2020 if the situation is not reversed by mitigation." There are complex reasons behind the dwindling of Bali's water resources, but it is hard not to blame the surge in tourism and golf courses for the sharp fall in the island's water table. "With over 77,000 registered hotel rooms, plus online booking platforms promoting thousands of Bali villas for rent — and recent announcements of increasing tourist targets to 30 million by 2029, the sustainability of Bali's water has now passed the tipping point," warned Florence Cattin of the IDEP Foundation. Journalist Anton Muhajir told *Al Jazeera*[3] that he believes Bali is in real danger. "Some of my friends have had to move from their ancestral homes in Denpasar because the water in their wells has turned salty," he said.

The rise of tourism as the island's main money-spinner is having an invidious impact on land use, once dominated by paddy fields but increasingly being diverted toward tourism. Student researchers at the University of Notre Dame (UND)[4] estimate that the tourist industry draws significant amounts of water averaging around 3 million litres a day. "With the growing development, the public water supply quickly became insufficient, causing hotels to draw significant amounts of ground and well water," the Notre Dame study found.

> *The rise of tourism as the island's main money-spinner is having an invidious impact on land use, once dominated by paddy fields but increasingly being diverted toward tourism.*

---

[2] The BWP team is drawn from the University Politeknik Negeri Bali (PNB) and the IDEP Foundation.

[3] Ian Lloyd Neubauer, "Bali: The Tropical Indonesian Island that is Running out of Water", *Al Jazeera*, 2 December 2019.

[4] Laine Asbury, "Bali's Water Crisis", undergraduate Capstone Project, College of Science, University of Notre Dame, 2014.

"Thus, the massive tourism development in southern Bali has excessively exploited the island's main water resources in the centre and the north. It is also negatively impacting the agricultural sector." UND estimates that over 750 hectares of prime paddy fields are sold-off every year to be converted into tourism-related projects. Since it no longer profitable to live off the land, a majority of Balinese are giving up on agriculture and moving to more viable jobs in mass tourism. This is a vicious cycle as conversion of greater parcels of farmland into hotels and villas places acute pressure on the island's water aquifers.

Tourism Bounty

Bali's economic growth has traditionally been higher than other provinces, including Java and Sumatra, because of the tourism bounty the island has enjoyed over the past few decades. Tourism today contributes over 80 percent to the island's economy, the parallel with Saudi Arabia is not off the mark. However, there is a dark side to this bounty as the easy earnings from mass tourism have given Balinese little incentive to upgrade their skills. On Jalan Legian in over-crowded Kuta or Jalan Raya Ubud in Ubud, there are literally thousands of Balinese employed as low-wage masseurs, shop assistants, waiters, and other assorted tourism-dependent professions. These are the Bali version of urban cowboys and cowgirls, who have been hurt the most due to the pandemic.

Due to its strategic location, sandwiched between Australia and other parts of Asia, Bali could be a hub for higher-value IT services. There are a few IT firms attempting to build on the location advantage, but it has not reached critical mass. In any event, these firms are run by expats with little opportunities for Balinese. However, getting the locals to work in key positions would require a dramatic shift in emphasis on education and skills development. To put it bluntly, Bali needs more engineers, fewer masseurs. Sooner or later, Bali's water crisis will upend the lives of thousands of Balinese. Tourist preferences are notoriously fickle, and it is arguable whether Bali will continue to be a magnet for global travellers as they seek out newer and less crowded destinations.

Bali's tourism industry can still be saved if local authorities and rapacious resort developers take a step back and focus on the future sustainability of the island. Perhaps Covid-19 will provide the trigger. The UN's World Tourism Organisation (UNWTO)[5] warned in a June 2019 report that while countries are integrating sustainability into their tourism policies, "evidence" on the results of their implementation remains limited. "Sustainability and competitiveness go hand in hand. Destinations and businesses can flourish while making a meaningful contribution to sustainability in several ways, including through the efficient use of resources, promoting biodiversity conservation, and taking action to fight climate change," the UNWTO's Secretary General notes in the report. Bali needs to focus on "regenerative tourism," the newest buzzword in the travel industry, where the philosophy is that tourists should not cause damage and actually leave the destination in a better place for future generations.

> *Bali's tourism industry can still be saved if local authorities and rapacious resort developers take a step back and focus on the future sustainability of the island.*

From the humid climes of Bali, it is a 3900-mile journey to the Mongolian capital of Ulaanbaatar (UB for short), where a brief summer is book-ended by extreme and near-winter conditions. For Asians living in the continent's tropical zone, it is hard to fathom the depth and coldness of the winter season in Ulaanbaatar, which has the dubious distinction of being the coldest capital city in the world. Average winter temperatures range from -20 to -45 degrees C and to note that it is bitterly cold would be a classic

---

[5] UNWTO, "Baseline Report on the Integration of Sustainable Consumption and Production Patterns into Tourism Policies", prepared in collaboration with UN Environment and with the support of the Government of France.

For Asians living in the continent's tropical zone, it is hard to fathom the depth and coldness of the winter season in Ulaanbaatar, which has the dubious distinction of being the coldest capital city in the world.

understatement. Over centuries, hardy Mongolians have figured out ingenious ways of coping with the harsh weather. But the country has also been given a poor hand in geopolitics. Blame it on geography as Mongolia has had to deal with Russia to its north and China to its south — two extremely large, intemperate, and mercurial nations which have impacted Mongolia's destiny in the 20th and 21st centuries. During the Cold War, Mongolia hitched its fortunes with the Soviet Union, angering China. With Russia's economy in terminal decline, Mongolia has more recently mended fences with Beijing. It is a delicate dance, but it must be said that the shoe was of course on the other foot during the millennia prior to this with Genghis Khan and his successors controlling large swathes of Europe, Central Asia, China, and Siberia.

I first heard about Mongolia's extraordinary climate-induced winter droughts (or dzud in the local lexicon) at Davos in 2000. I was working at the IMF and we met with then Prime Minister Nambaryn Enkhbayar (who went on to become President and Speaker of Parliament). To be immodest, I have attended many meetings with heads of state during my IMF and banking careers. They tend to be rigidly formal with a battery of interpreters translating the back and forth between the two principals. The meeting with Prime Minister Enkhbayar was remarkably different in terms of location (a noisy coffee shop without interpreters), tone, and substance, which is probably why I can vividly recall the discussion. Speaking in perfect English, the Prime Minister spoke about a changing climate and shifting herding practices, which had contributed to the country's worst ever dzud in 1999-2000 (repeated in 2010 and 2018). He described how the population of livestock and herding in Mongolia's vast steppes was controlled during the Soviet era, which enabled traditional nomadic families to practice their centuries-old trade without much disruption. However, Mongolia's post-Soviet democratic era had ushered in new freedoms to the country's 2.8 million people and a deregulation in herding had led to a proliferation in the livestock population. The new generation of herders, the Prime Minister said, were city slickers from UB and did not possess the collective wisdom of the traditional nomads, where knowledge flowed from generation to generation and sustainable farming was practised long before the phrase was coined. Mongolia's clash between modernity and tradition reached a crescendo in 1999 when the country recorded its worst-ever drought in decades. The United Nation's Office for the Coordination of Humanitarian Affairs issued a dramatic situation report[6] in September 2000 outlining the drought in dramatic terms: "In 1999-2000, the Mongolian population experienced their worst-ever drought since 1968, in the form of 'multiple dzud' which has been the cumulative result of the summer 1999 drought, dubbed the 'black dzud', and of last winter's huge ice cap: the 'iron dzud' and heavy snowstorms, 'white dzud'," OCHA reported.

Mongolia's tragedy is that climate change-induced drought has accelerated since 1999 and the country has faced at least two equally severe crises in the period since then as the following report from 10 October 2018 illustrates: "Overpopulation of livestock and the effects of climate change mean grass on the steppe, which animals eat to survive, is becoming thinner year on year," according to Henry Wilkins of *Al Jazeera*. "The nomads who

---

[6] "Mongolia – 'Multiple Dzud' and Drought OCHA Situation Report No. 10", September 2000.

> *Warm summers followed by extremely harsh winters are the lethal combination which delivers Mongolia's deadly dzud.*

have herded animals on horseback for centuries are finding it harder to keep their animals, the main source of their livelihoods, fed properly." It is estimated that over 700,000 livestock perished in the punishing cold in 2017 (estimated at -58 degrees C) and a million livestock the year before. With the steppe in climate distress, the new and traditional herders are moving back to UB in large numbers and congregating in the capital city's "ger[7] districts." These climate refugees today account for over 50 percent of UB's population and huddle together in difficult conditions. *The Guardian* newspaper reported that over the past 70 years, the average temperature in Mongolia has risen by 2.07 degrees, more than double the average global increase of 0.85 degrees over the past century. Warm summers followed by extremely harsh winters are the lethal combination which delivers Mongolia's deadly dzud. This should hold important lessons for tropical and temperate Asia, where the absence of rainfall is the immediate consequence of extreme warming conditions, leading to climate distress and emigration from rural to urban areas.

Climate Distress

How severe is developing Asia's environmental crisis and should we regard the examples illustrated from Bali and Mongolia as outliers or the norm? I am going to assert that adverse climate change impacts in the region are a reality and a humanitarian crisis is unfolding. Let's look at South Asia and Southeast Asia in turn, drawing from research conducted by the World Bank and other organisations. In a 2019 World Bank book[8] researchers warned that average temperatures in South Asia have risen over the past six decades

---

[7] A traditional yurt or ger is a round tent used by nomadic populations in Mongolia and Central Asia. The ger is insulated against the harsh winters by strategically placed animal hide.

[8] Muthukumara Mani et al., *South Asia's Hotspots: The Impact of Temperature and Precipitation Changes on Living Standards* (World Bank Group, 2019).

and will continue to rise: "Over the 2050 horizon, it predicts more warming inland and less warming in coastal areas," the book notes. "Changes in precipitation patterns have been more mixed, and this diversity will persist in the future. These weather changes are expected to result in a decrease in living standards in most countries in the region, compared with a situation in which current weather conditions are preserved."

Compared with more developed parts of Southeast Asia, India and its South Asian neighbours are more dependent on the annual monsoon season — which provides immediate relief from the severe heat of the summer season and more crucially to irrigate farmland. Over the past decade as summer temperatures have inched higher, the rainy season has become more unpredictable. As a long-time resident

Over the past decade as summer temperatures have inched higher, the rainy season has become more unpredictable.

of Mumbai and a journalist in the 1980s, I recall the anxiety in the city every June as the clouds darken and the promise of rain is literally in the air. The city's business and financial elites are painfully aware that fortunes could be made and unmade depending on the intensity of the rains every year. Mumbai also feels the damage to the hinterland from a drought as ever more migrants make their way to the city, living in uninhabitable conditions as discussed in Chapter 6. World Bank researchers[9] note that average temperatures in South Asia have already inched up over the past five decades — rising by 1.0 degree C to 3.0 degrees C in western Afghanistan and southwest Pakistan between 1950 and 2010. During the same period, parts of India, Sri Lanka, Nepal, and north Pakistan experienced increases of between 1.0 degree C to 1.5 degrees C. "Increasing average temperatures and changing seasonal patterns are already having an effect on agriculture across South Asia," the report notes. "Low-lying Bangladesh and the Maldives are increasingly vulnerable to flooding and cyclones in the Indian Ocean.

---

[9] "South Asia's Hotspots", report by the World Bank, 28 June 2018.

The scientific literature suggests that such events will grow in intensity over the coming decades. Dhaka, Karachi, Kolkata, and Mumbai — urban areas that are home to more than 50 million people — face a substantial risk of flood-related damage over the next century."

South Asia's vulnerability to climate change is by no means an outlier in Asia. Neighbouring Southeast Asia is also in the crosshairs of climate distress, albeit less from a rise in temperatures and more from rising sea levels. The United Nations Development Program (UNDP)[10] estimates that average temperatures in the region have risen more modestly compared with Mongolia and South Asia in the last seven decades. Between 1951-2000, the region witnessed temperature increases of between 0.1 degree C to 0.3 degrees C per decade, with projections showing much higher increases in the next few decades. What does this translate to in terms of impact and what does the region need to do? The UNDP makes three recommendations: conservation of water resources as the region is likely to face water stress; measures to build climate resilience in agriculture as the region is likely to face sharp variability in rainfall patterns; and coastal resource management as there is uncertainty about the precise degree to which sea levels will rise.

> South Asia's vulnerability to climate change is by no means an outlier in Asia. Neighbouring Southeast Asia is also in the crosshairs of climate distress, albeit less from a rise in temperatures and more from rising sea levels.

In many parts of Southeast Asia, the projected sea level rise is no longer an uncertainty. Journalist Amit Prakash provides an interesting anecdote[11] about how Vietnam is coping with the unpredictability of climate change. He

---

[10] "Climate Change Adaptation, South-Eastern Asia", UNDP report.

[11] Amit Prakash, "Boiling Point", *Finance & Development magazine*, published by the IMF, September 2018.

writes about the Blue Dragon, a riverfront restaurant in Hoi An, where on damp-stained walls the owner marks the level of annual floods that submerge the popular UNESCO World Heritage town, renowned for its bright yellow-painted buildings. A few weeks before the November 2018 leader's meeting of the Asia-Pacific Economic Cooperation (APEC) grouping, which was held at nearby Da Nang, Prakash reports that water levels at the Blue Dragon rose to 1.6 metres (5.25 feet). "Every time we get big rains or typhoons, it floods, and everything shuts down for three to four days," the restaurant owner said in the article. "Last year people had to escape in boats because the water was too high." Vietnam, Myanmar, and the Philippines feature prominently in the list of vulnerable countries to rising temperatures and sea levels. "Southeast Asia faces a dual challenge. It not only must adapt to climate change caused largely by greenhouse gases emitted over decades by advanced economies — and more recently by developing economies such as China and India — it must alter development strategies that are increasingly contributing to global warming. The region's growing reliance on coal and oil, along with deforestation, are undermining national pledges to curb emissions and embrace cleaner energy resources," Prakash writes.

Dominance of Coal

If politicians in developing Asia are all at sea in understanding the impact of AI on jobs, they are clearly out of their depth in figuring out that climate change is here and has real consequences for their citizens, particularly the poor. Part of the problem, as we discussed in Chapter 4, can be blamed on the origins and miseducation of the political

If politicians in developing Asia are all at sea in understanding the impact of AI on jobs, they are clearly out of their depth in figuring out that climate change is here and has real consequences for their citizens, particularly the poor.

class. The political and climate cycles operate under different rhythms and natural disasters are regarded as an act of god. There has been sharper convergence in the two cycles in recent years, but the dominant political narrative is that climate change originated in the developed West (which is true), there should be substantial financial transfers to poor nations to help deal with climate mitigation and adaptation (which is unobjectionable). However, Asia's political class are reluctant to take full national responsibility for dealing with the impending crisis, as the following comment from Bangladesh Prime Minister Sheikh Hasina[12] makes clear. Speaking at the Munich Security Conference in February 2019, the Prime Minister said that the world possessed an "enormous" amount of science, technology, innovation, and finance to address climate change. "We only need the will of the richer segments of societies everywhere to act ambitiously." To be fair to the Prime Minister, she does go on to articulate that as a country most vulnerable to a rise in sea levels, Bangladesh had taken several policy steps to address the challenge. This included the invention of flood-resistant, salt-tolerant, and drought-tolerant rice varieties, "mainstreaming" climate action and disaster management, and allocating 1 percent of the country's GDP to address climate change impacts.

However, in a clear sign that the Prime Minister's rhetoric is not always matched by action, Bangladesh continues to develop coal-fired power stations to meet rising electricity demand in one of the fastest growing economies in Asia, even at the expense of damaging the environment. Surely, the most egregious example is the development underway of the coal fired Rampal power station on the fringes of the Sundarbans, a cluster of low-lying islands abutting India and Bangladesh which are the world's largest single block of mangrove forests in the world and are listed as a UNESCO heritage site. Notwithstanding the environmental damage, the project is proceeding as a joint venture between Bangladesh and India. Environment group Greenpeace has agitated against Rampal, arguing that the debate over

---

[12] "Hasina appeals to rich to fight climate change", *Dhaka Tribune*, 17 February 2019.

the thermal power plant since its inception has been completely unconstructive.[13] "The voices of the local people who were reluctant in giving away their right over the land for this power plant have been suppressed. They used to produce thousands of metric tons of crops and fish every year; some of this is already lost and likely to get impacted further, severely. Countless complaints have been filed on substandard compensation and human rights violation.

Environment group Greenpeace has agitated against Rampal, arguing that the debate over the thermal power plant since its inception has been completely unconstructive.

To make matters worse, many flaws and self-contradictions have been found in the Environmental Impact Assessment (EIA) report put together by one of the government's own bodies," Greenpeace says.

Projects in Asia such as Rampal raise three immediate concerns: the region's over-reliance on coal as a feedstock for power generation; the ongoing debate about the role of the West in providing financial assistance to developing nations to deal with climate mitigation and with providing "climate space": the impact on the poor from coal emissions and its link with devastating climate change, which is misunderstood by Asia's political

Asia's dependence on coal is world-beating according to the International Energy Agency (IEA).

class. Asia's dependence on coal is world-beating according to the International Energy Agency (IEA).[14] "Coal's shift to Asia continued in 2018. The growth in demand for coal took place in only some countries in Asia — China, India, and a few countries in South and Southeast Asia — primarily because of the increasing demand for electricity in these countries, for which coal generally outcompetes gas,"

---

[13] Mowdud Rahman, "Sundarbans: World's Largest Mangrove Forest is at Stake", Greenpeace Report, 25 June 2017.

[14] "Global Energy and CO2 Status Report: The latest trends in energy and emissions in 2018", IEA, 26 March 2019.

according to the IEA. Coal power demand in China increased 5.3 percent in 2018 (compared with a 4 percent decline in America), in India by 5 percent, and there were similar increases in Indonesia, Vietnam, the Philippines, and Malaysia. Why does coal continue to be an attractive feedstock to generate power in Asia? For starters, it is in abundant supply both above and below the ground. Coal mines also provide employment to several million people across developing Asia and local politicians are reluctant to upset the status quo.

More to the point, the continued dominance of coal is completely at odds with promises made by the region in the context of the Paris Agreement on climate change. "Over 80 percent of global coal power capacity under construction is in this region," according to Kaveh Zahedi of the United Nation's Economic and Social Commission for Asia and the Pacific (ESCAP).[15] "Our region is still the one where the greatest new investments are being made in coal and clearly that is incompatible with the ambitions of Paris." UNESCAP estimates that over 40 percent of the region's existing energy supply comes from King Coal. Asia, particularly China, is making significant headway in investing in renewables (which we will get to later) but the Asian narrative about coal use is politically expedient and damaging to the environment. China's much talked about Belt and Road Initiative (BRI), for example, is dominated by the funding of coal-fired power projects in Asia, Africa, and the Middle East. For many sceptics, this is confirmation that the trillion-dollar BRI, China's equivalent of the Marshall Plan, is nothing more than an attempt to export the country's surplus capacity.

Arguments about coal in Asia invariably revolve around Bangladesh Prime Minister Sheikh Hasina's key point that rich nations should take the lead in dealing with climate change, provide significant levels of financial assistance to developing nations for mitigation and adaptation, and to provide the

---

[15] Trudy Harris, "Asia undermining efforts to reduce coal dependence", *Eco-Business*, 10 September 2019.

space for developing nations to continue to use coal because their economic growth depends on it. The 2015 Paris Agreement on climate change restated an earlier commitment that rich nations should assist poor nations to the tune of $100 billion a year by 2020. To date, Oxfam[16] notes in a scathing report that only $48 billion has become available and there remains some ambiguity on whether the money disbursed is actually meant to deal with climate change. "People in poorer countries are on average five times more likely than people in rich countries to be displaced by extreme weather events. Adaptation costs in developing countries are expected to be $140-300 billion a year by 2025/30. By mid-century, the costs of climate change to developing countries are estimated to exceed $1 trillion per year, even if global average temperatures remain below 2 degrees C," says Oxfam, adding that the rich nations should develop a common set of rules and methodology in designating climate-related financial assistance. At the moment the definitions are somewhat lax, making it difficult to quantify the actual level of aid provided.

Sheikh Hasina and other Asian leaders are absolutely right in advocating for greater levels of climate-related financial assistance from the West. This is not charity or reparations, as some sceptics have argued, and will not perpetuate aid dependence on the part of developing Asia and indeed Africa, the Middle East, and Latin America. There is a strong *moral* case because emissions and climate change accelerated during the long period that America and Europe have dominated the world economy. That dominance may well be coming to an end, but the developed West still has the moral responsibility to bear a significant share of the financial and mitigation burden, with one caveat. The caveat being Asia should *not*

---

[16] Tracy Carty and Armelle Le Comte, "Climate Finance Shadow Report", Oxfam, 2 May 2018.

be allowed to continue to burn coal. Former U.S. Vice President Al Gore, a Nobel laureate for his climate change advocacy, paints a stark picture about the dramatic and unprecedented rise in CO2 emissions. "Overall we are releasing CO2 into the atmosphere much faster than at any time in at least the last 66 million years," Gore said in a 2017 presentation at the Australian climate summit. "....The cumulative amount of global warming pollution that is resident in our atmosphere today traps as much extra heat every day as would be released by 400,000 Hiroshima class atomic bombs exploding every 24 hours."

Rogue's Gallery

While there is a causal link between the rising use of coal and the foul air which people breathe in Beijing and other Asian cities, this is only half the story. There is a veritable rogue's gallery contributing to the region's air pollution problems, posing a systemic risk for public health. This surely includes the phenomenal and unsustainable rise of cars, two-and-three-wheelers on Asian roads. China is today the world's largest producer of automobiles and India and Indonesia also feature amongst the top 20,[17] with car ownership becoming a powerful status symbol for the region's rising middle and lower middle class. So far so good. The dirty secret is that car ownership in Asia is heavily subsidised by the state, albeit indirectly via rising fuel subsidies. These subsidies are ostensibly targeted at the poor but in reality, end up as a massive tax rebate to the rich and the middle class. Don't take my word for this. The IMF[18] estimates that fossil fuel subsidies "typically

> *There is a veritable rogue's gallery contributing to the region's air pollution problems, posing a systemic risk for public health.*

---

[17] India produced around 5 million automobiles in 2018, securing the fourth spot. Indonesia was further down the ranking in the 17th spot with production of 1.34 million.

[18] IMFBlog, "Fuel for Thought: Ditch the Subsidies", 14 August 2019.

benefit the rich more than the poor" and if removed could release over 4 percent of global GDP "to invest in people, growth, and help protect the most vulnerable."

The IMF says the subsidies – which it says amount to 6.5 percent of global GDP annually – include expensive government funding to artificially reduce the price of energy below cost, the under-taxation of fuel consumption (6.1 percent of global GDP), "because energy consumption contributes to global warming, local pollution, increased traffic congestion and more accidents." To get your head around these staggering numbers, the World Bank estimates global GDP in 2018 to be around $88 trillion. At 6.5 percent of global GDP, annual fuel subsidies worldwide alone consume around $6 trillion. To place things in context, developing countries are pleading with rich nations to part with a piffling $100 billion annually to deal with climate change mitigation and adaptation. This proves that once distortions in national fuel policies are addressed, there will be plenty of money available to address the climate crisis.

> *This proves that once distortions in national fuel policies are addressed, there will be plenty of money available to address the climate crisis.*

We have so far taken a top-down approach in looking at the deteriorating environment in developing Asia. Let's take a look from the ground up, focusing on the challenges faced by Beijing and New Delhi, capital cities of China and India respectively, and two of Asia's mega cities with a population in excess of 20 million each. Singapore Prime Minister Lee Hsien Loong is believed to have angered China's leadership when he related the following joke about Beijing and Shanghai's air pollution and water quality: "Beijing residents' joke that to get a free smoke, all they have to do is open their windows. In Shanghai, if you want some pork soup, you just turn on the tap," the Prime Minister told a Washington D.C. audience in April 2013. The later reference was about water contamination from thousands of pork carcasses found floating in China's rivers. Lee was merely restating a popular joke heard in Beijing, but his comment hit hard because it drew global attention to China's worsening environmental record, just when President Xi Jinping assumed power in 2012.

It is useful to contrast Beijing's mixed record in tackling air pollution with that of New Delhi, which has unsuccessfully battled smog for the last few years. Defenders of Beijing and Delhi note that smog and deadly pollution are a direct result of the two capital cities' unique geography. "Beijing is backed up against tall mountains which tend to act as a barrier for any smog to clear out," according to AccuWeather meteorologist Jason Nicholls.[19] Prashant Kumar, a researcher at the University of Surrey[20] notes that as a landlocked mega city, Delhi has limited avenues for flushing air pollution out of the city. "Coastal megacities such as Mumbai have at least a chance to 'replace' polluted air with relatively unpolluted sea breezes, whereas Delhi's surrounding regions are sometimes even more polluted than the city," Kumar writes. Like other parts of Asia, Delhi residents have been enjoying a Covid-19 climate dividend as industrial and human activity went into lockdown at the beginning of March 2020. For Asian youth born in any of the region's mega-cities after 1990, this was probably the first time they inhaled fresh air and glimpsed clear blue skies.

> *For Asian youth born in any of the region's mega-cities after 1990, this was probably the first time they inhaled fresh air and glimpsed clear blue skies.*

Blaming poor geography for the deteriorating air quality would seem to be unfair since active human intervention could help turnaround the situation. In Beijing and China overall, at least during President Xi's first term, there appeared to be strong political resolve to tackle the worsening environment.

---

[19] "What factors contributed to Beijing's 'red alert' smog levels?" Accuweather.com, January 2016.

[20] "Underlying causes of Delhi's air pollution problems", *ScienceDaily*, 29 October 2015, with reference to Prashant Kumar et al.,"New Directions: Air Pollution Challenges for Developing Megacities like Delhi", *Atmospheric Environment* 2015.

This is a one-party state after all and the popular narrative has it that that when Beijing demands action, the rest of China would surely obey. This worked according to plan until the beginning of 2019. "China's record improvements in air quality since 2012 have shown how enforcing strong emissions standards and shifting away from coal can reduce pollution and save lives," Greenpeace reported in May 2019. "The next step is long-term planning away from coal and heavy industry. Future air quality gains are dependent on successfully reducing reliance on coal through accelerated clean energy investment and by setting strong coal reduction targets in energy plans and targets beyond 2020."

> *The rebalancing of China's economy, away from capital over-investment, low-cost manufacturing, and trade in favour of consumption and services will be the defining feature of the global economy over the next decade.*

China's strongest case for complying with the Paris climate accord is its stated commitment to reduce industrial over-capacity in key sectors such as steel and aluminium, which burn coal, and in achieving a more diversified economy. The rebalancing of China's economy, away from capital over-investment, low-cost manufacturing, and trade in favour of consumption and services will be the defining feature of the global economy over the next decade. This strategy appeared to be working according to plan until President Trump arrived on the global stage in 2016 and started demanding substantive changes to China's bilateral terms of trade with America. The accelerating tariff war has damaged China's growth prospects, forcing the hand of the authorities. It is no surprise that bad habits have returned — air pollution in Beijing in 2019 showed a dangerous return to pre-2012 levels mainly due to a fiscal boost, which provided incentives to factories to produce more. This cycle is likely to continue into the near future as China rebuilds after the pandemic. As a direct result, pollution readings in Beijing and neighbouring provinces have risen significantly by an estimated 8 percent, according to the Ministry of Ecology and Environment. "The readings assessed the amount of airborne particulate matter measuring less than 2.5 microns, known as PM2.5, which is considered one of the most dangerous pollutants because it can penetrate deep into the lungs and cause respiratory illnesses," *Reuters* reported in May 2019. In a perverse way, the accelerating trade war between America and China is forcing ordinary Chinese to breathe foul air and suffer serious health damage. In Beijing, the orange alert, which is the second highest in the capital's four-tier warning system, has made a decisive return and the health costs on ordinary Chinese will rise significantly in the years ahead.

Toxic Punchbowl

A similar crisis is unfolding in New Delhi as Prashant Kumar's study at the University of Surrey, cited earlier, shows. "Delhi has the dubious accolade of being regularly cited as the most polluted city in the world, with air pollution causing thousands of excess deaths in a year," the researcher explains. "Whilst it might be easy to blame this on increased use of vehicles, industrial production, or a growing population, the truth is that Delhi is a toxic pollutant punchbowl with myriad ingredients, all of which need addressing in the round." India's poor record in protecting its citizens from negative environmental impacts can be directly attributed to political dysfunction. Unlike in Beijing, when New Delhi mandates change, India's powerful states tend to ignore diktats from the centre. This also plays out in the Indian capital, which is ruled by the opposition Aam Aadmi Party (AAP, known as the Common Man's Party), and environmental issues become hostage to petty politics. Delhi Chief Minister Arvind Kejriwal, an engineering graduate from the country's elite IIT, has innovated with public policy to reduce air pollution in the city. In 2016, he introduced an "odd-even" rule restricting cars and two-wheelers with odd and even licence plate numbers to drive in the capital city on alternate days. The move was widely derided by New Delhi residents, although many of whom were not seriously impacted because they typically own more than one car. The policy was hastily withdrawn and is introduced sporadically during the winter months when pollution peaks.

Kejriwal's challenge demonstrates what happens in a mega-city when the interests of rich and middle-class citizens are misaligned with the majority of the population, who happen to be poor. New Delhi's elite cluster in the posh southern enclaves of the capital city and in Gurugram and Noida, sprawling suburbs with expensive high-rise apartments, manicured lawns, and shopping malls selling the Indian dream. Their air-conditioned existence contrasts with the living conditions of the poor, who cluster in shantytowns across the River Yamuna and in old Delhi. The AAP's campaign promise has been built on sensible steps to reduce air pollution in the city — measures include more tree planting, mechanised sweeping of roads, the mass distribution of facemasks, and the unpopular odd-even rule. However, the Common Man's Party cannot implement the rule because the capital city is an echo chamber of the rich and the powerful. Early in his political career, Kejriwal made news because he used public transport and was uncomfortable with elite trappings of power. Ultimately, he had to moderate his ambitions because the rich and the middle class dominate the airwaves daily while the poor only get to express their voice once in five years at the ballot box. Kejriwal's singular challenge in the next 18-months, warn ecologists, will be in dealing with a severe water crisis as the Upper Ganga Aquifer, which is the source of much of the water in the Indian capital, dries up. If this materialises, Delhi will become the second major Indian metro after Chennai to face an impending threat of a water crisis.

> *Kejriwal's challenge demonstrates what happens in a mega-city when the interests of rich and middle-class citizens are misaligned with the majority of the population, who happen to be poor.*

> *Another environmental drama is playing out in Indonesia, where parts of the country, Kalimantan and Sumatra notably, have become a massive palm oil plantation with over 7.8 million hectares under cultivation.*

Another environmental drama is playing out in Indonesia, where parts of the country, Kalimantan and Sumatra notably, have become a massive palm oil plantation with over 7.8 million hectares under cultivation. The WorldWatch Institute (WWI)[21] notes that the benefits of palm oil are difficult for Indonesia to ignore. "Once planted, the tropical tree can produce fruit for more than 30 years, providing much-needed employment for poor rural communities. And its oil is highly lucrative, due largely to the fact that the plant yields more oil per hectare than any other oilseed crop." Palm oil has also become an essential ingredient for cooking, cosmetics, and biofuel and is a vital ingredient in most consumer products sold globally. However, there is a dark side to this boom, as the WWI assessment notes. "Oil palm plantations often replace tropical forests, killing endangered species, uprooting local communities, and contributing to the release of climate-warming gases. Due mostly to oil palm production, Indonesia emits more greenhouse gases than any other country besides China and the United States." Indonesia is the world's largest producer of palm oil and together with Malaysia account for nearly 90 percent of world output.

The dramatic rise of palm oil is a relatively new phenomenon (1980s) and a surge in production can be directly linked to increasing consumer demand and a 2007 decision by the U.S. Energy Independence and Security Act. The American law was aimed at reducing the country's dependence on petroleum products and required[22] the replacement of a certain amount

---

[21] "Global Palm Oil Demand Fuelling Deforestation", WorldWatch Institute, September 2019.

[22] Abrahm Lustgarten, "Fuel to the Fire: How a U.S. law intended to reduce dependence on fossil fuels has unleashed an environmental disaster in Indonesia", *ProPublika*, 20 November 2018.

of petroleum products with ethanol from corn and sugar, and diesel with vegetable oils, mainly from soybeans. "Indonesian farmers who grow palm oil also contributed to the biodiesel supply but as soybean oil supplies around the world were used to support biodiesel in the United States, the food industry, which uses vegetable oils for lots of different purposes, went to palm oil instead," explains ProPublica reporter Abrahm Lustgarten in the report. I mention this because commentators rightly blame greedy Southeast Asian tycoons for unsustainable practices in the palm oil industry but ignore the hidden American hand behind the rise in demand. To develop truly sustainable palm oil will require action on the ground by Indonesian authorities, ensuring that the rights of small-holder farmers are protected, that the major plantations are in full compliance with internationally recognised standards in clearing forest land, in reforestation, and in paying a fair wage to plantation workers, many of whom are migrant labour with limited rights.

My own experience, in covering the palm oil industry as a journalist and more recently in banking, is that the notion of truly sustainable palm oil is pie-in-the-sky thinking. The incentive structure is skewed heavily in favour of expanding the amount of land under palm oil cultivation, not for its sustainable use. If left unchecked, it is easy to predict that the rainforests will disappear in a few decades and oil palm will be the only plant on the Indonesian side of Borneo. Huge forest fires, the direct result of annual clearing operations to make way for a new harvest, have already become a public health hazard in Malaysia, Singapore, and parts of Indonesia over the past three decades. Perversely, the Indonesian capital of Jakarta does not feel the impact from the forest fires, with Singapore and Kuala Lumpur bearing the brunt of the foul air. On a bad day due to the haze, Singapore's air quality can be as bad as that of New Delhi or Beijing.

> *If left unchecked, it is easy to predict that the rainforests will disappear in a few decades and oil palm will be the only plant on the Indonesian side of Borneo.*

What can be done to reverse the destruction of valuable rainforests and damage to public health in the region? International pressure will certainly help, including the fledgling global campaign against the use of palm oil. Multinational corporations like Unilever, which uses a phenomenal 1 million tonnes of crude palm oil annually in its products, has an out-sized role to play in changing behaviours in the entire palm oil supply chain, which includes growers, millers, and other intermediaries. Indonesia's own commitment to protect the Borneo rainforests and the overall environment should be held to account. Here the country's climate change mitigation efforts have been timid, poorly coordinated, and lack political will. In his second Presidential term (2019-2024), President Joko Widodo has committed to protecting the rainforests and to go after major palm oil firms for breaches in environmental and social rules. International and national pressure on Indonesia will have an impact but will not work fully unless politicians on the ground act on local concerns.

Human Dimension

There is a human dimension to Asia's unfolding environmental crisis as low-income communities across the region are displaced from their homes, forced to become climate refugees, and suffer serious health problems. They are collateral damage to the rise of palm oil as *the* world's essential food commodity, to the rise of coal as the essential feedstock for generating energy, and suffocating air pollution from the rise of the automobile as the essential mode of transport. If the humble motorcycle was the visible symbol of social mobility in the 1980s and 1990s, it is the gas mask, worn today by millions of Asians across the region, as the most visible manifestation of the

There is a human dimension to Asia's unfolding environmental crisis as low-income communities across the region are displaced from their homes, forced to become climate refugees, and suffer serious health problems.

worsening environmental crisis, pre-dating Covid-19. The World Health Organisation (WHO) identifies air pollution as the primary threat for the Asia-Pacific region as a whole: "Air pollution is the most lethal environmental threat in our region, and it affects people in middle-income countries at a much higher rate than those in high-income countries," says Dr Shin Young-soo, WHO Regional Director for the Western Pacific "....we need urgent action across energy, agriculture, transport, housing and beyond to ensure a healthy and sustainable future."

Who will lead this call to action if governments are ignoring the human impact and the corporate sector is part of the problem rather than the solution? While my assessment may be bleak, many analysts point toward the dramatic investments which China and India have made in recent years in renewables. China has mandated that it wants the country's car fleet to be completely electric by 2030 and its global competitive edge in building solar panels has made solar-sourced power generation cheaper than coal for the first time ever. India is also placing massive bets in solar and wind energy and has innovated by subsidising the public use of energy saving light-emitting diode (LED) bulbs. This is all for the good but old and bad habits die hard and the urgency to deal with the climate crisis is absent in the two Asian giants.

Asia needs a grass-roots revolution, *a la* Greta Thunberg, the Swedish teenage girl who has single-handedly done more to raise urgent, international attention to climate change than any summit of the United Nations. It should be a revolution led by young people because they will be inheriting a future filled with smog, contaminated water, and an unpredictable rise in temperatures. Thunberg started her protests by skipping school every Friday and launched a solo protest at Stockholm, holding a placard and drawing attention to the urgency of the climate crisis. "Even though this movement has become huge and there have been millions of children and young people who have been school striking for the climate, the emission curve is not reducing and of course that is all that matters." There is a model for young Asians to emulate. In 2019, Hong Kong's seemingly endless reserves of young protestors, led by the likes of Joshua Wong and Nathan Law, took to the streets and bravely battled against the introduction of an extradition law, which served as a proxy for their collective grievance against a range of issues. Asia needs a million young girls and boys to lead the charge on climate. The problem, as we will discover in the next chapter, it is not easy to be a teenage girl in a rising Asia.

Chapter 9

To Be a Teenage Girl in a Rising Asia

Our sixth circle of hell is the widening gender disparities in Asia and how it impacts disadvantaged teenage girls.

reta Thunberg and Malala Yousufzai are world's apart in terms of background and upbringing. Thunberg, 17, was born into relative privilege in egalitarian and welfare-rich Sweden. Her mother is an opera singer and father an actor. In *Scenes from the heart*,[1] the autobiography penned by the Thunberg family, Greta challenges her parents to reduce their carbon footprint by turning vegan and reducing international travel. She started skipping school every Friday in August 2018 by launching a valiant solo protest, "School Strike for Climate," which soon received global attention and adulation. The rest is history and Thunberg's actions generated the momentum for a genuine grass roots and youth-driven protest movement calling urgent attention to climate change. Thunberg's harsh words to global political grandees at the September 2019 U.N. Climate Action Summit was the defining moment of an otherwise torpid summit, full of platitudes and very little in terms of substance. "This is all wrong. I shouldn't be up here. I should be back in school on the other side of the ocean. Yet you all come

---

[1] Malena Ernman and Svante Thunberg, *Scener ur hjartat*, (Bokforlaget Polaris, 2018).

to us young people for hope. How dare you?" she thundered, adding that leaders had "stolen" her dreams and her "childhood" with empty words. I have waited for a long time for someone to deflate the hot air and pomposity of global summitry, which Thunberg accomplished effortlessly.

I have waited for a long time for someone to deflate the hot air and pomposity of global summitry, which Thunberg accomplished effortlessly.

In contrast to Thunberg's relatively privileged upbringing, new Oxford graduate Malala Yousufzai, 23, was born in Pakistan's achingly beautiful Swat Valley, the heartland of the country's rigidly conservative Pashtun community. Malala grew up in the aftermath of 9/11 and in the shadow of deadly conflict. The Pakistan branch of the Taliban, not to be mistaken with the deadlier Afghan clan, dominated the Swat Valley and sought to impose their medieval brand of religious doctrine, which severely restricted women's rights and access to education. The young Malala, then only 11 years old, spoke up by penning a pseudonymous article for BBC's local Urdu service advocating for girl's empowerment, their right to attend school, and became well-known, particularly after the Army stepped in and ejected the Pakistan Taliban. On 9 October 2012, two Taliban gunmen entered a public bus in which Malala was travelling with other girls. They were returning from school. Recounting the ordeal in a BBC interview a few years later,[2] Malala said that two Taliban boys stopped the bus on the pretext of searching for their sister. "The one who came at the back, he was young, he was not old. He had a gun here (gestures to hip) …. Then he said, who is Malala? All the girls were terrified. Some of the girls think he might be a journalist. They were not expecting, because we never thought it would happen." The young Taliban shot Malala in the head, fortunately not fatally, and she was flown to the UK for reconstructive surgery. Malala survived the assassination

---

[2] Ben Bryant, "Malala Yousufzai recounts moment she was shot in the head by Taliban", *The Telegraph*, 13 October 2013.

attempt and is indeed thriving as a powerful advocate of girls' rights. For her advocacy, she received the Nobel Peace Prize in 2015; Thunberg is surely likely to receive hers sooner rather than later.

The fact that two schoolgirls living in different corners of the world have captured the world's imagination over the past decade is both reflective of the uncertain times we live in, and the fact that socially conscious young women are acutely aware that we are facing a crisis and doing something about it. Comparing the background and circumstances of Greta and Malala is also important for one simple fact. In many parts of developing Asia, there are a hundred million Malalas — disadvantaged teenage girls facing social strictures, sanctions, and seemingly insurmountable barriers as they attempt to educate themselves and access economic opportunity just like their male peers.

> *These girls are unheralded, largely ignored by political and business elites, including I dare say by more privileged women who are pre-occupied with securing their own position in society.*

These girls are unheralded, largely ignored by political and business elites, including I dare say by more privileged women who are pre-occupied with securing their own position in society. Asia's disadvantaged teenage girls have become the region's silent and forgotten minority, just like urban cowboys and cowgirls, forced to play second or third fiddle by virtue of their gender and rarely feature in the international discourse. To be sure, there are multiple well-meaning global forums and UN summitry focused on lifting the "girl child." We will get to that later, but nothing quite squares with the grim reality of what the girls face daily to remind ourselves that the task at hand is daunting. Let's visit ground zero.

Collateral Damage

I was visiting a charity a few years ago in a busy corner of one of India's major urban centres. The charity's primary objective was to provide teenage girls from poor families with after-school skills training — to position them for jobs in the country's then booming economy. It was a state-run school and the classrooms were shabby but functional. Going by the enthusiasm with which we were greeted, the school population was eager to engage and learn new skills. The charity worker matter-of-factly told me that the biggest risk faced by the girls was not at school or at the after-school activities.

The risk to the girls, the charity worker told me, was sexual assault. The teenage girls were easy targets in the busy neighbourhood with narrow lanes abutting an open field.

These were safe places compared with the danger they faced in negotiating their neighbourhood to and from school every day. A majority of the girls hailed from a trading community which transacted business from home, selling their wares to visiting businessmen who came from across the country. The risk to the girls, the charity worker told me, was sexual assault. The teenage girls were easy targets in the busy neighbourhood with narrow lanes abutting an open field. Worse, the charity worker said, families of the victims seldom went to the police or sought the help of social workers. Their reasoning was shocking. Beyond the obvious fear of reputation damage, the families apparently feared a loss of business. Complaining to the police would scare customers away, they reasoned, damaging their economic prospects. Although the charity worker did not quite put it this way, the families probably regarded their girls to be collateral damage. Something to be accepted perhaps as the normal cost of doing business in India. There is a silver lining to this story, albeit a very thin lining, in that the charity worker told me that girls attending this school and the after-school activity have developed greater confidence and are able to advocate for themselves, even pushing back against sexual predators and going to the police.

While the girls going to school in the example cited above at least have the agency to protect themselves, the fate of thousands of girls in rural Thailand,

Cambodia, Myanmar, and Laos is even more tragic. In the early 1990s, when Thailand's economy was booming, international attention was focused on Bangkok's notorious sex trafficking industry. An overwhelming majority of girls were trafficked from rural areas, often with the consent of their parents. A *Los Angeles Times* article[3] reported from a remote mountain village around 460 miles north of Bangkok: "Now when girls finish sixth grade, the last mandatory grade in Thailand, teachers go out to try to persuade parents not to sell them into prostitution — at age 11," the paper reported. "Authorities send monks to the mountains of the north, where the practice is most common, to counsel parents it is wrong to sell their flesh and blood." Thai academic, Chakrapand Wongburanavart, quoted in the same article said that the once isolated villagers are increasingly sacrificing their daughters to pay for the luxuries of the modern world. "This is the shortest way to upgrade their social status," he said.

Over 26 years have elapsed since that article appeared and I was expecting to see a dramatic reduction in human trafficking in Thailand and Indochina. After all Thailand, despite suffering many economic ups and downs over the past two decades, has become a solid middle-income country with better prospects for the country's 60 million people. Thailand's neighbours, with the possible exception of Myanmar, have also come a long way due to rising incomes. My supposition was wrong. Here is an article from the *Bangkok Post*[4] on how an illegal "matchmaking" service in Laos hatched a plot to sell underage girls to Chinese men, facilitated by traffickers based in Bangkok. The newspaper cited the example of a 15-year old girl who was sold to the "matchmaking" service by her own father for around $310, a fortune in rural Laos. "It's her duty," the father was quoted as saying. "She is a daughter and that's what she is supposed to do — work and bring home some money. Moreover, she will have a better future married to a foreign man." The father's

---

[3] Sheila Mcnulty, "Thais Selling Daughters Into Prostitution", *Los Angeles Times*, 13 November 1994.

[4] Chaiyot Yongcharoenchai, "Lifting the veil on virgin brides for sale", *Bangkok Post*, 16 October 2016.

brutal assessment of his daughter's seemingly better prospects was belied when she was denied entry into China, because immigration officials rightly believed she was underage, and she was eventually rescued by an NGO in Vientiane. "I don't want to go home," the girl told the newspaper. "I know my father will be disappointed and he will try to find a way to send me away again. I don't want to go through that anymore."

> *Bangkok's sex trafficking industry has become a global hub — attracting middle-aged men from Europe, America, the Middle East, and other parts of Asia.*

While the spotlight in this story was on Chinese men seeking underage girls, they are by no means singularly guilty. Bangkok's sex trafficking industry has become a global hub — attracting middle-aged men from Europe, America, the Middle East, and other parts of Asia. It is both a shadowy and very visible industry — lightly regulated and dominated by criminal groups with the tacit support of law enforcement and the political class. The United Nations Office on Drugs and Crime reported in 2017[5] that of the 1,248 "detected" victims of trafficking for sexual exploitation in the 2014-2017 period, "almost 70 percent" were underage girls. However, Thailand's Attorney General only prosecuted 36 of these cases for reasons which are hard to fathom. Or not, if you understand the impunity with which sex trafficking rings operate in the country.

A few years ago, Thailand was outraged when *Newsweek* magazine declared that the country's fundamental strengths were "sex and golf courses."[6] When that report came out in 1999, at the height of Thailand's economic woes, I thought the characterisation was unfair. However, two decades later as the country has prospered, Thailand's leaders have shown little determination in stamping out Bangkok's laissez-faire sex trade. General Prayuth Chan-ocha,

---

[5] UNODC, "Transnational Organised Crime in Southeast Asia', 2017 report.

[6] George Wehrfritz, "Beyond sex and golf", *Newsweek*, 11 July 1999.

Thailand's Prime Minister was forced to act on human trafficking only over the threat of international sanctions. The most closely awaited report in Bangkok is the annual U.S. State Department's Trafficking in Persons annual report which had placed Thailand on a watchlist a few years ago. More recently in 2019, the State Department upgraded Thailand's ranking to Tier 2 over improved law enforcement. "The Government of Thailand does not fully meet the minimum standards for the elimination of trafficking but is making significant efforts to do so,"[7] the State Department said, listing efforts in identifying more victims, and sentencing convicted traffickers and complicit officials to significant prison terms as steps taken. The Thai Government has also reported a record increase in the number of rescued human trafficking victims, not only in the sex trade but also in lightly regulated industries such as fishing.

> *However, two decades later as the country has prospered, Thailand's leaders have shown little determination in stamping out Bangkok's laissez-faire sex trade.*

Unjust Disparity

To return to my original thesis about the seemingly pre-ordained fate of teenage girls in developing Asia, let's look at the structural, social, and demographic barriers which perpetuate bias and discrimination. Sri Mulyani Indrawati is a rare exception to the rule that all finance ministers in Asia have to be men.[8] She was a prominent academic in Indonesia before becoming a technocrat — running the World Bank's operations out of Washington D.C. in between terms as Finance Minister. In an eloquent article in *The Straits Times*[9] Sri Mulyani and a co-author argue that it is "deep unjust gender

---

[7] U.S. Department of State, "Trafficking in Persons Report 2019", Thailand section.

[8] The only other female Finance Minister in Asia today is India's Nirmala Sitharaman.

[9] Sri Mulyani Indrawati and Anne-Birgitte Albrectsen, "Asia: The Future is Female", *The Straits Times*, September 2018.

disparity" which is holding Asia back and offer three of the biggest issues which deserve the attention of business, governments, and civil society. To quote them in full:

> *"The first is challenging and changing everything in Asian societies that keeps women and girls from reaching their full potential in the work-force. We need to upend the gender norms that mean women take on the bulk of unpaid labour and care work. We must also end the culture of fear for girls in Asia's cities. Part of this is changing attitudes, but it's also about building more safety infrastructure. In an era of increased urbanisation, with girls and young women in cities having more opportunities for work and education than ever before, it is intolerable that they cannot leave their homes without fear of harassment, abuse or exploitation. The final thing we need to do is ensure girls have the right role models and mentors so they can really be the ones leading the way. If girls see more women in positions of leadership either in the boardroom, in senior management, or in elected offices, this starts to challenge the preconceptions of the types of jobs that girls should aspire to.*

The first is challenging and changing everything in Asian societies that keeps women and girls from reaching their full potential in the work-force.

Sri Mulyani's article is soaring with high purpose and exhortation for Asian governments to do a better job in protecting girls from abuse at home and in the workplace and in nurturing their full potential to contribute to society. The original sin in many Asian societies is the explicit social bias which favours boys over girls and hard-wires prejudice for life, which Sri Mulyani refers to as "challenging and changing" everything in Asian societies acting as a barrier for girls and women. There are examples from the recent past in Asia, perhaps outliers from the last century, where state and society treated women fairly and equitably — China under Mao and Afghanistan before the brutal civil war and rise of the Taliban. Tragically these gains have evaporated in recent years because of the primacy of the boy child in China and the resurgence of hardened social attitudes in Afghan society. The popular mythology of Mao's rule is that the great helmsman was absolutely wrong on almost every aspect of economic

There are examples from the recent past in Asia, perhaps outliers from the last century, where state and society treated women fairly and equitably — China under Mao and Afghanistan before the brutal civil war and rise of the Taliban.

and social policy in China in the 1950s and 1960s except for one — the role of women. Mao famously said in 1955 that women hold up "half the sky." Social policy analyst Helen Gao writes[10] about her grandmother's stories from her career as a journalist in the early decades of the People's Republic of China. "She recalls scrawling down Chairman's Mao's latest pronouncements as they came through loudspeakers and talking with joyous peasants from the newly collectivised countryside. In what was her career highlight, she turned an anonymous candy salesman into a national labour hero with glowing praises for his service to the people." Street photographs of Beijing and Shanghai during that era shown an army of men and women on bicycles, equal partners in the revolution. "The Communists did many terrible things," Gao quotes her grandmother as saying, "But they made women's lives much better." There are stinging critiques of course which challenge the proposition that Chinese women flourished during the Mao era. Commentators have pointed out that women still held a subordinate position at home and were expected to carry out all the household tasks. Although there were women in prominent positions of political power — Mao's own second wife was the architect of the disastrous Cultural Revolution — the Politburo and provincial party officials were predominantly men.

---

[10] Helen Gao, "How Did Women Fare in China's Communist Revolution?" *The New York Times*, 25 September 2017.

Afghanistan by contrast was truly a progressive society. It is hard to imagine that Kabul in the 1960s and 1970s was South Asia's ultra-hip capital city with high levels of girls' education and women holding prominent positions in business and politics. There are sepia-toned photographs from that era which show women holding their own well before a rigidly conservative society was born. Amnesty International reports[11] that until the conflict of the 1970s, which was triggered by toppling of the monarchy and the Soviet invasion, there was a steady progression in women's rights in the country. As a historical footnote, Afghan women earned the right to vote in 1919, a year after women in the UK and a year before America. In the 1950s, the government abolished purdah, the separation of men and women in social gatherings and society at large, and the country's new constitution protected women's rights. Afghanistan's progress toward a more egalitarian society has unfortunately been halted by a prolonged civil war, which accelerated under the Taliban's brutal rule. The restrictions against girls and women imposed under the Taliban are well-known but worth repeating — they were banned from going to school or studying, banned from working, banned from leaving the house without a male chaperone, banned from being involved in politics or speaking publicly. It is perhaps small comfort that no country in Asia today restricts women's rights quite on the scale of Afghanistan under Taliban. However, this is a back-handed compliment because the Taliban are an extreme example and what represents normal in developing Asia today is still worse than the global norm.

> *It is perhaps small comfort that no country in Asia today restricts women's rights quite on the scale of Afghanistan under Taliban.*

What can Asia learn from its recent past — utopian Afghanistan and China — to reverse the alarming slide in protections and rights for girls and women. A starting point should be demographics and the deification of boys over girls

---

[11] "Women in Afghanistan: The back story", Amnesty International UK, 25 November 2014.

in traditional societies. South Asia is a true laggard. In a damning report on gender equality in South Asia, UNICEF[12] reports that a preference for sons means that the girl child must struggle twice as hard to survive and fulfil her potential. "If the girl child manages to overcome health issues and gets a basic education, it is unlikely she will escape child marriage — in the region, 1 in 2 girls are married before the age of 18. Bangladesh has the highest rate of child marriage at 52 percent, followed by India at 47 percent, Nepal at 37 percent, and Afghanistan at 33 percent," UNICEF reports. The UN agency added that girls are also systematically disadvantaged across the region as "structural inequalities" and the low status of women affect their rights. "Social norms in South Asia prioritise a son receiving higher education, so the girl child often loses out on continuing her education," UNICEF notes. "This is seen in the stark differences in the girl-boy ratio in secondary level classrooms across the region. Women make up less than 5 percent of the police force and less than 10 percent of judges in South Asia — reflecting the strength of social norms and the disparity in justice systems."

To be born a girl in many parts of India and Asia is still regarded as a burden, even a curse. Developing Asia has made impressive strides in a range of socio-economic indicators, but the region still has some way to go in terms of gender equality and rights. I was born and raised in South India, as noted before, in a region noted for matriarchal-led societies which was an exception to the horrible patriarchy which prevails in the rest of the country. Norms and prejudices are embedded into individuals and conventional wisdom has it that women enjoy greater agency and freedoms in the south compared to the more medieval northern parts of the country. As I discovered sifting

> *Developing Asia has made impressive strides in a range of socio-economic indicators, but the region still has some way to go in terms of gender equality and rights.*

---

[12] UNICEF South Asia, "Introduction to gender equality program".

through health and gender data, my assumption was a simplistic one. Rapid economic development does not necessarily lead to egalitarian outcomes as evidenced, for example, with rising inequality at a time of high growth. Similarly, higher incomes do not translate into progressive gains for women and other oppressed segments of society. To paraphrase what Pramod told me in Chapter 3, men in Asia live in heaven and a significant majority of women live in hell. Dante himself, who idolised Beatrice although his views on women were regressive, would still be shocked with the dystopian situation faced by many women and girls in Asia today.

Son Meta-Preference

The modern version of *Inferno* is perhaps a chapter in India's annual Economic Survey for 2017-2018, which provides scathing evidence about what it describes as the country's "son meta-preference" which skews the sex-ratio at birth.[13] The survey notes that the "biologically determined" natural sex ratio at birth is 1.05 males for every female. Any significant deviation from this is on account of human intervention — specifically sex-selective abortion. "In the case of China, the one-child policy interacted with the underlying son-preference to worsen the sex ratio to 1,070 in 1970 to 1,156 in 2014. India's sex ratio during this period also increased substantially even without the one-child policy from 1,060 to 1,108, whereas if development acted as an antidote, it should have led to an improvement in the sex ratio." Looking at Indian state level data yields richer insights on

> *The modern version of Inferno is perhaps a chapter in India's annual Economic Survey for 2017-2018, which provides scathing evidence about what it describes as the country's "son meta-preference" which skews the sex-ratio at birth.*

---

[13] *Economic Survey 2017-2018*, Volume I, Chapter 7 "Gender and Son Meta-Preference: Is Development Itself an Antidote?"

the extent of anti-female bias pervasive throughout the country. The sex ratio in Punjab and Haryana, two of India's richest states is 1,200 males per 1,000 females, the highest in the country. The other lagging performers, unsurprisingly, are states to the north and centre of the country. Southern states, with the exception of Andhra Pradesh, perform considerably better.

Although India banned the practice of parents determining the sex of the child before birth, the practice is widely prevalent. The Economic Survey also highlights that the policy has created unintended consequences. In states where the regulation is effective, this has led to the perverse practice of the "son meta- preference." Quite simply, with the ban in sex determination in place, many Indian parents continue to have children until a son is born. Families where a son is born are also more likely to stop having children than families where a girl is born. "A son meta preference — even though it does not lead to sex-determined abortion — may nevertheless be detrimental to female children because it may lead to fewer resources devoted to them," according to the Survey. Under this scenario, adolescent and teenage girls are deprived of access to education, healthcare, and nutrition because of explicit bias in the household towards boys. In 1990, Indian economist Amartya Sen had calculated that due to the skewed ratio of females to males globally, he estimated that nearly 100 million women were "missing" in the world, almost 40 million in India alone at the time.[14] The missing women are a result of human intervention in terminating pregnancies and the son meta preference. Using similar methodology, the Economic Survey calculates that the stock of missing women in India, as of 2014, was nearly 63 million and "more than 2 million women go missing across age groups every year, either due to sex selective abortion, disease, neglect, or inadequate nutrition."

We should let these words sink in — a stock of 63 million missing women and more than 2 million women going missing across age groups every year. As context, this is equivalent to the entire population of France, and larger than

---

[14] Sen's analysis initially appeared in an essay he authored for *The New York Review of Books*.

We should let these words sink in — a stock of 63 million missing women and more than 2 million women going missing across age groups every year.

the population of South Korea. Successive Indian governments have attempted to address the endemic discrimination and social practice on the reasonable belief that higher incomes and better social outcomes go hand in hand. Prime Minister Modi launched his *Beti Bachao, Beti Padhao* campaign in 2015, which translates to save the daughter, educate the daughter, with the following pledge. "Let us celebrate the birth of the girl child. We should be equally proud of our daughters. I urge you to sow five plants when your daughter is born to celebrate the occasion." Key pillars of the BBBP campaign are tighter enforcement against sex-determined abortion and the mobilisation of communities at district level to reduce the unfortunate stigma and prejudice which exists on the arrival of a baby girl in the household. Indian demographic data shows that fast-growing states with socially progressive policies, in the south and west of the country, are aging faster compared with the states in the northern hinterland with low growth and high population rates. Journalist Samar Halarnkar[15] describes this as India "slowly cleaving" into two countries — the old south and the young north. Fertility rates in four southern Indian states have fallen to 1.7 to 1.9 per women, well below the replacement rate of 2.1, and match levels of advanced Western European countries like the UK, Sweden, Holland, and Norway. "In contrast, women in the cow-belt states of Rajasthan, Uttar Pradesh, Bihar, and Madhya Pradesh are popping out three children or more; Chhattisgarh and Jharkhand are just below three. These fertility rates are in line with countries like Haiti, Lesotho, and Guatemala," Halarnkar writes. Many of these children are a result of the son meta-preference.

India is by no means the only Asian country facing demographic and social practices which favour boys over girls. China's case is even more

---

[15] Samar Halarnkar, "India is slowly cleaving into two countries – the old south and the young north", *Quartz India*, 29 June 2016.

stark because the country is aging far more rapidly than India and state intervention, in the form of President Xi scrapping the unpopular one-child policy, is unlikely to reverse several decades of gender discrimination. The origins of the one-child policy have a lot to do with Deng Xiaoping's 1979 reform agenda.[16] Alarmed with Malthusian warnings about the country's exploding population, then at 970 million, Deng introduced the policy as a temporary measure and was initially targeted at the majority Han population in urban areas.

China's case is even more stark because the country is aging far more rapidly than India and state intervention, in the form of President Xi scrapping the unpopular one-child policy, is unlikely to reverse several decades of gender discrimination.

However, as with any centrally directed policy emanating from Beijing, the provinces aggressively implemented the rule by requiring women to have abortions if they had more than one child and forced sterilisations if anyone violated the rule. To say it as it is, the one-child policy was anti-female because it forced Chinese parents to make a choice. Their overwhelming preference for boys over girls has played out against the backdrop of dizzy economic growth since 1979. Health experts have documented a sharp rise in out-of-country adoption, where parents were willing to give away their girls to retain the option of having a boy child. There has been an increase in the adoption of girls from mainland China since 1979. The journal Adoption Quarterly estimates that since 1992, when China allowed foreign adoptions, around "70,000 primarily female infants" have been adopted by American parents. Statistics on adoption of Chinese girls into other countries are hard to come by and they certainly do not account for all of China's own missing girls. While most medical advances have helped society, the development of

---

[16] Much before China introduced its one-child policy, India attempted forced sterilisations on a mass scale between 1975 and 1977 under Emergency rule imposed by Prime Minister Indira Gandhi. The programme was hugely unpopular and was partially responsible for Mrs Gandhi's electoral defeat in 1977.

the sonography has played a detrimental role in China, India and elsewhere, in giving parents the access to determining the sex of the child before birth. Abortion levels in China since the one-child policy was introduced, going by formal and informal estimates,[17] is between 300-400 million and these are primarily female foetuses. The 400 million figure may well be over the top but even a 100 million abortions are an excessive amount. Strangely enough, the National Health and Family Planning Commission, which brutally enforced the policy estimates that it's "good policies," i.e. restricting Chinese parents to having one child, have resulted in 400 million fewer births since 1981.

President Xi overturned the one-child policy in 2016 and Chinese couples are today allowed to have two children, a policy relaxation which has come too little and too late. After heralding the policy change as a major piece

> *President Xi overturned the one-child policy in 2016 and Chinese couples are today allowed to have two children, a policy relaxation which has come too little and too late.*

of social reform, China's leadership has suddenly turned silent on the topic. "The absence of family planning references in the National Day parade is a strong signal that family planning has done more harm than good to this country and has never been a so-called great accomplishment," Mu Guangzong, a professor from Beijing's Institute for Population Research told the *South China Morning Post*.[18] The newspaper estimates that China's labour force, defined as those aged between 15 and 59, has declined by 40 million over the last seven years, painting a gloomy demographic picture that adds pressure on Beijing to abandon birth restrictions and encourage births. New births have also dropped to 14.6 million in 2019 and the birth rate plummeted to 10.48 per 1,000, estimated to be the lowest number since the revolutionary days of 1949.

---

[17] China's Health Ministry disclosed in 2013 that there were an estimated 336 million abortions since the one-child policy was introduced in 1979. Unofficial estimates are higher.

[18] Zhou Xin and Cissy Zhou, "China's 'awkward silence' as lack of family planning slogans from 70th anniversary parade could signal policy shift", *South China Morning Post*, 2 October 2019.

Brides Shortage

China's rapid population ageing and the huge gender divide has created an industry of experts in Beijing and beyond who fret about social cohesion and what they impolitely refer to as a "brides shortage." Sitting in his elegant think-tank office in a leafy Beijing suburb, one of China's prominent security specialists painted a stark picture about the country's demographic choices in the future. This was in 2016, the year when China hosted the G20 to pomp and pageantry, and secured accolades for advancing the global economic agenda. The security specialist told me that nation-states have historically gone to war over securing natural resources or defending their territory. His prediction is that in the distant future, China's stark gender gap will force the leadership to consider an invasion of a different kind — for brides, as the country runs out of marriageable women and a surplus of men posed a fundamental challenge to political stability. "The genesis of the Arab spring was that you had too many unemployed young men who had nothing to do," the specialist told me. "They revolted out of frustration. Now multiply the number of young men in the Arab world by a factor of a hundred and you have China." The specialist then pulled out a notebook and proceeded to draw a crude map of Asia. "India will be in the same situation as China in a few years," he said, striking out South Asia, noting that the region was under India's sphere of influence. "In our immediate neighbourhood, all the countries are ageing rapidly. So, we have to look further afield — in Southeast Asia and Central Asia as the source." China and India combined have a population of close to 2.8 billion, with at least 100 million "extra" men who will be desperately seeking a partner in the next decade. The consequences for domestic and regional instability are likely to be profound and little understood by the region's political class.

> *China's rapid population ageing and the huge gender divide has created an industry of experts in Beijing and beyond who fret about social cohesion and what they impolitely refer to as a "brides shortage".*

The security specialist's somewhat crass and unexpected candour startled me. China think-tank officials are usually very guarded in their interactions with foreigners. However, I may have met him when this issue was uppermost on his mind and he decided to take me into his confidence. Fretting about a brides shortage is not a uniquely Chinese phenomenon. All over developing Asia, the sharp rise in human trafficking has been linked with a rise in bride trafficking, which can have tragic consequences on the girls as we discussed earlier. "There is irony here," *Human Rights Watch* noted in a recent report.[19] "When there are too many women, women lose. When there are too few women…women again lose. But the truth is we all lose. We know that skewed sex ratios are already having harmful consequences and we do not fully understand what other long-term consequences there may be for societies affected by these disparities."

Given the huge social barriers that girls face in accessing school education, one can assume that they probably under-perform compared with boys on a full set of metrics. This assumption is not only wrong but reinforces social stereotypes endemic in many Asian societies about the learning abilities of girls.

There is a panoply of global research as to why girls outperform boys at school through college, regardless of nationality and region. "From elementary school through college, girls are more disciplined about their schoolwork than boys: they study harder and get better grades. And

> *There is a panoply of global research as to why girls outperform boys at school through college, regardless of nationality and region.*

yet men nonetheless hold a staggering 95 percent of the top positions in the largest public companies," writes clinical psychologist Lisa Damour,[20]

---

[19] Heather Barr, "You should be worrying about the woman shortage", Human Rights Watch, 4 December 2018.

[20] Lisa Damour, "Why Girls Beat Boys at School and Lose to Them at the Office", *The New York Times*, 2 July 2019.

citing data from American schools and colleges. *The Economist cites*[21] an OECD study which looked at school outcomes of 15-year old boys and girls across 23 rich countries in reading, mathematics, and science. The core results showed that boys still score somewhat better at maths, and in science the genders are roughly equal. However, the study showed that when it comes to students who really struggle, the difference is "stark": boys are 50 percent more likely than girls to fall short of basic standards in all three areas. Overall, girls outperform boys in school for three principal reasons:

However, the study showed that when it comes to students who really struggle, the difference is "stark": boys are 50 percent more likely than girls to fall short of basic standards in all three areas.

- Girls read more than boys. Reading proficiency is the basis upon which all other learning is built.

- Girls spend more time on homework. Researchers suggest that doing homework set by teachers is linked to better performance in maths, science, and reading.

- Peer pressure plays a role. Boys are likely to be more disruptive in class, egged on by their peers, which fosters negative teacher perceptions (and lesser scores).

High Scores

Scanning the global literature, I was curious to analyse if the high school scores for girls versus boys translated to developing Asia, particularly since the girls faced significantly higher social barriers and prejudice. The answer

---

[21] "Why girls do better at school than boys", *The Economist*, 6 March 2015.

Singapore is the gold standard in Asian school education, and educators are actively intervening to narrow the gender gap to ensure that girls and boys perform well in secondary and tertiary education.

is an emphatic yes. Let's start with Singapore which is internationally recognised for doing a superb job in educating girls *and* boys. Statistics[22] from the Ministry of Education showed that girls in the city-state tend to outdo boys academically at a younger age although this gap closes as they enter their late teens and early 20s. "The disparity in performance between boys and girls is a complex issue that depends on various factors, such as subject matter, students' education level, motivational level and behaviours and the education systems," explained a spokesperson for the Ministry of Education in the article. Singapore is the gold standard in Asian school education, and educators are actively intervening to narrow the gender gap to ensure that girls and boys perform well in secondary and tertiary education.

Let's move to the hyper-competitive city of Mumbai, where families put their children veritably through the grind to secure high scores in the annual school leaving exam. To give you a sense of scale, look at the sheer number of students who appear in these exams — the 2019 cohort in the western Indian state of Maharashtra alone amounted to over 1.7 million students. Three students from Mumbai, which is Maharashtra's capital, featured amongst the top ten at the national level in 2019. Two of the three students were girls and girls overall performed significantly better than the boys. At the state level, the girls outshined the boys by a hefty pass percentage of 10 percent — 82 percent for the girls compared with 72 percent for the boys. This is by no means an urban phenomenon since schools in semi-urban and rural areas performed better than urban centres. With some variation,

---

[22] Amelia Teng, "Girls lead in primary school, but boys catch up: MOE study", *The Straits Times*, 2 January 2017.

these outcomes are replicated on a national level, seemingly giving girls a significant academic advantage as they prepare to go to college. The tragic aspect of this story is that there is a sharp fall in the drop-out rates of girls at two levels — when they turn 12 and when they pass the school leaving exams. A majority of the girls never make it to college, giving men a significant advantage in the workplace. Although India has passed a progressive Right to Education Act, giving all citizens free access to a school education, social restrictions and expectations about a girl's "place" at home is having an adverse impact. *Time magazine*[23] interviewed a 11-year old girl Nehi who had to drop out of school to help with housework. "My brother and sister are very small. My grandmother is old and ill. If I don't help my mother, she will not be able to manage especially during the harvest season…," she said, a phenomenon not unique in a country where girls are placed on a lower social pedestal compared with boys.

We next turn to another major Asian country, Indonesia, to see whether it was doing a better job than India in girls' education. On the face of it, the metrics are better. Rates of women literacy and school enrolment are significantly higher compared with India. One of the signature achievements of President Suharto's early tenure was in social development and those gains have remained constant despite the vicissitudes of the Asian Financial Crisis, which impacted the country the most. These gains have held steady and a blog in The Borgen Project[24] reports that student enrolment in Indonesia is no longer influenced by gender. Citing UNICEF data, it added that 92.8

One of the signature achievements of President Suharto's early tenure was in social development and those gains have remained constant despite the vicissitudes of the Asian Financial Crisis, which impacted the country the most.

---

[23] "School has been a right for girls since 2009. So why aren't they going?" *Time magazine*, 27 July 2019.

[24] "Top Ten Facts about Girl's Education in Indonesia", The Borgen Report, January 2019.

percent of Indonesian girls and 92.7 percent of boys were enrolled in primary school, with the percentage falling to 62.4 percent of girls and 60.9 percent of boys at secondary school level. "In Indonesia, girls are more likely than boys to drop out of school," the blog noted "…one of the primary reasons for this is early marriage and the stereotypical mind of society."

Womenomics

What can be done to overcome social conventions and stereotypical minds across developing Asia? The problem is certainly not a lack of financial resources since countries are devoting ever more resources to improving education and health outcomes. The deployment of these resources could of course be gender-focused in as much as the increased spending is doing little to overcome social prejudice. To use public policy phraseology, two fundamental challenges stand in the way of improving educational and economic opportunities for girls in society. The first problem, which we have discussed at length, has to do with the *pipeline*, i.e. they aren't enough girls completing school and entering college for them to access quality jobs and fulfilling careers. The data from Indonesia on secondary school drop-out rates for girls is symptomatic of an Asia-wide problem of ensuring equitable education outcomes for both sexes. It matters little if Asia is creating millions of manufacturing and service sector jobs if these roles are primarily going to qualified men.

No government, including dictatorial ones, can simply mandate that education is a human right and expect a dramatic transformation in hardened social attitudes.

The region's second problem has a lot to do with delivering sensible policy outcomes at *the last mile*. Asian policymakers talk a good talk in national capitals and in global forums about their commitment to strengthening gender equality and to girl's education. However, even the most caring bureaucrat and local politician fails at ground level because high purpose collides with social reality at the last mile. No government, including dictatorial ones, can simply mandate that education is a human right and expect a dramatic transformation in hardened social attitudes. Although not a developing country, Japan's experience in the last five years under former Prime Minister Shinzo Abe is instructive.

In 2013 and in the face of international criticism, Abe articulated his "womenomics" strategy to increase female participation in the country's ageing workforce and to build a more equitable society. Japan's demographic challenges are well known but what was perhaps less well known was the persistently low female participation in the workforce. Unlike developing Asia, Japan does not have a pipeline problem. Education levels for men and women are very high, befitting its status as Asia's richest nation. However, Japan's masculine and patriarchal workplace was uncaring and discriminatory towards women. Highly qualified women in their twenties and thirties were relegated to work as "coffee ladies" in giant corporations with the implicit expectation that they would eventually become housewives.

In response, many educated women flocked to work for foreign companies based in Japan, where their skills were recognised and pathway to senior positions was assured. One of them, who rose through the ranks of global investment banking was Kathy Matsui, formerly in a senior Japan leadership role at Goldman Sachs and who coined the phrase "womenomics." In the six years since it was launched, the female participation in the Japanese economy has inched up and is currently at a higher level than the United States. However, there are persistent social barriers which are hindering further progress and Abe's vision of a truly egalitarian workplace. "Analysis of the success of womenomics finds areas of progress but also persistent challenges," reports the Council on Foreign Relations (CFR).[25] "Government policies to

---

[25] "Japan introduces "womenomics" to counter the country's aging workforce and boost GDP" — Spotlight on Japan, CFR.Org, 2019.

increase women's labour force participation have had little immediate effect on the strong cultural pressures that dissuade many Japanese women from staying in the workforce." Japan has introduced truly progressive tax benefits and childcare, aimed at the retention of professional women in the public and private sectors. Japan can afford to do this despite having one of the highest debt-to-GDP ratios in the world. Since most of the debt is denominated in yen, it reduces the chances of the country facing a traditional financial crisis.

Offering generous fiscal incentives could be a bridge too far for developing Asia as finance ministers juggle competing demands for resources. In any event, more money is not necessarily the panacea for improving the social conditions and economic opportunity of Asia's teenage girls. Money of course will be helpful, but no amount of money can deal with deeply entrenched social attitudes and prejudice. Developing Asia needs social transformation on a dramatic scale, a true cultural revolution, led by women and supported by fathers, brothers, sons to agitate for change and deliver results on the ground. In what form and shape will this revolution take?

> *Developing Asia needs social transformation on a dramatic scale, a true cultural revolution, led by women and supported by fathers, brothers, sons to agitate for change and deliver results on the ground.*

It will be hard to mandate from the top — Asia's gerontocratic leadership lacks the stamina and the will to bring about sudden social change. It requires committed citizenry to look within themselves and campaign for change, perhaps on the scale of recent protests by young Hong Kongers, although they should eschew violence. Which brings me back to Malala Yousufzai and Greta Thunberg. These young ladies have defied the odds by championing change against formidable odds. Their examples could provide the playbook for a girl's revolution. Hopefully they don't have to take to the jungle, as militants in our next chapter have been forced to do.

Chapter 10

A Million Internal Mutinies

Our seventh circle of hell is Asia's raging internal insurgencies,
a potent cocktail of isms, separatism, and religious identity.

I was at a dinner with a South African diplomat a few years before East Timor separated from Indonesia in the bloody 1999 referendum, when it was not so obvious that independence was within reach. The diplomat had been in the "bush" during South Africa's long years of apartheid rule and had come into contact with many freedom fighters from East Timor, currently serving in leadership positions in Dili. I pushed back against his assertion that East Timor was about to separate, noting that Indonesia would never give up its territory. With a twinkle in his eye, the diplomat told me that it was my relative youth and inexperience which was speaking. He added that the main difference between Asian and African governments in fighting domestic insurgencies was that "Asia did not quite know when the game was over." He said that even South Africa's notoriously racist apartheid government did not take long in the early 1990s to conclude that White rule was unsustainable. "Given your ethnic and religious diversity, it is very hard for majoritarian leaders to compromise, until it is too late," he said.

If Asia's insurgencies were a contiguous land mass, it would probably comprise the fourth largest country after China, India, and Indonesia, with the impacted population in the 200-300 million range.

The diplomat's words are ringing in my ear as I focus attention on the region's million internal mutinies. If Asia's insurgencies were a contiguous land mass, it would probably comprise the fourth largest country after China, India, and Indonesia, with the impacted population in the 200-300 million range. From the high mountains of Indian-occupied Kashmir to the low plains of the Gangetic delta, a diverse group of Indian insurgents have waged an uninterrupted low-intensity war against the state for decades. China's restive and remote western half of the country, with Tibet and Xinjiang as the epicentre, has been in the throes of insurgency for just as long. The sprawling archipelagic state of Indonesia has faced bloody separation, in East Timor as noted above, now independent Timor Leste after the 1999 referendum; sporadic unrest in Aceh before the region was provided autonomy; Papua, and Maluku; and a major threat from Islamic extremism. In the southern Philippines, a rag-tag but lethal band of insurgents from the New People's Army, the Moro Islamic Liberation Front, and the more extremist Abu Sayyaf group have wreaked havoc with successive governments in Manila simultaneously waging war and peace. Thailand faces an Islamic insurgency on its heel and neighbouring Myanmar is renowned for its pot-pourri of insurgent groups who have battled the Bamar majority-dominated government for decades.

Majoritarian Instincts

In a sure sign of the majoritarian instincts of Asia's leaders, Myanmar's Aung San Suu Kyi, recently deposed in a coup, has destroyed her global reputation by standing firmly on the side of the Myanmar generals in their vengeful pogrom against the Rohingya. The once revered pro-democracy icon even appeared before the International Court of Justice (ICJ) in the Hague in December 2019, defending her government's actions and insisted that claims of atrocities had been either exaggerated or misconstrued. "Genocidal intent cannot be the only hypothesis," she told the ICJ, without referring to the Rohingya, and pushed back against suggestions that Myanmar was not capable of addressing the issue. Like much of the international community, I admired Daw Suu's courage and tenacity during her long years in detention, but was cautioned by friends who knew her well from her days as a student in New Delhi that she was first and foremost a Burmese nationalist, like her revered late father Aung San. Defending and articulating majority Bamar rights would be her primary objective, they said, and she is eager to make peace with the Army. This cynical strategy has failed because the Army never quite trusted the lady and moved aggressively to remove her from power.

The insecurities of the Myanmar military and the Bamar elite is perhaps understandable given the country's state of permanent conflict. Writing in the London Review of Books,[1] historian and former UN official Thant Myint-U notes that since the Japanese bombing of Rangoon began in December 1941, Myanmar hasn't had a "single year" of peace. "In the uplands, minority communities established their own militias, to protect themselves and enforce their demand for self-rule," he writes. "The communist insurgency is long over, but more than two-dozen 'ethnic armed organisations' still exist, plus hundreds of smaller groups. No one knows how many people have died in this, the longest of all wars in the world; perhaps half a million, with millions more displaced."

Asia's melting pot of different ethnicities, tribes, and religious affiliations is one of the region's great strengths. At the dawn of

> *Asia's melting pot of different ethnicities, tribes, and religious affiliations is one of the region's great strengths.*

---

[1] "Not a Single Year's Peace — Myint-U Thant on Burma's Problems", *London Review of Books* 41, no.22 (21 November 2019).

independence in the mid-1940s, leaders drew strength from diversity and attempted to curb the worse majoritarian instincts of the dominant ethnic group like the Han Chinese in China, or religious majorities in India and Indonesia. That strategy is fraying as majoritarianism has made a decisive comeback and in every economically successful Asian country, there is an insurgency or two as separatist groups invoke Marxism, nationalism, cultural identity, and religion to battle the all-powerful state. In the age of hyper-nationalism and nativism, secular values which bound Asia together in a web of tolerance for centuries are showing signs of stress. The consequences for developing Asia has been increased militancy, violence, and the state using all of this as a pretext to assume greater powers. This is a battle which Asia's new generation of strongmen are relishing as they are no big fans of domestic peace building.

Writer and peace mediator Michael Vatikiotis has written a powerful book[2] on Southeast Asia's struggles in balancing fast economic growth with the inability of the political class to promote inclusive policies. "The gun is never far removed from the political arena in Southeast Asia," he writes. "For a part of the world that has made so much social and material progress, that regularly tops charts of economic growth and investment, why do so many countries plumb the bottom of international indices measuring freedom and good government? Why does the region continue to struggle with democratic transition?" Vatikiotis adds[3] that in his book he has identified the "perpetual selfishness" of urban ruling elites, their reluctance to share the fruits of growth and development, resolve chronic conflicts, and resistance to accountability as exerting a "considerable" drag on social and political progress.

As a member of the urban elite which Vatikiotis refers to, I must confess to have been completely oblivious to the troubles and terrors faced by the

---

[2] Michael Vatikiotis, *Blood and Silk: Power and Conflict in Modern Southeast Asia* (Orion Books, 2017).

[3] Michael Vatikiotis, guest post in Asian Books Blog, 21 July 2017.

poor in the rural parts of my country. I grew up in urban, cosmopolitan Hyderabad, now capital of newly constituted Telangana state, where our pre-occupations, at least that of a majority of us in the 1970s and 1980s, was on very mundane thoughts of career progression, rising up the middle-class ladder, and buying the elusive first home. While urban

> *While urban Hyderabad slept, one of modern India's great and bloody insurgencies was literally flaring up at our doorstep with the direct support of more than a few of our middle-class brethren.*

Hyderabad slept, one of modern India's great and bloody insurgencies was literally flaring up at our doorstep with the direct support of more than a few of our middle-class brethren. The insurgents are called Naxalites, named after the Naxalbari district in eastern India where the rural poor went up

> *At its peak in the mid-2000s, the "red corridor" controlled by the Naxalites straddled ten Indian states, a staggering 180 districts, and total population of over 200 million.*

in arms in 1967. It is an urban-rural insurgency with financing, ideology, and strategy provided by a group of middle-and-upper class Indians disaffected by the Indian state. The Naxalites fight with and on behalf of the poor in rural India with the objective of establishing an independent Marxist-Maoist enclave in a big chunk of eastern, central, and southern India. At its peak in the mid-2000s, the "red corridor" controlled by the Naxalites straddled ten Indian states, a staggering 180 districts, and total population of over 200 million. The actual number of Naxal fighters, aligned with at least a dozen splinter groups of the original Communist Party of India (Marxist–Leninist) is believed to number around 20,000. Their governing ideology is Maoism blended with home-grown beliefs.

While the actual number of fighters is disputed, the Observer Research

Foundation (ORF) notes[4] that the Indian state has had to deploy a counter-insurgency strategy (COIN) to combat the rise of Naxalite insurgency, modelled on what U.S. forces did against Islamic extremists in Iraq and Afghanistan. "Various COIN initiatives have been an amalgamation of both population-centric and enemy-centric approaches, combining law and order mechanisms and development instruments," the ORF paper said. "Given that law and order is under the purview of the states or provinces, the most crucial counterinsurgency efforts are in the hands of state-level leadership." Indian states have been ham-handed in the way they have managed the Naxalite menace. While the Naxal attacks on state targets have led to heavy-handed intervention, little attention has been paid to improving the lot of the rural poor.

In Naxal Territory

The roots of this insurgency and indeed of the Naxal moment itself have received considerable attention in India and other parts of South Asia. Rather than plough through old history, let me offer you a glimpse of what made a group of urban intellectuals take up arms against the Indian state and wage a decades-long insurgency. More critically, India does need to worry about a new generation of disaffected urban intellectuals, raised amongst spectacular riches but living in relative poverty, launching a million new mutinies of their own against rising inequality, stalled social mobility, and political obsolescence. The Modi government has even coined a new phrase, urban naxals, to describe and

> *The Modi government has even coined a new phrase, urban naxals, to describe and deride any opposition to its rule from urban intellectuals, implying that it is only a matter before they take up arms and challenge the status quo.*

---

4 Niranjan Sahoo, "Half a Century of India's Maoist Insurgency: An Appraisal of the State Response", ORF Occasional Paper, June 2019.

deride any opposition to its rule from urban intellectuals, implying that it is only a matter before they take up arms and challenge the status quo. The concentration of these urban naxals is in media, civil society, and educational institutions like the Jawaharlal Nehru University in New Delhi.

My personal experience is several decades old but remains relevant as the Naxalite insurgency rages on, with its own peaks and troughs. In 1987, I was a journalist working in Bombay when a senior representative of a Naxal group operating out of Hyderabad invited me and a group of journalists to undertake a "field trip" to a remote part of Telangana to witness rural distress for ourselves. It was a tempting invitation to visit my own backyard, of which I knew so little. The assignment would also take me away from my day job at a business magazine covering India's business elite, a privileged walled-off world where the currency at the time was earnings per share and the subversion of India's suffocating economic rules.

My first shock was soon after our arrival into Hyderabad. We were received by the son of a prominent local lawyer and taken to his home in an affluent part of the city. I was simply unaware of the tentacles and reach of the Naxal movement amongst the elite in the state. The young man and his father were steeped in privilege, but they were risking it all by lending support to

Familiar quotes of the Great Helmsman we heard from the young Naxals was that "power flows through the barrel of the gun" and "armed struggle" was the only way of meeting the aspirations of the country's "teeming millions".

what they regarded as unjust depredations that the rural poor were being subjected to. The second shock was not the relative comforts of the house, which had all the trappings of upper-class India, but the language and discourse. A few of my journalist colleagues in the group had leftist leanings, not at all surprisingly for India at the time. They were comfortable with Karl Marx thought, which they debated each evening at the Bombay Press Club over rum and instant noodles, but even they struggled to debate the merits of Maoism and class warfare, which the young man and his associates effortlessly cited as proof of India's many inequities. Familiar quotes of the Great Helmsman we heard from the young Naxals was that "power flows through the barrel of the gun" and "armed struggle" was the only way of meeting the aspirations of the country's "teeming millions."

For the next five days as we made our way through rural parts of the state in a plush white van, to escape being noticed was the reason offered, we were challenged by our hosts about our beliefs and convictions about Indian democracy. During a particularly heated argument over dinner, the young man coldly informed that my head would be on the chopping block "when the revolution came." I was regarded as a member of the "petty bourgeoise" who was supporting the status quo. The ideological debate over dinner was all about seizing private property and business on day one of the revolution, creating revolutionary committees at every Indian village, and jailing and executing the bourgeoise. I felt that the debate, fortified by cheap alcohol, was taking place in a parallel universe. The young man and his associates were no armchair Maoists or Marxists like many of my fellow journalists. They were prepared to go to battle on behalf of the rural poor and indeed they showed much empathy in our meetings at several dirt-poor villages during the following days. What we witnessed at ground level in rural India, far away from the concerns and pre-occupations of urban citizens, was that life was particularly hard for the poor because of mass exploitation by rich farmers with the tacit support of the state. In one district, a majority of people worked in beedi[5] factories, delicately wrapping thousands of tendu leaves for 12-15 hours a day with limited wages and no labour protections. A majority of the workers were women.

During research for this book, I went back to a few primary and secondary sources to look at the state of the Naxal movement in Telangana. To my

---

[5] A beedi is a traditional Indian cigarette wrapped in a leaf from the Coromandel ebony tree, known as tendu locally, which curiously enough grows in parts of South and East India where the Naxal movement is powerful.

disappointment, I learnt that India's economic reforms since the early 1990s has accelerated rural distress and the Naxal movement is alive and well, albeit under a new generation of leadership. In 2006, then Prime Minister Manmohan Singh even declared that "Naxalism" represented the "single biggest internal security challenge every faced by India." The Naxalites have been targeted Indian police and para-military forces as part of their terror campaign, killing over 2000 since 1989. While the Naxals themselves have been targets of the state, civilian deaths still constitute the largest share of the 12,000 deaths. Writing about the anguish of the rural poor, legal scholar Raman Dixit writes[6] that "sometimes", there is a limit to what people "can brook." "Their faith in the legal system fails them, the popular government becomes a toy in the hands of the industrial bourgeoise and capitalist entrepreneurs, they lose the power to govern even the aspects of their own lives and there is a sense of simmering anarchy. This is not a passing mood — it has been born out of a strong sense of being wronged and alienated amidst their land and property."

The rise of the Naxal movement in India is not only due to the stickiness of Marxist or Maoist thought, which ironically has been discredited after the fall of Communism in the late 1980s. It also represents the spectacular failure of governance on the part of successive Indian governments in implementing land reform and in ensuring that the rural poor also benefitted from a rise in national incomes. "The credit for the survival of the movement for over 40 years must go to the government, which has failed abysmally in addressing the causes and conditions that sustain the movement," Dixit adds. The

> *The rise of the Naxal movement in India is not only due to the stickiness of Marxist or Maoist thought, which ironically has been discredited after the fall of Communism in the late 1980s.*

---

[6] Raman Dixit, "Naxalite Movement in India: The State's Response", *Journal of Defence Studies* 4, no.2 (April 2010).

Land rights and eminent domain are a striking example of this unfinished business, particularly in a resource-rich country like Indonesia.

problem lingers on and the lot of beedi workers has not substantially improved since my visit over three decades ago. Years after my visit, I also read that the young man who was our guide during our 1987 trip was tragically killed in what Indian security forces euphemistically describe as an "encounter killing."[7] Was the death of this privileged young man in vain? While I am repelled by the home-grown "Maoist" ideology which he and his supporters lived and died for, I can't help but think that his heart was in the right place. Given his wealth and privilege, the young man could have become a successful lawyer or corporate executive. Yet he preferred to advocate for the cause of the rural poor whom he barely knew. His death, and that of hundreds of idealistic young men and women in the Naxal movement, reminds us that beneath the gloss and veneer of modern Asia, there lurks ugly, unfinished business which will continue to haunt the region. Land rights and eminent domain are a striking example of this unfinished business, particularly in a resource-rich country like Indonesia.

Pain in Papua

From Naxal-infested rural India, we turn our attention toward the island of New Guinea, the western half of which belongs to Indonesia.[8] There are three striking geographical facts about New Guinea, of which the Indonesian provinces of Papua and West Papua are a part, which are worth mentioning.

---

[7] Encounter killings in India and South Asia happen when security forces claim that they killed a suspect in self-defence. For good reason, they are also known as extra-judicial killings because their legal basis is suspect.

[8] Papua was a Dutch colony until 1962, after which control was temporarily transferred to Indonesia under an international agreement that required a UN-mandated referendum to be held by 1969. The controversial referendum did take place with over a thousand Papuans selected by the Indonesian Army voting in favour of accession.

It is the world's second largest island after Greenland. The Indonesian side has mountain peaks which rival the Himalayas and the Andes. And the province's dense forest cover, which is unfortunately eroding, is incredibly rich in biodiversity. It is also far away from the Indonesian capital Jakarta, which is over 2,000 miles and two time zones away.

I have travelled to many parts of Indonesia but my visit to Papua's provincial capital of Jayapura was the most memorable. I visited in the late 1990s when Papua was known as Irian Jaya, which has since been split into two provinces. There is an otherworldliness to Papua which can best be described as the logical setting on earth for the Hollywood blockbuster *Avatar*. The

> *There is an otherworldliness to Papua which can best be described as the logical setting on earth for the Hollywood blockbuster* Avatar.

parallels with the movie are striking not least because of Papua's mineral resources —around 260 miles south west of Jayapura is the Grasberg mine, which has the distinction of being the world's largest gold and second largest copper mine. American mining company Freeport McMoRan has long controlled the mine and its profits, but majority control was recently ceded to the Indonesian Government as part of President Jokowi's campaign of resource nationalism. Papua is sparsely populated, around 4.6 million, and the local population is an anthropologist's delight – it is home to over 300 distinct tribes and an equal number if not more languages are spoken across the sprawling province. It is perhaps predictable that both the Indonesian authorities and Freeport have struggled to negotiate land rights with the local tribes and have often resorted to violence and extortion. "For years, critics have held up Freeport's operations in Irian Jaya, the Indonesian half of the island of New Guinea, as a poster child of neo-colonialism," wrote journalist Peter Waldman of *The Wall Street Journal* in 1998.[9] "The mining has

---

[9] Peter Waldman, "Hand in Glove: How Suharto's Circle, Mining Firm Did So Well Together", *The Wall Street Journal*, 29 September 1998.

generated billions of dollars for New Orleans-based Freeport since it arrived in 1967, and billions more for the Indonesian government. But, critics say, the mining has brutalized one of the world's most pristine ecosystems and done little to lift local tribes, just decades removed from Stone Age isolation, out of poverty and primitiveness."

In 1996, in what must have been one of the most dramatic encounters between a modern multinational corporation and an indigenous tribe anywhere in the world, a senior Freeport official met with the leader of the Amungme tribe, whose land on which the Grasberg mine rests. As protest, the tribal leader who subsequently accused Freeport of "cultural genocide," emptied the contents of a basket in the presence of the official, signifying in local custom that he longer regarded the American official and the mining company as a trusted friend and was removing them from his life. When modernity clashes with tradition, as has been happening at Papua for decades, it becomes the real-life version of *Avatar*. If you are looking for a cardboard and tone-deaf villain, here is Freeport's former Chairman Jim "Bob" Moffett declare to *The Wall Street Journal* that "if we are not there, what do these people have," adding that the company's opponents "don't see what these people looked like before we got there. If they had, they wouldn't like what they saw." I guess the Amungme and other Papuan tribes would share a similar sentiment about Moffett's assertion. In the two decades since Indonesia emerged as a vibrant democracy, Freeport and the government have definitely improved governance at the mine and there is more attention paid to environmental and social standards. But for locals, this still does not diminish the fact that copper and gold are being extracted from land which they regard as sacred. This is not a uniquely Indonesian problem as even developed Australia with its vast mineral resources has done a terrible job in interacting with and negotiating land rights with Aboriginal Australians, a painful sore which has festered for centuries.

The battle over Grasberg and its riches has taken place against a backdrop of a latent separatist movement lead by the Free Papua Movement (OPM) and allied insurgency groups. They have been unsuccessful in their core demand – independence- although the two provinces enjoy greater autonomy and share of financial resources since sweeping democratic reforms were introduced in post-1998 Indonesia. Unlike their counterparts in Aceh, still a part of Indonesia but enjoying greater

> *The battle over Grasberg and its riches has taken place against a backdrop of a latent separatist movement lead by the Free Papua Movement (OPM) and allied insurgency groups.*

autonomy, and East Timor, now-independent Timor Leste, who waged a united and successful decades-long campaign to separate from Indonesia, the OPM and its many splinter groups are hopelessly disunited and disorganised. From time to time, they remind the Indonesian authorities that they remain a force to reckon with. In December 2018, members of the Papuan Liberation Army, a separate group from the OPM, attacked and killed up to 31 people in a remote corner of the province. Most of the dead are believed to be Indonesian soldiers although this has been contested by other sources which claim that many local workers were amongst the victims. This claim is impossible to verify because as in Indian-occupied Kashmir or China's restive Xinjiang province, Papua and West Papua are out of bounds for journalists and human rights groups. Credible and well-sourced information is hard to come by and the Indonesian Government's dominant narrative is that the Papua insurgency groups are involved in a terror and separatist campaign, a contention difficult to disagree with. Indonesia, particularly the Armed Forces (TNI), is not blameless either and has in fact been complicit in its assertion of control over the mineral-rich province at the expense of recognising its ethnic and cultural diversity. The dominant Javanese and Sumatran ruling class view the Papuans with disdain and barely concealed racist overtones. Located on the other side of the fabled Wallace Line[10] which

---

[10] English naturalist Alfred Russell Wallace drew the famous line after his name to distinguish the recorded differences between the flora and fauna between the western and eastern parts of the Indonesian archipelago.

> *The Papuans will always be regarded by Jakarta's ruling elite as the "other," which explains why there is still an independence movement.*

divides Asia from Melanesia, the integration of Papua and other eastern Indonesian provinces, neighbouring Maluku province is another example, into the mainstream has eluded Indonesia's political leadership. The Papuans will always be regarded by Jakarta's ruling elite as the "other," which explains why there is still an independence movement.

Benny Wenda, the head of the United Liberation Movement for West Papua, another breakaway faction of the OPM, is an advocate for a negotiated settlement with the Indonesian authorities. He lives in exile in the UK, has an active Twitter feed, and also appeared in London's Hyde Park during the height of the pandemic to deliver an impassioned speech. "We don't want any bloodshed; we want Indonesia to come to the international table to discuss and we can agree to a referendum. That's what our campaign is about," he told *The Guardian* newspaper after the December 2018 terror incident. Wenda has launched an impressive campaign to advocate for an UN-mandated referendum but his appeal has largely fallen on deaf ears by the international community. In 2017, Wenda claimed to have gathered the signatures of over 1.7 million Papuan and West Papuans demanding another independence referendum. However, the UN's "decolonisation" committee, one of the many toothless, bureaucratic organs of the gargantuan UN system, refused to consider the petition because Papua was apparently outside the scope of its mandate. With its small population and lack of global sympathy or attention, it is difficult to see how Papua's independence campaign can ever gain momentum. But as my South African diplomat friend reminded me years ago, nothing is ever set in stone.

Restive Xinjiang

From Naxalite India to a rag-tag band of Melanesian freedom fighters in Papua, our insurgency review would be incomplete without analysing China's restive Xinjiang province, where the Turkic–Uighur ethnic group have been fighting their own independence battle with limited success for decades. The most dramatic example of Uighur terror came on 28 October 2013 in Beijing's heavily fortified Tiananmen Square when a SUV vehicle deliberately rammed into the

The most dramatic example of Uighur terror came on 28 October 2013 in Beijing's heavily fortified Tiananmen Square when a SUV vehicle deliberately rammed into the crowd near the Gate of Heavenly Peace, in fact right under Chairman Mao's iconic portrait.

crowd near the Gate of Heavenly Peace, in fact right under Chairman Mao's iconic portrait. Five people died in the attack, including three inside the SUV and two bystanders and over 30 people were injured. The attack was a huge embarrassment to Chinese intelligence and security forces. Tiananmen Square and a few square miles around it is where China's leadership project national power and influence, as they have done for thousands of years. To have a terror attack take place on its doorstep was a sign perhaps of complacency or lax security. "The SUV burst through the security barriers lining the square and drove through a crowd of pedestrians before slamming into one of the stone bridges leading to the former imperial palace known as the Forbidden City," Beijing police said on their official microblog.[11]

Chinese officials identified the perpetrators as members of the banned East Turkestan Islamic Movement, a UN-mandated terrorist organisation with established links with regional terror networks and Al-Qaeda. What caught my eye was the identity of the passengers in the vehicle which rammed into innocent bystanders. The driver was identified as Usmen Hasan and his co-passengers were his wife and mother. What drives a family to head to Tiananmen Square with an intent to kill? I am not an expert on China's

---

[11] As reported by The Washington Post, 29 October 2013.

restive Uighur community and have relied on experts to guide me through the origins of the little-known insurgency in western Xinjiang province, at least until recently, which deploys different tactics compared with largely peaceful groups in neighbouring Tibet. The Uighur's are officially recognised as belonging to one of China's minority groups and number around 12 million. Very much like Papua, Xinjiang province's capital Urumqi is far away from Beijing, around 1,700 miles, and lies at the heart of central Asia.

An abbreviated history of the community comes from Usaid Siddiqui of the TV network Al Jazeera. "The Uighur struggle for self-rule arguably dates back to the 18th century, when the Qing dynasty conquered the Xinjiang province and incorporated it into China. Uighur nationalists organised several uprisings against the dynasty, which ruled China until the early 20th century," Siddiqui writes. "In 1949, Mao Zedong's forces thwarted Uighur aspirations by imposing total control over Xinjiang, setting off protracted tensions that have characterised Uighur-state relations to date."

During a different historical epoch, when Marco Polo made his famous trek to China, he encountered the Uighurs who were the biggest contributors to and beneficiaries of trade along the Silk Road.

For a brief period in the 1930s, there was an independent Republic of East Turkestan which has become a footnote in history as the region became an integral part of China after Mao's revolution. During a different historical epoch, when Marco Polo made his famous trek to China, he encountered the Uighurs who were the biggest contributors to and beneficiaries of trade along the Silk Road. "Unlike many of the nomadic tribes of Central Asia, the Uighurs are an urban people whose identity crystallized in the oasis towns of the Silk Road," writes Ishaan Tharoor in *Time magazine*.[12] "A walk through the bazaars of old Uighur centres such as Kashgar, Khotan, or Yarkhand reveals the physical legacy of a

---

[12] Ishaan Tharoor, "Brief History of the Uighurs", Time magazine, 9 July 2009.

people rooted in the first trans-continental trade route: an astonishing array of hazel and even blue eyes, with blonde, brown, or black hair — typically tucked beneath headscarves or customary Uighur cap." In short, the typical Uighur man or woman is radically different in appearance compared with a Han Chinese. Uighurs stand out in China as the "other."

Long before their emergence as global entrepots in the globalisation era after the last World War, it was Kashgar which was the Singapore and Hong Kong of an earlier era of booming trade. That bygone world has moved on tragically and the Uighurs are today marooned in a land-locked, economically backward, and politically unstable part of Central Asia. The Uighurs speak a Turkic language which is not spoken within China and indeed the rest of Asia. Their choice, like the Tibetans have been forced to as well, has been to either make peace and accept that the region is an integral part of China or fight to preserve their cultural identity and homeland. To play devil's advocate, the former proposition — integration with China — should be attractive for Uighurs and other minority groups. During the excesses of the Mao era, the minorities suffered along with the majority Han community. However, all of China, including the outlying provinces, have prospered since 1979 in the era after Deng Xiaoping. China's official Xinhua agency[13] asserts that Xinjiang has "seen rapid economic growth" in the past few years, with infrastructure projects bringing the region closer to China. Growth has exceeded 7 percent in the last few years, higher than the national average, and per capita incomes have also soared. China's fabled infrastructure development will bring the restive region closer to the rest of the country through investments under the Belt and Road Initiative. "The

> *Long before their emergence as global entrepots in the globalisation era after the last World War, it was Kashgar which was the Singapore and Hong Kong of an earlier era of booming trade.*

---

[13] "Economic development in Xinjiang on fast lane", Xinhua news agency, July 2017.

Alaska-sized region borders eight countries and serves as a crossroads for a railway link to London and a route to the Arabian Sea through Pakistan, where China is financing a $62 billion port and transportation corridor," Bloomberg reported in January 2019. Here is Kashgar's opportunity to once again become the crossroads of global trade. However, Covid-19 is likely to derail some of these infrastructure plans.

The origins of Uighur anger against Beijing can partially be traced to the brutal way their homeland was subsumed by Mao's revolutionary government.

Why is there so much of anger within the Uighur community as Xinjiang appears to be benefitting from China's rising economic tide? The origins of Uighur anger against Beijing can partially be traced to the brutal way their homeland was subsumed by Mao's revolutionary government. That is the past, one may argue, but Beijing has made matters worse more recently by implementing a policy built on the will of the majority population. This majoritarianism approach to building national cohesion is not unique to China. India (in Kashmir) and Indonesia (in Papua and other eastern Indonesian provinces) have also pursued a similar path. To put it simply, Uighur's and Tibetans feel that the benefits of China's economic prosperity have mainly flowed to the majority community who have resettled in large numbers in the two provinces. In Xinjiang and Tibet, unofficial estimates suggest that the Han community is close to a majority and play a dominant role in local politics and business. This is part of a deliberate Chinese government strategy for reasons which could be benevolent (rebalancing growth) or sinister (swamping restive provinces with the majority population) or both.

It is a sense of social and political dislocation which has fuelled Uighur anger and militancy, that accelerated after the emergence of terror group Al-Qaeda in neighbouring Afghanistan. Young Uighur men by the thousands have become radicalised and have fought alongside Al-Qaeda and more recently ISIS in the Middle East. The rest of China is facing their wrath as the terrorists return home with radical ideas to seek greater autonomy or independence, manifested spectacularly in the suicide attack on Tiananmen Square in 2013 and other equally dramatic incidents.

Mass Surveillance

It would appear that winning over Uighur hearts and minds should be a logical part of Beijing's strategy as it prepares to invest massively in Xinjiang's future. Unfortunately, China's majoritarian instincts in Xinjiang have followed a narrower path of repression and a significant attempt is underway to "deradicalise" the Uighur community via a massive re-education programme euphemistically called Vocational Education and Training Centres. In its scope and ambition, the programme is truly Orwellian. How to de-radicalise an estimated 1 million Uighur men appears to have consumed China's leadership since President Xi came to power

Unfortunately, China's majoritarian instincts in Xinjiang have followed a narrower path of repression and a significant attempt is underway to "deradicalise" the Uighur community via a massive re-education programme euphemistically called Vocational Education and Training Centres.

in 2012, which coincided with a sharp increase in terror attacks originating from Uighur groups. "The Chinese government has built a vast network of re-education camps and a pervasive system of surveillance to monitor and subdue millions from Muslim minorities in the Xinjiang region," reported *The New York Times*.[14] The newspaper, which is banned in China, said that the Chinese authorities were essentially deploying two approaches to tame militancy in Xinjiang.First, building a network of "re-education" camps across the province with the ostensible reason of providing "vocational

---

[14] "China's Prisons Swell after Deluge of Arrests Engulfs Muslims", *The New York Times*, 31 August 2019.

training" to youth and their families. An estimated 800,000 (lower end) to 2 million (higher end) Uighurs have gone through these involuntary training camps. In 2017, the *Reuters* news agency estimates that China spent over $3 billion in building these camps. Second, human rights groups have alleged that there has also been a sharp increase in arrests and prosecutions of Uighurs across the province, swelling the ranks of the prison population.

Since I have mainly cited Western sources on this issue, it is useful to look at the other side of the story — to look at China's own explanation of what is taking place and the considerable sympathy or silence that the detentions have drawn from the Muslim world. Xinjiang's Governor Shohrat Zakir, who is a native Uighur, dismissed allegations that the detention camps were permanent. "Most of the graduates from the vocational training centres have been reintegrated into society," Governor Shohrat told journalists in July 2019. "More than 90 percent of graduates have found satisfactory jobs with good incomes." With the lack of a truly independent news source, it is difficult to verify the Governor's assertions. There have also been reports that the Uighurs were not allowed to practise their religion in the camps, which another local official confirmed in an article in Al Jazeera[15] as being a temporary measure, i.e. they were allowed to practise Islam once they returned home but not at the camps. A Singapore journalist Ravi Velloor, who was my former colleague, visited the camps in July 2019, along with a group of foreign journalists, and reported that "it is hard to fault China for wanting to rehabilitate the Uighur if their ideology is anathema to the Chinese state and hostile to other communities."[16] More critically, there has been deafening silence from the Islamic world on the detention of Uighurs and the re-education camps. This perhaps signals that countries like Saudi Arabia, Egypt, Pakistan, which face Islamic radicalisation challenges of their own, are content to allow the Chinese to repress their religious brethren.

---

[15] "China: Most People in Xinjiang camps have 'returned to society'", *Al Jazeera*, 30 July 2019.

[16] Ravi Velloor, "Speaking of Asia: Inside those Uighur re-education camps", *The Straits Times*, 5 July 2019.

> *The "Xinjiang model" has wider implications for the rest of Asia. It is likely to be replicated elsewhere as governments attempt to tame insurgencies and other social ills.*

The "Xinjiang model" has wider implications for the rest of Asia. It is likely to be replicated elsewhere as governments attempt to tame insurgencies and other social ills. What makes the Xinjiang model attractive are two fungible factors. The first is the rise of surveillance and facial recognition technologies which makes it easy to scale state surveillance. China is certainly a global leader in AI and facial recognition technologies, as its great firewall provides the authorities with a national database recording the daily activities of citizens. China has also announced plans to launch a social credit score for every citizen, which will reward or penalise them for their success or failure in complying with the rules. Covid-19 has provided China with the perfect opportunity to pilot some of these apps for contact tracing and using cell-phone data to identify virus hot spots. Other Asian nations are eager to learn more about China's technological edge in surveillance. The second factor is the assumption of sweeping legislative and legal powers by many Asian governments to deal with insurgencies and their extension to resolve other social problems — the campaign against illicit drug gangs in Thailand and the Philippines being notable examples. For a man with a hammer, everything is a nail. Similarly, for every Asian government keen to tame domestic insurgencies, political opposition, and societal ills, access to surveillance technologies and legislative over-reach is a licence for abuse of power.

Leader with a Hammer

In the Philippines, President Rodrigo Duterte is an outstanding example of an Asian leader with a hammer. The country has been waging an insurgency in the southern half

> *In the Philippines, President Rodrigo Duterte is an outstanding example of an Asian leader with a hammer.*

of the country for several decades and the President is right in saying that the groups pose a threat to internal security. The insurgency has several independent strands. There is the one led by communist groups aligned with the New People's Army (NPA), which, like India's Naxalites, has been battling a long-running insurgency against the state for several decades. Security analysts believe that the NPA is degraded as a force, but the group continues to target the state. The second group in the southern Philippines is the Moro National Liberation Front, the Moro Islamic Liberation Front, and breakaway groups who have fought for an independent Mindanao homeland for decades and recently settled for greater autonomy under a new 2019 agreement. This agreement, which creates an autonomous Bangsamoro region, is under risk from an ongoing threat for the Philippines from radical Islamic groups, often under the Al-Qaeda and ISIS umbrella, who have out-witted the Army in the southernmost tip of the country. In 2017, the Army waged a five-month battle against terrorist groups to lift a siege in the city of Marawi. This was a hugely embarrassing moment for President Duterte and the Army. The terrorists were battle-hardened and lifting the siege by the Army resulted in considerable loss of lives and morale.

The International Crisis Group (ICG) notes[17] that the establishment of the Bangsamoro Autonomous Region should represent the "end" of the Moro struggle for self-determination and the resolution of the conflict between Moros and the Philippine state. "The region has a long history of separatist fronts fracturing when peace deals are reached and splinter groups taking up arms again against the state and their former allies," the ICG report said. "Such fragmentation, if repeated, could create new recruiting opportunities for Islamist militants, including those associated with ISIS." Given that insurgencies pose a real national security threat to the Philippines, should we overlook President Duterte's overzealous approach in dealing with some of the country's other domestic problems? The drug war, which the President

---

[17] "The Philippines: Militancy and the New Bangsamoro", *Asia Report* no. 301, International Crisis Group, 27 June 2019.

has waged with extra-judicial zest, is a stunning example of how counter-insurgency tactics plays out in a battle against the country's drug lords. Even before he was elected President, Duterte was plain-spoken about what he intended to do. "Forget the laws on human rights. If I make it to the Presidential Palace, I will do just what I did as mayor. You drug

The drug war, which the President has waged with extra-judicial zest, is a stunning example of how counter-insurgency tactics plays out in a battle against the country's drug lords.

pushers, hold-up men and do-nothings, you better go out. Because I'd kill you. I'll dump all of you into Manila Bay and fatten all the fish there." Like a good politician, President Duterte believes in keeping his electoral promises and his war against drugs has proceeded at a furious pace since he took office in 2016. The problem, to put it mildly, is that the Duterte's drug war is like the battle for Marawi, with little or no adjustment made for the fact that the government was battling a social menace, not terrorists. Citing data from the Philippines Drug Enforcement Agency (PDEA), Human Rights Watch (HRW) said in a report[18] that over 4,948 suspected drug dealers and users died during police operations between July 2016 and September 2018. However, these casualty figures do not include the thousands of others killed by unidentified gunmen. According to the Philippines National Police, 22,983 such deaths since the "war on drugs" began are classified as "homicides under investigation." HRW said: "The exact number of fatalities is difficult to ascertain because the government has failed to disclose official documents about the 'drug war', the report said. "It has issued contradictory statistics, and in the case of those 'homicides under investigation', stopped releasing the figures altogether."

It is useful to pause here to consider the horrific impact of President Duterte's war on drugs. There are allegations that some, if not most of the killings have been carried out by shadowy groups acting on behalf of the President's

---

[18] Human Rights Watch, "The Philippines: Events of 2018".

supporters. This is again difficult to verify because of the atmosphere of fear which the President has fostered in the country, in particular targeted against domestic critics of his drug strategy. To be sure, drug trafficking and addiction are societal ills which need to be tackled by a combination of tough law enforcement and sensible social policies. The Philippines is by no means a perfect democracy, but it has an established legal framework to deal with the issue, until President Duterte decided that previous governments had been too timid, and a tough new approach was needed. Two of the President's fiercest critics on the drug war and who have faced bitter retribution happen to be women, one is a prominent politician now under arrest and the other an international journalist who runs a local news site, which has been targeted by the government for everything from tax evasion to working for the CIA. Senator Leila de Lima and Maria Ressa

> *He regards any dissent or criticism to his rule as a national security threat, pushing the Philippines dangerously back in time to the Ferdinand Marcos era.*

are respected and highly regarded in the Philippines for their probity, commitment to the rule of law, and for advocating for the rights of citizens. Yet in conflating their legitimate actions with that of a dangerous insurgent, President Duterte has become the man with the ultimate hammer. He regards any dissent or criticism to his rule as a national security threat, pushing the Philippines dangerously back in time to the Ferdinand Marcos era. It is no coincidence that the Marcos family has made a return to the national mainstream under Duterte, with the late dictator's son Bongbong Marcos seen as a viable future contender to the Presidency.

President Duterte is a savvy user of social media, in the same league as Trump and Narendra Modi, and he and his supporters have weaponised fake news, making it difficult for ordinary Filipinos to distinguish between fact and fiction on the drug war. "It is hard to gauge public reaction when exponential lies laced with anger and hate spread faster than facts," Maria Ressa told

Poynter.[19] "They AstroTurf the government's narrative and coordinated attacks against alternative views help create a bandwagon effect." Ressa added that the goal was to "cripple" any beliefs in institutions – journalists and newsgroups are systematically attacked — so "there is no challenge" to President Duterte's powerful voice. "This is a case study of how democracies around the world are being destroyed: without facts, you can't have truth. Without truth, there is no trust," she said.

To return to the themes we explored in Chapter 4, political accountability in developing Asia is being diminished across the spectrum — in countries with one-party rule, nominal democracies, or even democratically elected governments — because the leader in charge believes that he or she is infallible. There is no distinction any more between the state's fight against insurgencies and separatist groups, which tend to enjoy strong domestic support, with a more sinister effort to consolidate political power and control by silencing domestic critics. New surveillance technologies and social media tools have become powerful enablers. If Asian leaders regard every internal threat as a threat to their rule, they will face a million new mutinies as the political opposition and the man on the street will begin to act like an insurgents. Nowhere is this more evident than in Hong Kong when the authorities disregarded public objections to an unpopular extradition bill which has since ballooned out of control. It is arguable whether the obsession of Asian leaders to pursue command and control methods to consolidate political power at home will work when they face a genuine cross-border

> *If Asian leaders regard every internal threat as a threat to their rule, they will face a million new mutinies as the political opposition and the man on the street will begin to act like an insurgency.*

---

[19] Cristina Tardaguilla, "Legal battle between President Duterte and Maria Ressa's Rappler shows the Philippines 'dark reality' and sends some fact-checkers to therapy", Poynter.org, 2 August 2019. The Poynter Institute is a journalism school based in Florida.

security threat from external forces. After a long period of peace and prosperity, Asian regional insecurity is no longer a theoretical possibility. It is fuelled in part by a new Cold War between the U.S. and China, which we turn to in the next chapter.

Chapter 11

Lessons from Stora Latina

Our eighth and final circle of hell is Asia's fragile geopolitics.
A new Cold or actual war between an incumbent and rising
superpower could have disastrous consequences.

Asia's national security and foreign policy establishment have a lot on their minds these days — a pitched battle for economic and political supremacy between America and China, continued North Korean intransigence, a prolonged border stand-off between India and China, and the virulent spread of the Covid-19 pandemic. There is no shortage of official meetings on these topics with regional and global counterparts either — to fret about these challenges and to make high-minded statements about regional security. Asia's security czars meet routinely and regularly at a veritable alphabet soup of regional meetings — the ASEAN Regional Forum, the annual Shangri-La Dialogue (SLD) in Singapore, and smaller, more informal gatherings to discuss regional security, geopolitics, and increasingly cyber and data resilience. I appreciate that their inbox and meeting calendar for the year are full, albeit with face-to-face interactions minimised due to the pandemic. When the world opens up, I would like to suggest a radically different venue for the next meeting of the ARF or the SLD — Sarajevo.

Why on earth would I suggest holding a meeting focused on Asian security in the troubled Bosnian capital city, at least 6,000 miles away from Singapore? In a word — to learn the lessons of World War I and how unprepared world powers were when they stumbled into it over a hundred years ago, with the inciting incident coming on 28 June 1914. On that fateful morning in the Bosnian capital, then part of the sprawling Austro–Hungarian empire, a young Serbian rebel Gavrilo Princip walked to the city's Latin Bridge or Stora Latina, to wait for the motorcade carrying Archduke Franz Ferdinand and his wife. The 50-year old Archduke was the heir apparent to the Austro-Hungarian throne, which ruled over Bosnia amongst other sprawling European territories, and his visit to restive Sarajevo was described as routine. On hindsight this was a catastrophic mistake, not least because that day marked the 525th anniversary of the defeat of Serbia at Kosovo, a powerful, emotional day for Serbian nationalists to strike against the empire. The Archduke had arrived by train that morning from Vienna and security was light, even after the Austro–Hungarian royal's motorcade faced a botched assassination attempt earlier in the day. By historic accounts, Princip positioned himself at Stora Latina with only the vague expectation that the royal motorcade would pass him by. When it did, only because the Archduke's driver had lost his way, Princip was standing opposite the bridge and managed to shoot the royals at point-blank range.

It was a shot heard around the world as the assassination of Archduke Franz Ferdinand at Sarajevo was the trigger for the mother of all unintended wars

> *It was a shot heard around the world as the assassination of Archduke Franz Ferdinand at Sarajevo was the trigger for the mother of all unintended wars — World War I, which reshaped geopolitics, launched modern warfare, and has the dubious distinction of being one of the deadliest conflicts in human history.*

— World War I, which reshaped geopolitics, launched modern warfare, and has the dubious distinction of being one of the deadliest conflicts in human history.

The four-year war between 1914 and 1918 lead to over 40 million casualties, smaller than the more geographically spread World War II which followed two decades later, but more lethal given that Europe was the primary theatre of conflict. Visitors to a military museum in Vienna can still view the Graf & Stift four-cylinder, Double Phaeton open-top limousine which carried the Archduke that morning and his bullet ridden, blood-stained military uniform. Historians have speculated ever since if the war which followed could have been avoided had the Archduke travelled with greater security and survived the assassination attempt.

Silent Witness

I visited Sarajevo last summer and spent a few days in the city's historic quarter, walking along lanes and by-lanes which have stood silent witness to history's bloodiest confrontations over the past century. Sarajevo was not only the epicentre of World War I, but the Bosnian capital has seen much bloodshed more recently. At the height of the Yugoslavian conflict in the 1990s, Sarajevo was under a brutal siege which showed the worst and best qualities of humanity. Stora Latina itself was a disappointment. The bridge is not much of a bridge but a small concrete link over the Miljacka River which criss-crosses the city. On such banality was built the horrors of World War I which followed the 28 June 1914 assassination near Stora Latina.

> *The bridge is not much of a bridge but a small concrete link over the Miljacka River which criss-crosses the city. On such banality was built the horrors of World War I which followed the 28 June 1914 assassination near Stora Latina.*

In the centenary after World War I, historians accumulated overwhelming evidence that it was fragile politics, missed opportunities for dialogue, and massive misunderstandings and miscommunication between the incumbent powers of the era that lead to the humanitarian tragedy. Even the circumstances which lead to the rise of Hitler and World War II two decades later have their roots in the war and the unfair political settlement of 1918, which saw a defeated Germany humiliated into paying financially unsustainable reparations to the victorious French and British authorities.

> *He added that he saw eerie parallels between the geopolitics of 1914 and today and the key lesson is that "bad stuff" can happen very fast and the international community needs to build structures that can avoid "naked, armed conflict".*

The end of World War 1 was not a time for celebration either because the world was soon engulfed by the Spanish flu pandemic. A fragile global order was ill-equipped to deal with that pandemic, just as the fragmenting world of 2020 has discovered with Covid-19. Australian historian Christopher Clark, who has written a masterful book about the origins of World War I[1] has said that the War could have been avoided if European powers looked at the bigger picture and compromised. "In the end, we're looking at a Europe inhabited by great powers, each of which was, in a very egotistical and autistic way — without respect, really, to the interests of the others — pursuing its own interests and each of which was willing, for the sake of the pursuit of its own interests, to take the risk of a major conflict," Clark said in a 2014 interview with *Radio Free Europe*. He added that he saw eerie parallels between the geopolitics of 1914 and today and the key lesson is that "bad stuff" can happen very fast and the international community needs to build structures that can avoid "naked, armed conflict."

---

[1] Christopher Clark, *The Sleepwalkers: How Europe Went to War in 1914* (Harper Perennial, 2014).

What has any of this got to do with contemporary Asia, you may well ask. "Those who cannot learn from history are doomed to repeat it," the philosopher George Santayana once said, and the parallels between Asia today and the world of the pre-1914 era are striking for four reasons.

First, the period between 1870 and 1914 was an era of relative peace *within* Europe. Major conflict between regional powers had subsided, ushering in a period of regional political stability, not very different from Asia before 2016. With the exception of the protracted India-Pakistan conflict that has raged on for decades, there is relative peace *within* Asia at least since the end of the Vietnam-China conflict of 1979. A long period of peace and stability lulls policymakers into complacency about the costs of war.

Second, 1870-1914 marked the "high water mark" of 19th century globalisation, according to researchers at Oxford University.[2] "Nineteenth century globalisation involved increasing transfers of commodities, people, capital, and ideas between and within continents," the Oxford paper notes. Asia's own globalisation era, which started with the rise of Japan in the 1950s and accelerated in the following decades, has striking parallels with this era.

Third, 19th century globalisation saw the speedy introduction and diffusion of new technologies — the telegraph which revolutionised communications, the steamship and rapid passage via the Suez Canal which accelerated the speed of shipping goods across the world, the development of international finance, and deadly new weapons. Not very different from the world of today with the explosion of social media, rise of the smartphone, e-commerce, drone warfare, and AI.

Finally, the movement of people across borders. Due to stunning economic growth in the late 19th and early 20th century, there was a dramatic increase

---

[2] Matthias Morys, Guillaume Daudin, and Kevin H. O'Rourke, "Globalization, 1870-1914", University of Oxford Discussion Paper Series no.395, May 2008.

> *This has parallels with the rapid migration of our urban cowboys and cowgirls to meeting growing labour demand in a rising Asia although their wages in real terms have not kept pace.*

in the free movement of people. *The Economist*[3] marvels at the stunning pace of emigration from and into Europe during those heady years when peace and prosperity appeared guaranteed. Migration rates were remarkable. In the decade 1901- 1910, 5 percent of those from Austria-Hungary left the country, more than 6 percent of Britons, 7 percent of the Irish, 8 percent of Norwegians, and nearly 11 percent of Italians. Argentina added another 30 percent to its population, in immigrants alone, in that decade. "Europe had lots of workers: the new world not so many. So, as the workers moved, real wages nearly doubled during the period compared with a 50 percent rise in America." This has parallels with the rapid migration of our urban cowboys and cowgirls to meeting growing labour demand in a rising Asia although their wages in real terms have not kept pace.

Asian Vulnerability

At the cusp of World War I, economist John Maynard Keynes, who belonged to that era of globalisation boosters famously remarked: "The inhabitant of London could order by telephone, sipping his morning tea in bed, the various products of the whole earth, in such quantity as he might see fit, and reasonably expect their early delivery upon his doorstep; he could at the same moment and by the same means adventure his wealth in the natural resources and new enterprises of any quarter of the world, and share, without exertion or even trouble, in their prospective fruits and advantages." Substitute the London of 1914 with Beijing or Singapore or Seoul in 2020 and you get a sense of *déjà vu*. Asia's greatest vulnerability today is that its economic dynamism, which has done much to lift billions out of poverty,

---

[3] "1914 Effect: The Globalisation Counter-reaction", *The Economist*, 14 June 2017.

has bestowed upon the continent too many contenders for regional supremacy. In this, Asia resembles the pre-World War I era of great power rivalry.

Asia's greatest vulnerability today is that its economic dynamism, which has done much to lift billions out of poverty, has bestowed upon the continent too many contenders for regional supremacy.

The Asian inventory of great powers jostling for supremacy includes the incumbent power (America) attempting to contain or at least slow the pace of a rising one, China. Sprinkled across the Asia-Pacific region is an array of regional or pseudo-regional powers — Japan, Korea, India, Australia, Indonesia — who are keen to retain their own sphere of influence. Below this head-table are smaller countries, ASEAN ex Indonesia, South Asia ex India, who in the memorable words of Singapore Foreign Minister Vivian Balakrishnan don't want to be forced into making "invidious" choices of taking sides, particularly in a contest of wills between China and the U.S.

The formal security alliances which underpin regional security have a huge American bias, understandable given the superpower's dominance since the 1950s. The inventory of American security alliances includes bilateral pacts with Japan, Korea, Australia, the Philippines, and security partnerships with Taiwan and Singapore. Underpinning these alliances and partnerships is a deep commitment on the part of America, resolute and unshaken until very recently, to be the region's guardian and policeman. In addition to the security alliances, America also works closely with India, Australia, and Japan, the so-called Quad nations, on regional security, a development regarded with great suspicion by Beijing — even Vietnam appears to have inched closer to America because of an assertive China.

The rhetoric of successive American Presidents about preserving peace and security in East Asia has been backed up by the presence of over 100,000 soldiers permanently stationed in Japan and Korea and smaller numbers across the region. American aircraft carriers routinely patrol the South China Sea on freedom of navigation patrols, a putative conflict zone which we will turn to shortly. It is no surprise that in a unipolar world, America was Asia's Big Brother and sole guarantor of stability. Singapore diplomat and writer Kishore Mahbubani has written[4] that the "biggest strategic gift" that America has made to the world is to "spark" the rise of Asia by generously sharing its wisdom and best practice with millions of Asians. "It is dangerous to over-simplify history, but some crude facts are undeniable," he wrote. "If the American dream had not been discovered and created, and Europe had continued to dominate world history, Asian societies may not have awoken from centuries of slumber so quickly and smoothly. American generosity saved Asia."

The provision of American security insurance to East Asia, during and after the Vietnam War, gave governments the space to develop their economies and not worry about regional security. This is a fact that is little understood or appreciated by educated Asians who assume that peace and stability in the region happened miraculously due to a mix of Asian values and tolerance. With the recent rise of China and America's seeming indifference to the region, which predates the Trump administration I should add, Asian countries are struggling to figure out a viable path forward. Much can change of course under President Biden, but the new administration will be consumed with dealing with domestic issues during the first year. U.S. diplomat Douglas Paal writes that America's allies in the region, who have long benefitted from the prosperity enjoyed under the Pax Americana, now are watching nervously to see how Washington will

> *The provision of American security insurance to East Asia, during and after the Vietnam War, gave governments the space to develop their economies and not worry about regional security.*

---

[4] Kishore Mahbubani, "America's Conflicting Destinies", *The New York Times*, 19 November 2009.

decide its future role. "These countries also are watching Beijing uneasily and are sensing its growing strength and influence, yet they are still eager to seize the opportunities that China presents," Paal writes.[5] "In effect, U.S. regional partners are anxious over the classic dilemma of neither wishing to be entrapped in an unwanted conflict nor abandoned to an uncertain dependence on and vulnerability to a powerful neighbour, in this case, Beijing." China of course views the exercise of its influence in the region very differently and has a red line in the form of Taiwan and Hong Kong in determining when and how it will intervene militarily. Xi Jinping has denied suggestions that China is nurturing regional aspirations to dominate Asia. Speaking in May 2019 on the 40th anniversary of the launch of market reforms, Xi dismissed the idea of a clash of civilisations between the West and China. He also called upon Asia to maintain peace as a "precondition" of economic growth. "All countries should conduct exchanges beyond borders of state, time, and civilisations, and work together to protect the peaceful time we have, which is more precious than gold." Western analysts have dismissed Xi's pledges and China's overall stance as platitudes which masks a more sinister world view of dominance.

Thucydides Trap

The drama which unfolds at the annual Shangri-La Dialogue in Singapore, cancelled in 2020 due to the pandemic, where harsh words are exchanged at the podium between Chinese and American security officials, is symptomatic of a much bigger problem — barring one or two, there are few historic precedents of a successful transition between an

This is the so-called Thucydides trap, named after a Greek historian who 2,500 years ago observed upfront the dramatic tensions between a rising power (Athens) and an incumbent one (Sparta).

---

[5] Douglas Paal, "America's Future in a Dynamic Asia", Carnegie Endowment for International Peace, 31 January 2019.

incumbent and rising power. The two recent exceptions are the smooth and peaceful handing of the baton between the UK and America at the end of World War II and united Germany's emergence after reunification in 1990, which vaulted Germany into a position of regional influence in Europe. Harvard University's Belfer Center for Science and International Affairs analysed the historical record and concluded that in 12 of 16 cases of a tussle between a rising and ruling superpower over the past 500 years, the result was war. This is the so-called Thucydides trap, named after a Greek historian who 2,500 years ago observed upfront the dramatic tensions between a rising power (Athens) and an incumbent one (Sparta).

Writing in *The Atlantic*,[6] scholar Graham Allison of the Belfer Centre, explains that Thucydides went to the heart of the matter of the tussle between Athens and Sparta, focusing on the "inexorable" structural stress caused by a rapid shift in the balance of power between two rivals. The Greek historian identified two key drivers of this dynamic, Allison notes: the rising power's growing entitlement, sense of its importance, and demand for greater say and sway, on the one hand, and fear, insecurity, and determination to defend the status quo this engenders in the established power, on the other. In the end, the 30-year Peloponnesian War which followed these structural stresses ended up bankrupting Sparta, the nominal victor, and Athens. Are America and China destined to face a similar fate 2,500 years later, two powers marching toward inevitable war? Some Asia watchers I have spoken to assert that the Thucydides trap is an ancient Greek and Western construct which has little relevance to conflict and power in modern Asia. They point out that in the

> *Some Asia watchers I have spoken to assert that the Thucydides trap is an ancient Greek and Western construct which has little relevance to conflict and power in modern Asia.*

---

[6] Graham Allison, "The Thucydides Trap: Are the US and China Headed for War? "*The Atlantic*, 24 September 2015.

millennia during which Asia dominated the world, there was a great deal of collaboration between great powers and regard the current debate as very biased. A reading of history does show that there was a cross-fertilisation of contact and ideas between China and India, long before European colonial rule. Yet recent history on great power rivalries is far less encouraging.

This is where Asian policymakers and America will benefit from a re-reading of the lessons of World War I. Geopolitics in 1914 was dictated and determined by major European powers — with the empires of Germany and Austro-Hungary forging a Triple Alliance with Italy. The Ottoman Empire which dominated eastern Europe and the Middle East would take the side of the Triple Alliance after hostilities broke out. The dominant power of the time, Great Britain, was keen to forge alliances of its own and built the Triple Entente with France and Russia. Embedded in these rival alliances was an explicit commitment that members of the Alliance and the Entente would be prepared to go to war should any of their allies be threatened with aggression, the early 20th century version of NATO's Article 5.

When Gavrilo Princip assassinated Archduke Ferdinand in June 1914, war was not inevitable but became so because regional powers acted irresponsibly. Russia's defence of its Serbian kinsmen was pitted against German and Austro–Hungarian determination not to lose the Balkans. Great Britain, alarmed with the rise of Germany as a regional power, saw that the conflict was perhaps inevitable and possibly the only way to reduce the influence of Berlin. In a bare 37 days after the assassination, full-scale war broke out. "The lamps are going out all over Europe, we shall not see them lit in our life-time," remarked British Foreign Secretary Edward Grey on the eve of war on 3 August 1914.

To return to Christopher Clark, the historian notes that the first world war "unleashed" the demons of political disorder, extremism, and cruelty that "disfigured" the 20th century. "It destroyed four multi-ethnic empires (the

Russian, the German, the Austro–Hungarian, and the Ottoman)," he writes[7] ".... It disorganised the international system in immensely destructive ways. Without this conflict, it is hard to imagine the October Revolution of 1917, the rise of Stalinism, the ascendancy of Italian Fascism, the Nazi seizure of power, or the Holocaust. It was, as the historian Fritz Stern put it, "The first calamity of the 20th century, the calamity from which all other calamities sprang."

As Asian policymakers look at regional security today, they should seek to avoid the second calamity of the 21st century — the first one being Covid-19. Their overwhelming concerns boil down to two strategic questions. Can America be relied upon to provide security insurance as it has done so ably in the past, or, do countries need to hedge their bets by staying passively neutral or align closely with China? There is no simple yes or no answer to these thorny questions because American and Chinese rhetoric on peace and stability is literally all over the place. Former Malaysian Prime Minister Mahathir Mohamad took a pragmatic approach in dealing with Beijing when he briefly returned to power. "When China was poor, we were frightened of China. When China is rich, we are also frightened of China. I think we have to find some way to deal with China," he told the *South China Morning Post* in an interview in March 2019. The Malaysian leader also spoke about American unpredictability in the age of Trump and the historic fact that China over millennia "never sought to conquer or colonise other Asian nations, in a way that the Europeans had since coming to the region in the 15th century. In the aftermath of Joe Biden's victory, America's elder statesman Henry Kissinger warned that America and China should do everything possible to prevent conflict. "Unless there

> *As Asian policymakers look at regional security today, they should seek to avoid the second calamity of the 21st century — the first one being Covid-19.*

---

[7] Christopher Clark, "The First Calamity", *London Review of Books* 35, no.16 (29 August 2013).

is some basis for cooperative action, the world will slide into a catastrophe comparable to World War 1", he told the Bloomberg New Economy Forum in November 2020.

Scenario Planning

How will Mahathir's Malaysia or indeed other regional leaders behave and act if there was a breakout in hostilities or outright war between America and China? In private conversations, Asian policymakers admit that they are ambivalent about taking sides. A former senior minister of an ASEAN country told me that his team had undertaken detailed scenario planning for precisely such a development and had soberly concluded the following: "The very possibility of war between China and America would be the end of Asia as we know it," he told me, preferring to remain anonymous because of his stature. "Today's alliances would fall apart and every nation will decide on its own if it wished to side with the status quo power or a rising one." In his telling, a possible war would be the final act *after* America and China took steps to scale back on bilateral trade, decouple supply chains, and sought to build competing spheres of influence in the region. "The dominoes in the region which will side with China are a very short list — Laos, Cambodia, possibly the Philippines if a Duterte-type leader is in place, and Myanmar," he said. "ASEAN's middle powers — Singapore, Thailand, Malaysia, and Indonesia stand to lose out the most from either Chinese or American economic disengagement. How will we act? I wish I could tell you. I simply don't know."

> *In private conversations, Asian policymakers admit that they are ambivalent about taking sides.*

Since Asian policymakers are either confused or reluctant to be drawn into public discussion on possible war scenarios, I have decided to construct three possible scenarios which would draw America, China, and other Asian powers into possible conflict in the future. The scenarios themselves are drawn from headlines *du jour*. First, a conflict in the South China Sea over China's island building and domination of regional sea lanes. Second, we turn to the India–China boundary conflict and the inter-linked and historic India-Pakistan tensions, described by analysts as the world's most "dangerous" region because both countries possess nuclear weapons. Finally, we will look at North Korea's perennial attempts to gain global legitimacy by simultaneously pleading for aid and threatening the international community with nuclear calamity if aid was not forthcoming. In each of these scenarios, both America and China are critical power players. They are nominally on the same side on the North Korean crisis, directly opposed in the case of the South China Sea, and China has a distinct Pakistan slant when it comes to the crisis on the Indian sub-continent.

The South China Sea first and China's position on island building. Speaking at the 2019 edition of the Shangri-La Dialogue in Singapore, China's Defence Minister General Wei Fenghe was crystal clear about the country's strategic position on extending and expanding its territorial claims across the South China Sea. "…is China's construction on its South China Sea islands and reefs militarisation?" he asked. "It is the legitimate rights of a sovereign state to carry out construction on its own territory. China built limited defence facilities on the islands and reefs for self-defence. It is only when there are threats will there be defences. In the face of heavily armed warships and military aircraft, how can we not deploy any defence facilities." General Wei also dismissed concerns that China's aggressive island-building imperilled freedom of navigation in the South China Sea — which without exaggeration is Asia's economic lifeline as much of the region's oil imports and commerce

> *General Wei also dismissed concerns that China's aggressive island-building imperilled freedom of navigation in the South China Sea – which without exaggeration is Asia's economic lifeline as much of the region's oil imports and commerce sails through these waters.*

sails through these waters. "Over 100,000 ships sail through the South China Sea every year," he said. "None has been threatened. The problem, however, is that in recent years some countries outside the region come to the South China Sea to flex muscles in the name of freedom of navigation."

This is not hypothetical by any means because Vietnam and China came close to a serious conflict in May 2014, a few weeks before the 100th anniversary of World War I

The General was obviously taking a swipe against America as the outside power meddling in the region. However, what about the perspective of countries located *in* the South China Sea, which are parties to the conflict with China? Here Vietnam offers a striking example of a country whose initial reluctance to take sides was overcome by what it regarded as aggressive Chinese incursions into its territorial waters. This is not hypothetical by any means because Vietnam and China came close to a serious conflict in May 2014, a few weeks before the 100th anniversary of World War I, when state-owned China National Offshore Oil Corporation (CNOOC) deployed its *Haiyang Shiyou* 981 oil rig, or HYSY 981 for short, near the Triton Islands in the Paracel Islands chain in the South China Sea, which is disputed territory claimed by China, Taiwan, and Vietnam. This is a dry run, say military analysts and historians, on how an unintended future war could be triggered.

CNOOC with the explicit support of China's Navy deployed a flotilla of vessels near the islands, which according to international law falls within a grey zone claimed by the two countries. Although it did not receive much global attention at the time, the Vietnam and China tussle over the oil rig was the first full-blown regional security crisis in East Asia outside of North Korea's nuclear threats. The Chinese objective was to conduct oil exploration and drilling, ostensibly to mark the grey zone as falling in its territorial waters and future proofing against any competing claims from Vietnam or Taiwan. It was also an attempt by China, analysts say, to test the resolve of an Asian neighbour to stand up to a rising power. In June 1914, it took the lone action of a Serbian nationalist to trigger World War I. A hundred years later, geopolitical analysts wonder if a Chinese oil rig would play a similar unintended role in sparking conflict in East Asia.

Blow by Blow

The Asia Maritime Transparency Initiative (AMTI)[8] has published a paper which provides a blow-by-blow account, albeit from an American perspective, of the deployment of the oil rig on 1 May 2014 and the resultant Vietnam reaction. "Vietnamese Coast Guard and Fisheries Resources Surveillance (VFRS) forces were immediately dispatched to intercept HYSY 981," the AMTI note says. "Their mission in the words of a navy official, was to make a 'show of force' to prevent the oil rig from 'establishing a fixed position.'" There was an immediate escalation in the stand-off as the number of naval vessels deployed by the two sides rose sharply,

> There was an immediate escalation in the stand-off as the number of naval vessels deployed by the two sides rose sharply, demonstrating that a tussle over maritime territory does not take long to become a security crisis.

demonstrating that a tussle over maritime territory does not take long to become a security crisis. "Violent collisions occurred almost immediately," according to the AMTI report. "Beijing claimed the Vietnamese deliberately rammed Chinese vessels, with video showing a VFRS cutter striking two Chinese Coast Guard (CCG) ships."

Date-check: On 4 May, barely four days after the oil-rig deployment, China expanded its defence perimeter from one to three nautical miles to "better shield" the oil rig. On 6 May, the Obama administration intervened in

---

[8] Michael Green et al., "Counter-Coercion Series: China-Vietnam Oil Rig Standoff", Asia Maritime Transparency Initiative, CSIS, Washington D.C., 12 June 2017.

the crisis by describing Beijing's actions as "unilateral, provocative, and unhelpful." Undeterred by Washington's carefully calibrated diplomatic language aimed at China to back-off, China sharply increased the number of naval vessels to protect the oil rig. The deployment of naval power resembled a war game between friendly powers, but this was no game and it is difficult to describe Vietnam and China being enemies despite their shared past as hostile neighbours. They are more like *frenemies*, not quite friends or enemies but both dependent on each other in regional supply chains, where Vietnam is a viable competitor to China's status as the final assembly point, and in growing business links. Vietnam took aim at the growing commercial relationship between the two countries by shoring up domestic support for its position.

Date check: On 13 May, China's actions triggered massive anti-China protests all over Vietnam, targeting China-owned businesses and the ethnic Chinese community. "Popular unrest spiralled out of state authorities' control on May 13," AMTI reports. "Across Vietnam, rioters 'spontaneously'" vandalized hundreds of foreign-owned businesses thought to belong to Chinese companies (many other foreign firms were also targeted accidentally)." This led to deaths of at least four Chinese nationals which resulted in China evacuating its nationals from Vietnam and issuing grim travel warnings. This was a bare 13 days after China's initial provocation in deploying a rig in contested waters.

Pumping up domestic support through nationalist rhetoric is time-tested political theatre in the region — China is guilty of the same when it whipped up rhetoric and local protests against Japan, most recently in 2012, and we will soon discuss the implications of fraying Japan–Korea ties. However, it is hard to establish if the protests in one-party states like Vietnam were spontaneous, as the authorities claimed it was, or was triggered by state backing, as independent news reports on the topic have made clear. Although the anti-China protests were soon contained, they have a tendency in lots of other cases to spiral out of control. What would have been China's reaction

> *We will never know the answers to these questions, but my point is that it has become quite easy to build realistic scenarios about a future conflict in South China Sea.*

if the death toll of its nationals were in the hundreds rather than the four reported? Would this have provoked the People's Liberation Army (PLA) into launching a full-out ground assault against Vietnam a la 1979? We will never know the answers to these questions, but my point is that it has become quite easy to build realistic scenarios about a future conflict in South China Sea.

Date check: On 17 May, in the real China–Vietnam stand-off, there were reports from China which claimed that Vietnam had deployed over 60 ships around the oil rig and had instigated "500 rammings." From Vietnam's perspective, Beijing had deployed over 130 vessels and there were rumours, actively spread via social media, of Chinese troop mobilisations in provinces close to the Vietnam border.

How did Vietnam's neighbours in the ASEAN grouping respond to the unfolding maritime saga? In a major development, ASEAN foreign ministers came out in support of Vietnam in a statement on May 11, expressing "serious concern" and urging "all parties concerned" to exercise self-restraint and avoid actions which could undermine peace and stability. This was an important development and its significance should not be understated. While there is no ASEAN doctrine equivalent to NATO's (North Atlantic Treaty Organisation) Article 5 which states that an attack on one member is an attack on all of its members, the Southeast Asian grouping was clearly rattled by China's incursion. On 27 May, in full view of the region, Chinese tugboats pulled the contentious oil rig out of the disputed waters, a full 27 days after the initial deployment. A senior Chinese official also visited Hanoi a month later to further de-escalate tensions. But China has not entirely given up on its maritime ambitions as the oil rig has made regular reappearances in Vietnam waters, most recently in the summer of 2019.

What lessons has Vietnam drawn from this encounter? For one, it has made the possibility of a future conflict with its giant northern neighbour a real possibility as the country's 2019 Defence White Paper validates. It reinforces *pro forma* Vietnam's long-standing position of "three no's" — no military alliances, no foreign bases and usage of the territory for military activities, and no siding with one country against the other. But there is sharper language in the White Paper on the country's emerging security risks. "New developments in the East Sea, including unilateral actions, power-based coercion, violation of international law, militarization, change in the status quo, and infringements upon Vietnam's sovereignty, sovereign rights, and jurisdiction as provided in international law have undermined the interests of nations concerned and threatened peace, stability, security, safety, and freedom of navigation and overflight in the region," the White Paper asserts.[9] Elsewhere in the Paper, there is favourable language welcoming "vessels of navies, coast guards, border guards, and international organisations to make courtesy or ordinary port visits," which implicitly supports America's long-held position on such freedom of navigation visits and places ASEAN in a quandary as it negotiates with China on a formal Code of Conduct in the South China Sea.

It reinforces pro forma Vietnam's long-standing position of "three no's" — no military alliances, no foreign bases and usage of the territory for military activities, and no siding with one country against the other.

The Chinese position would be to obviously exclude "third parties" like America from interfering in a bilateral dispute with its neighbours. In a significant development, the Trump administration (most likely to be followed by the Biden White House) has become more aggressive in pushing back against China's maritime claims in much of the South China Sea. Secretary

---

[9] I have drawn from Huong Le Thu, "Vietnam Draws Lines in the Sea", an excellent analysis of the White Paper in *Foreign Policy*, 6 December 2019).

of State Mike Pompeo described China's expansive maritime claims as "completely unlawful" and cited a 2016 ruling by an international tribunal in a case brought by the Philippines which found China to be in violation of international law because of its island building activities. China pushed back by noting that Pompeo's accusations were "completely unjustified" and

> *Sooner or later, there will be a repeat of the HYSY 981 saga, involving Vietnam or one of the ASEAN claimants to islands occupied by China, which may be similar to or a more aggressive variant of the May 2014 incident, leading to full-scale war.*

that Beijing was "committed to resolving disputes through negotiation." Cui Tiankai, the Chinese Ambassador to America also reminded American viewers in a television interview[10] that the U.S. was not a signatory to the United Nations Law of the Sea Convention, which Pompeo had cited without irony in criticising China.

Sooner or later, there will be a repeat of the HYSY 981 saga, involving Vietnam or one of the ASEAN claimants to islands occupied by China, which may be similar to or a more aggressive variant of the May 2014 incident, leading to full-scale war. The lessons learnt by Vietnam are reflected in the assertive White Paper, which its ASEAN neighbours are likely to read with great interest. While the South China Sea conflict is at a relatively early stage, our next scenario has been a theatre of conflict for the last seven decades.

Nuclear Neighbours

Neighbours and perennial enemies India and Pakistan have waged four wars and multiple quasi-wars since 1947 over the disputed territory of Kashmir. Most recently in the spring of 2019, a suicide bombing of Indian para-military troops by a terror group with alleged links to the Pakistan

---

[10] Cui Tiankai interview with Fareed Zakaria, CNN, 19 July 2020.

Army led to an aerial bombardment by both sides. Pakistan downed an Indian jet and in a show of goodwill returned the pilot and offered to hold a peace dialogue. While there are various reasons for Indian Prime Minister Narendra Modi's sweeping re-election victory in May 2019, the tussle with Pakistan clearly played a leading role in appealing to the nationalistic instincts of the country's electorate. Since his election victory, the Modi administration has doubled down on nationalism by revoking Article 370 of the Constitution, which guaranteed a special status to the Indian side of Kashmir. India has decisively changed conditions on the ground without the consent of Kashmir's Muslim-majority population and the territory is in an effective state of siege with several political leaders detained.

These facts are all well-known and I don't intend to build a future war scenario between India and Pakistan since they have been at each other's throats multiple times for the past few decades and are likely to do so again. The worrying aspect of the Kashmir conflict is its regional dimension, drawing in Afghanistan, Pakistan, China, Russia, and India into a new Great Game — with America, Russia, India, and China replacing Great Britain and Russia as the primary regional power competitors. Over the past three years, the Trump administration has made it clear that it wants to pull American troops out of Afghanistan and has launched peace talks with the Taliban, with the current government being left out of the negotiations. Ahmed Rashid, the pre-eminent Afghan watcher writes that there is growing regional consensus for such a peace accord. "Despite the acute differences among the regional players — Iran and the Gulf states, India and Pakistan, Pakistan and Afghanistan — there is growing consensus on seeking an end to the

> *The worrying aspect of the Kashmir conflict is its regional dimension, drawing in Afghanistan, Pakistan, China, Russia, and India into a new Great Game — with America, Russia, India, and China replacing Great Britain and Russia as the primary regional power competitors.*

> *The interesting aspect of the Afghanistan-Pakistan crisis, or Af-Pak as it was once described, is how much India and China are players in the region.*

war in Afghanistan," Rashid wrote in early 2019.[11] "The long war has proved devastating to the neighbouring states as terrorist groups find sanctuary in an increasingly lawless Afghanistan and the implementation of economic infrastructure projects is hindered."

The peace talks proceeded in fits and starts, with the Taliban coming very close to visiting the Presidential retreat of Camp David near Washington D.C. to sign a peace accord but was called off by President Trump at the last minute because of a Taliban-supported terror attack which killed American soldiers. The agreement was finally signed between America and Taliban leadership in Doha in February 2020 with several unresolved issues, the most notable of them being the current Afghan government was not invited to the negotiations. When he served as Vice President under Obama, Biden was a strong advocate for a U.S. pull-back out of Afghanistan and this is likely to continue.

The interesting aspect of the Afghanistan–Pakistan crisis, or Af-Pak as it was once described, is how much India and China are players in the region. New Delhi has been resolutely close to the current and previous Afghan governments and has been a major provider of aid since the Taliban was ousted in the aftermath of 9/11. Meanwhile, China has doubled down in supporting its traditional partner Pakistan by investing in the strategic port of Gwadar on the tip of the Persian Gulf, and through the reported $700 billion China–Pakistan Economic Corridor (CPEC), part of Beijing's ambitious Belt and Road Initiative (BRI).

The view from Beijing is that India is a belligerent power in South Asia and New Delhi needs to do more to build bridges with Pakistan and other

---

[11] Ahmed Rashid, "This Man is Revered Among the Taliban. Can He End the Afghan War?" *The New York Times*, 28 January 2019.

neighbours. India of courses pushes back noting that it is a victim of terror acts hatched in Pakistan. These sharply differing world views suggest that chances of the next India–Pakistan war becoming a much bigger regional conflict are rising with America keen to withdraw its security footprint. Beijing is eager to extend its regional reach by providing a security blanket to Pakistan, and India is anxious to protect the status quo in South Asia, where it is the unchallenged big dog of the region but has done a terrible job in maintaining good relations with smaller neighbours.

Xi and Modi

To this combustible mix one must surely add border tensions between India and China which flared up in June 2020 at the height of the pandemic. A brief history first. Since India's independence in 1947 and China's own revolution in 1949, the

> *Since India's independence in 1947 and China's own revolution in 1949, the leaders of the two countries have been as different as chalk and cheese.*

leaders of the two countries have been as different as chalk and cheese. India's first Prime Minister Jawaharlal Nehru was an Anglophile and a democrat compared with his contemporaries Chairman Mao and Prime Minister Zhou, whose own background was steeped in Japan's rise as a major Asian power and the Russian Revolution. Although India was a strong advocate for China's entry into the United Nations in the early 1950s, relations have been poisoned ever since due to a protracted border dispute, triggered in part by British colonial administrator Henry McMahon's (thus the McMahon Line) controversial geographical rendering of the demarcation line between Tibet and India. The two countries share a long 2,167-mile border extending from the remote and frozen Himalayan terrain of Ladakh to India's northeast. In 1962, China invaded parts of this border in a brief war which India was found unprepared to wage. Prime Minister Nehru never recovered from the national humiliation which followed, and the war scarred the psyche of successive generations of Indians. In my frequent trips to China, India seldom features in the discourse with policymakers and academics. In contrast, China is an all-consuming obsession with the Indian elite, bolstered in recent years with growing trade, investment links and the teen addiction to Chinese apps like Tik-Tok, which the Indian Government banned after the recent border tensions.

Unlike Nehru and Mao, Narendra Modi and Xi Jinping are remarkably alike as aggregators and centralisers of political power and as leaders who do not tolerate dissent. They have met 18 times in the last six years, including two well-publicised one-on-one summits at Wuhan and most recently in southern India in late-2019. Beneath the bonhomie and the hugs, the latter being a signature gesture from Modi to all world leaders that he meets, there have been simmering border tensions which the two countries have been simply unable to resolve. Matters came to a head in April 2020 when by neutral accounts, soldiers from the People's Liberation Army entered the line of actual control (LAC) dividing the two countries at Pangong Tso, the highest salt water lake in the world at an elevation of 4,225 metres, and parts further north where the frozen borders of China, India, and Pakistan-Occupied Kashmir meet in a disputed junction along the Galwan River. China's strategic intent appears to be to deprive India direct access to restive Xinjiang province and to build its own growing transport links between Tibet and Pakistan-Occupied Kashmir along the Karakoram Highway and further into the Pakistan hinterland as part of its grand China–Pakistan Economic Corridor (CPEC).

Despite the friendly show of Modi–Xi summitry, it appears that China became suspicious of India's intentions vis-à-vis Kashmir, with the revocation of Article 370 in August 2019, which effectively changed the nature of India's hold over Kashmir, and the Army's considerable investments in infrastructure along the LAC of the two countries. Whatever the intentions on both sides, soldiers from the PLA and the Indian Army literally came to blows along the Galwan River on 15 June 2020 in the first violent confrontation between the two countries in several decades. We don't have Chinese media accounts of what took place that night and have to rely on Indian and international iterations. What has been confirmed[12] is that the fighting began on the night of 15 June after Indian soldiers set fire to a tent erected by the PLA on the Indian side of the LAC, which

The fact that this was a medieval battle in difficult terrain with fisticuffs and barbed wire batons was fortunate because both sides adhered to the protocol of not bringing deadly weapons along the LAC.

provoked a bloody hand-to-hand battle for several hours and cost lives on both sides, 17 confirmed by India including the commanding officer and an unspecified number from China, including the commanding officer. The fact that this was a medieval battle in difficult terrain with fisticuffs and barbed wire batons was fortunate because both sides adhered to the protocol of not bringing deadly weapons along the LAC. In the period since the15 June kerfuffle, China and India military commanders have met to disengage and de-escalate. They may well succeed temporarily but the die has been cast. After focusing on Pakistan as the only external threat for several decades, the China border clash re-opens a second front for India, in mostly hostile terrain and against a more formidable and well-funded PLA. Did China test India's resolve at the height of the pandemic by "teaching" New Delhi a lesson for its recent moves on Kashmir, as has been recently speculated? Or is the Chinese build-up a part of President Xi's masterplan, as Indian journalist Shekhar Gupta[13] has speculated, to remind India of the considerable costs involved in the permanent stand-off and in pushing New Delhi to negotiate a final settlement. Opinion is divided on this topic. What is clear is that border clash will lead to a strategic re-think on India's part of moving closer to America and other quad nations in jointly engaging with a rising China. India has been a reluctant partner of the Quad in recent years,

---

[12] From *The New York Times*, 17 June 2020.

[13] Gupta's assessment came in his popular *Cut the Clutter* video newsfeed on September 23, 2020.

hesitating to be seen as part of the anti-China Western brigade. If India indeed moves firmly to the American orbit, it may turn out to be a major miscalculation on the part of Xi Jinping, whose second term has been marred by the pandemic, escalating U.S.–China trade tensions, and the protests in Hong Kong. Xi Jinping's positioning of China as the next superpower and introduction of a more assertive diplomacy, dubbed "wolf warrior" after a popular Chinese action movie, is a game-changer for Asia and has raised the stakes for regional security. On its part, the Trump and most likely the Biden administration will continue to move forward in assembling a group of allies along the "Indo-Pacific", a regional security construct straddling countries along the Indian and Pacific oceans. If America wishes to re-engage with Asia, a positive signal would be via trade and the CPTPP, which could be repurposed as an Indo-Pacific Free Trade Area.

Kim Tactics

Our next theatre of conflict, North Korea, which has raged on for several decades also suffers from the presence of too many pivotal players. Besides America and North Korea, resolution of the regional conflict is impossible without the tacit participation and support of China, Russia, Japan, and South Korea, who participated in the now defunct six-party talks. Each of these players have differing strategic objectives when it comes to bringing Pyongyang to the negotiating table. "The other five participants in the six-party talks share an interest in

> *Our next theatre of conflict, North Korea, which has raged on for several decades also suffers from the presence of too many pivotal players.*

a denuclearised Korean Peninsula, while the North maintains a virtually opposite position," writes Korean researcher Jaebum Kim.[14] "Nonetheless, the other five also have differing positions and interests despite their agreement

---

[14] Jaebum Kim, "The North Korean Factor in East Asian Regional Security", *Journal of Global Policy and Governance*, September 2013.

on the overarching denuclearisation goal, and Pyongyang is apt to playing off the five against one another." He adds that North Korea avoids permanent mechanisms and cumulative agreements that could build durable regional security and stability regimes. This critical point appears to be lost on the Trump administration as it attempted to graft a bilateral peace deal with North Korea with other parties to the six-party talks relegated to the role of bystanders.

During an earlier era, as recently as the 1990s, it was quite possible for America to forge a deal with Pyongyang without the active participation of regional powers. However, those times have changed and it is the assertiveness of China, South Korea, Russia, and Japan that has provided Kim Jong Un, with every incentive to push for more

For a few North Korea experts, China may well be the major obstacle for such a deal because it is seen as the one country which has the greatest leverage on Pyongyang but has so far failed to change behaviours.

concessions from America, and for the bystanders to complicate matters by not matching their public rhetoric with action. Take China's public position on a resolution of the North Korea issue as an example. As recently as December 2019, Foreign Minister Wang Yi said in an interview with the *People's Daily* that the United States needed to take "concrete steps" to deliver on what was agreed between President Trump and North Korean leader Kim Jong Un at their Singapore summit in June 2018. The Foreign Minister added that he was encouraging the two parties to "work out a feasible roadmap" to establish peace and "realizing complete denuclearisation on the Peninsula."

For a few North Korea experts, China may well be the major obstacle for such a deal because it is seen as the one country which has the greatest leverage on Pyongyang but has so far failed to change behaviours. Indeed, besides his visits to Singapore and Hanoi to attend the summit meetings with Trump, the country which Kim Jong Un has visited most frequently is China, with four visits in 2018 alone. In geopolitical terms, China's security calculus is a reasonable one. True, it has considerable leverage over North Korea because over 90 percent of the impoverished country's trade passes through China. At the same time, China has real concerns that an implosion of the Pyongyang regime would send millions of poor North Koreans across its borders, a la Syria, and in its worst-case scenario the two Koreas would merge with Pyongyang's nuclear arsenal intact. A unified nuclear Korea on China's doorstep would dramatically alter the security balance in North Asia and could compel Japan to pursue the nuclear option as well. So, for Beijing, the central element of any resolution of the North Korean issue should include denuclearisation as the central feature. "China shares Washington's desires for North Korea's denuclearization but does not believe in it is achievable in the short term," said a report by the Washington D.C.-based United States Institute for Peace.[15] "Beijing regards a nuclear North Korea to be inherently destabilising because it provides a rationale for U.S. military deployments and possible intervention in the region, prompts regional actors such as Japan and South Korea to strengthen their defensive capabilities, and raises calls for the development of indigenous nuclear capabilities in these countries — all of which are inimical to China's interests and security."

School Bullies

To add to the already unstable relationship between Beijing and Washington over trade and other issues, which has serious spill-over effects on the region as discussed earlier, South Korea and Japan are squabbling like school bullies with little regard to the fact that they are both allies of Washington and house American

> *South Korea and Japan are squabbling like school bullies with little regard to the fact that they are both allies of Washington and house American troops on their soil.*

---

[15] "China's Role in North Korea Nuclear and Peace Negotiations", USIP Senior Study Group Final Report, 6 May 2019.

troops on their soil. The source of the current tensions between Seoul and Tokyo dates back to grievances originating in Japan's colonisation of Korea before World War II, and the brutal treatment meted out to slave labour and Korean "comfort women" who were forced into prostitution, deeply emotional issues which have forever hindered good relations between the two countries. At the same time, Japan and Korea are also major trading powers and are intrinsically linked in regional and global supply chains. The two countries are home to Asia's most global firms, Samsung, Sony, Toyota, Hyundai — economics should trump politics in bilateral relations, in theory at least.

However, Korea and Japan are currently engaged in a low-intensity trade war following a Korean Supreme Court ruling in 2018 ordering Japanese companies to financially compensate Koreans forced to work as contract labour during the Japanese occupation of the country. Japan retaliated by placing restrictions on the export of vital chemicals used in semi-conductors and Korea all but threatened to rescind a security relationship aimed at presenting a united response to the North Korean issue.

Japan and Korea are "geographically, historically, and culturally the closest neighbours as well as the most important, mutually beneficial partners in terms of human exchanges," South Korean President Moon told then Japanese Prime Minister Shinzo Abe at a regional summit. "Our relationship is one that cannot be made distant, even if there is temporarily an uncomfortable issue." This suggests that the trade tit-for-tat will simmer for a while but will eventually be resolved. But it will not go away and the persistent tensions between Seoul and Tokyo raise two immediate concerns. First, America's inability or indifference to placing pressure on its two allies to quickly resolve differences, given the graver threat they face from an unstable North Korea. Second, South Korea and Japan appear to have differing strategic security objectives and nationalist impulses which makes their behaviour in a real crisis very unpredictable. In opinion polls in South Korea, a majority of young Koreans respond emotively to historical grievances against Japan. No

Korean President can ignore powerful voices from the street, in particular from the youth. Young Koreans are also overwhelmingly in favour of a rapprochement with the North, indeed of a united Korea, which is not necessarily an outcome which Japan favours.

> *Young Koreans are also overwhelmingly in favour of a rapprochement with the North, indeed of a united Korea, which is not necessarily an outcome which Japan favours.*

To compound matters, South Korea's bilateral relationship with China has also deteriorated over Beijing's repeated objections over the deployment of the Terminal High Altitude Area Defence (THAAD), the American-made anti-ballistic missile defence system, which Beijing regards as being directed at China rather than North Korea. Japan, Korea and China are major economic trilateral partners. In a real geopolitical crisis, disentangling long-standing economic relationships by making hard political choices will test the resolve of East Asia's great powers. Nationalist voices emanating from the three countries suggests that emotion will overwhelm cold economic choices.

The three geopolitical scenarios that I have outlined are not water-tight and independent of each other. Resolution of the South China Sea islands dispute could become inextricably linked with a resolution of the North Korea issue, or exacerbate it further. A geopolitical crisis further west, in South Asia, could also compel China to make a choice on whether to harden its position toward India and exercise its growing political clout by engaging more deeply in South Asia and Afghanistan. Whichever way China reacts will transform Asian geopolitics forever, with divided opinion in the region on whether it will be for the better or worse.

Asia's economic miracle was built on predictable assumptions that regional stability was a pre-condition for economic advancement. Economic progress has rekindled nationalist, nativist sentiment which the region had bottled up for decades, very much like Europe had in the first era of globalisation.

In the summer of 1914, it was raw emotion that dictated how European powers reacted to the assassination of the Archduke. In 37 days after the assassination, Europe went up in flames in ways that no geopolitical pundit of the time had predicted. Asian powers should check their emotions at the door and visit Stora Latina. Or jeopardise it all by foolishly making war inevitable.

EPILOGUE

EPILOGUE

Chapter 12

An Asian Renaissance

"The darkest places in hell are reserved for those who maintain their neutrality in times of moral crisis."[1]

Dante Alighieri passed away in September 1321. Florence's ruling class regretted sending the late poet into humiliating exile and attempted to have his body returned for a ceremonial burial. His adopted city, Ravenna, refused and his remains are buried there to this day. It is questionable whether Dante himself would have appreciated the belated gesture, so angry he had become in exile about politics and society during the fading years of the late Middle Ages. He probably died a bitter and sad man. His crime in the eyes of the ossified establishment was his blistering critique of the Pope and push for change.

But fate and destiny have a strange way of restoring reputations. Precisely twenty-six years after Dante's death, in 1347, Italy and the world were struck by the bubonic plague known as the Black Death which came in several waves for the next four years and may have taken the lives of over 100 million worldwide, even 200 million if unreliable accounts from that century can be believed. What has all of this got to do with Dante? A lot as we will discover in this chapter.

---

[1] This is attributed to Dante but never appears in the full form quoted here.

Italian Professor Gianna Pomata told *The New Yorker*[2] that she saw parallels with Covid-19 and the plague which struck the world in the 14th century — "not in the number of dead but in terms of shaking up the way people think," she told the magazine. "The Black Death really marks the end of the Middle Ages and the beginning of something else." That something else, the author of the article Lawrence Wright wrote, was the Renaissance. "After the Black Death, nothing was the same," Pomata added. "What I expect now is something as dramatic is going to happen, not so much in medicine but in economy and culture. Because of danger, there's this wonderful human response, which is to think in a new way."

Dante may have died a sad man, but history has vindicated the old poet and philosopher. What followed the narrow mindedness and bloody rivalries of the Middle Ages, with the plague as its peak, was a flourishing of Europe's golden age — the Renaissance. Reason, rational thinking, scientific inquiry, and empirical evidence became the guiding posts of that era, just as Dante and many of his contemporaries had advocated for. The Renaissance was not all milk and honey, I must add. Two of the darkest moral stains on Europe's history, slavery and colonialism, originated during that era. Rational thinking and reason were also bound up with brutality and medieval attitudes towards the rest of the world, which Europe conquered and enslaved.

> *Dante may have died a sad man, but history has vindicated the old poet and philosopher. What followed the narrow mindedness and bloody rivalries of the Middle Ages, with the plague as its peak, was a flourishing of Europe's golden age — the Renaissance.*

---

[2] I highly recommend the article by Lawrence Wright, "How Pandemics Wreak Havoc – and Open Minds", *The New Yorker* – 13 July 2020, as well as his prescient novel, *The End of October: A Novel* (Penguin Random House, 2020) which maps out the spread of a deadly virus in our era and the world's failure to deal with it.

The broad point here is that pandemics, natural disasters, and even man-made disasters like the 2008 Global Financial Crisis have long-lasting impacts. They tend to reshape societal thinking, priorities, and concerns in a fundamental and profound way, which is not apparent in the immediate aftermath. Without the 2008 GFC, for example, globalisation and trade would have probably accelerated and there would have been no surge in nationalism and nativism, as we have witnessed in America with the rise of Trump, the UK Brexit vote, and emergence of hard-line leaders like Xi, Modi, and Erdogan. Over two decades ago, Southeast Asian politics was also shaken up by the Asian Financial Crisis with the ouster of President Suharto in Indonesia, the arrival of Thaksin in Thailand, and the beginning of the Anwar-Mahathir soap opera in Malaysia. Over 137 years ago, the Dutch colonial hold over Indonesia loosened after the spectacular Krakatoa volcanic eruption. "Krakatoa was not the cause of the birth of Indonesia, far from it," writer Simon Winchester[3] told *The Guardian* in 2005, "but it was a sign, a trigger, and it remains a significant moment in Indonesian political history for that very reason".

Catalyst for Change

What does Covid-19 mean for Asia? As I have argued in this book, Asia was rife for disruptive change long before Covid-19 made an appearance in Wuhan in late

> *The pandemic will serve as a catalyst for change, a trigger.*

2019. The pandemic will serve as a catalyst for change, a trigger. There was a time when Asia's long period of economic expansion lead to tangible gains for over 4 billion people. In fact, the region's singular contribution to humanity in the past century has been the opening up of Asian minds, economic opportunities, and positive social outcomes after a prolonged period of slumber. As we learnt in Chapter 1, Asia's rise after World War II

---

[3] Simon Winchester, *Krakatoa: The Day The World Exploded 27 August 1883* (Viking Press, 2005) is also recommended reading.

and colonial rule was not pre-ordained and was predicted to fail in the eyes of many cynical Western observers.

A few months before India's independence in August 1947, Jawaharlal Nehru convened an Inter-Asia Conference in New Delhi to signal to the world that Asia had woken up. "We stand at the end of the era and on the threshold of a new period of history," he said. "Standing on this watershed which divides two epochs of human history and endeavour we can look back on our long past and look forward to the future that is taking shape before our eyes. Asia, after a long period of quiescence, has suddenly become important in world affairs." Asia has fulfilled Nehru's vision, and that of other post-colonial leaders by becoming an engine of growth for the global economy. The only problem is that the growth engine is carrying a train which is filled with self-satisfied elites and hundreds of millions of people are stranded on the platform, unable to get in. The cost of entry to live the Asian dream is getting ever steeper.

For decades, our only measure of Asia's dynamism was the region's high rates of economic growth, something it is justly celebrated for. However, there are limits to what GDP growth alone can measure and what it says about the health and well-being of a nation. Bangladesh may have one of the fastest growing economies in Asia, but its health system has been found wanting as the Covid-19 pandemic rages across the country. India used to pride itself until very recently for having the fastest growing economy in the G20 but the internal migration of millions of migrants due to the lockdown has exposed the state's inability to provide an adequate safety net for the poor. In the Philippines, fairly robust economic growth over the past two decades has not stopped the emigration of millions of educated Filipinos in search of a better life.

> *However, there are limits to what GDP growth alone can measure and what it says about the health and well-being of a nation.*

The late Robert Kennedy was a famous critic of GDP and what it claimed to measure. The GDP, he said in 1968 in a speech at the University of Kansas "measures neither our wit nor our courage, neither our wisdom nor our learning, neither our compassion nor our devotion to our country, it measures everything in short, except that which makes life worthwhile". Nobel Laureate Joseph Stiglitz[4] notes with frustration that for the global economy it should be clear that, in spite of the increases in GDP, in spite of the 2008 crisis being well behind us, everything is not fine. "We see this in the political discontent rippling through so many advanced countries; we see it in the widespread support of demagogues, whose successes depend on exploiting economic discontent; and we see it in the environment around us, where fires rage and floods and droughts occur at ever-increasing levels."

Asia's GDP and growth obsession is fuelled wilfully by politicians eager to sell a message to people that life is good, by research arms of multilateral institutions and the private sector who talk up growth targets at the expense of everything else, and by the region's thought leadership mafia, a loose coalition of conference organisers, business media, consulting firms, writers, and business folks who have a vested interest in hyping up the Asia story. This is elite capture because none of the issues which I have highlighted in the eight circles of hell receives serious attention in the vast echo chamber of Asia boosters. During my long career, I have attended a fair share of conferences devoted to the generic topic of Asia Shining. Indeed, I am guilty of organising a few of these myself. These events are set pieces where the Asian and global elite come to celebrate their success and paint a utopian picture of the region in the future. It never

This is elite capture because none of the issues which I have highlighted in the eight circles of hell receives serious attention in the vast echo chamber of Asia boosters.

---

[4] Joseph Stiglitz, "It's time to retire metrics like the GDP. They don't measure everything that matters", *The Guardian*, 24 November 2019.

occurred to me until recently that the glass was not only half full, but it may not be a real glass at all, perhaps an optical illusion, of the stories the elite tells itself about progress and prosperity. If Pramod had been invited to speak at any of these events, indeed if any of our urban cowboys, disadvantaged teenage girls, climate refugees, and members of the lower middle class were present, we would have heard a different, less hopeful story about stalled mobility and narrowing opportunities in Asia.

Instead of obsessing about GDP growth forecasts, may I propose to the thought leadership mafia that they pay attention to the following three metrics which could provide a more balanced view of whether high rates of growth are translating into better lives for all. The first metric is the UN's annual Human Development Index, which we discussed in Chapter 3 and provides a snapshot of how the region is faring on an important set of socio-economic indicators. *As an aspiration, all of Asia should endeavour to be in the top 50 by 2030.* The second metric is tax-to-GDP ratios in developing Asia, which are abysmally low and on average range well below 20 percent according to OECD estimates, with Indonesia at the lower end of 11 percent. This metric is important not least because Asia's has the largest contingent of billionaires on earth who should be paying more than their fair share to finance development. If high rates of economic growth are not leading to buoyancy in tax revenues, there are likely to be serious distortions in tax policy and administration, leading to a reduction in social spending and long-term investments in infrastructure. The third metric is health and education spending by governments, the former being glaringly obvious after the pandemic exposed serious weaknesses in health infrastructure and delivery. In recent years, the state in Asia is behaving like an addict, getting high on accolades about economic growth and indifferent to building institutional capacity and social protections.

Covid-19, with all of the devastation it has wrought on lives and livelihoods, presents a real opportunity for a great reset in thinking on how better growth should lead to better outcomes. To critics who are likely to push back and

Covid-19, with all of the devastation it has wrought on lives and livelihoods, presents a real opportunity for a great reset in thinking on how better growth should lead to better outcomes.

say that GDP growth is a necessary precondition for better outcomes, which I don't necessarily disagree with, please listen to Jacinda Ardern. The New Zealand Prime Minister, who has received effusive praise globally for her efficient handling of Covid-19, criticised the tendency amongst countries to measure success by economic growth and GDP alone. "Economic growth accompanied by worsening social outcomes is not success," she said.[5] "It is failure."

Tharman Shanmugaratnam, one of Singapore and Asia's most thoughtful leaders, gave an important speech[6] during the height of the pandemic on how Covid-19 has raised the stakes and has the makings of a profound social crisis all over the world. "We are already seeing this happen elsewhere. It did not begin with the pandemic," he said. "Social divisions were already growing in these countries. But they are now getting even wider. Job and income losses have hit some groups much harder than the others. Children without well-off parents are falling behind, with their schooling disrupted and little done to help them. All of this is sharpening feelings of helplessness, and the sense that the system is stacked against those who are already disadvantaged. And it is bringing long-standing perceptions of racial injustice to a boiling point." The Senior Minister added that there are many societies which used to be cohesive but are now fragmenting, both in the West and in Asia. "No society remains cohesive simply because it used to be," he said. "The economic dangers we now face compel us to fortify our society and reinforce the strengths that we have developed over many years."

---

[5] The Prime Minister made these remarks at the Goalkeepers 2019 event organised by the Bill & Melinda Gates Foundation, 26 September 2019.

[6] Tharman Shanmugaratnam, "A Stronger and More Cohesive Society", National Broadcast, Singapore, on 17 June 2020.

Asian Values

What would this fortification look like in the current Asian context? I don't want to give a blithe response by saying better policies. Through the book, I have been parsimonious in offering specific policy advice to Asian governments because I recognise that all politics is local and good policies have to be built from the ground up, with input from people. Let's focus on values instead, good Asian values, which propelled the region's growth story for several decades. Over three decades ago when I first moved to Singapore, I heard that it was Asian values which was the secret sauce for the rise of East Asia. Singapore's founder Lee Kuan Yew and former diplomat Kishore Mahbubani were the intellectual drivers of the debate, asserting that it was Confucian virtues such as filial piety, family diligence, education, and obedience to authority which explained much of the economic success of the Asian tigers.

> *Let's focus on values instead, good Asian values, which propelled the region's growth story for several decades.*

This view was not universally shared, as can be expected, and many western critics conflated Asian values to mean an all-powerful state, lack of political debate, and individual liberties being subsumed by a communitarian ethos. "For Lee, the Chinese aphorism that best captured the uniquely Asian/Confucian view of the individual's role in society was:"*Xiushen, qijia, zhiguo, pingtianxia,*" writes scholar Orville Schell.[7] "Bringing peace under heaven first requires cultivating oneself, then taking care of one's family, and finally looking after one's country." Embedded in the Asian values debate of the 1990s, was the presumption that a majority of East Asians preferred tangible economic development and an improvement in their lives over airy-fairy notions of free speech and democratic dissent. On hindsight, this thinking was flawed because of the democratic transformation of Taiwan,

---

[7] Orville Schell, "Lee Kuan Yew, the Man who Remade Asia", *The Wall Street Journal*, 27 March 2015.

Korea, Indonesia, and the protests in Hong Kong. The Asian values debate also met its hubris with the Asian Financial Crisis two decades ago, where crony capitalism was widely blamed for the region's brief economic meltdown.

Values never go out of fashion and it is an appropriate time to revive the debate.

> *The Asian values debate also met its hubris with the Asian Financial Crisis two decades ago, where crony capitalism was widely blamed for the region's brief economic meltdown.*

Critics of the 1990s brand of Asian values, predominantly from Europe and America, have apparently changed their own minds as well. Many of them are looking at the social devastation in their own backyards and grudgingly acknowledge that values should be at the centrepiece of any discussion on national renewal. Writing in a different context about the U.S. elections, FT journalist Simon Kuper[8] asked politicians to lead with values, not policies. "Few voters still believe candidates' policy promises — especially in the U.S., where modern presidents struggle to get even piffling laws through Congress," he writes "…instead of promising policies, promise values. Values talk is more credible, it sounds human, and it explains your policies." David Brooks, a columnist for *The New York Times*, has written passionately about the role of values in rebuilding America after the pandemic. "In this atmosphere, economic resilience will be more valued than maximised efficiency," he writes. "We'll spend more time minimizing downside risks than maximising upside gains. The local and the rooted will be valued more than the distantly networked. We'll value community over individualism, embeddedness over autonomy."

All of this suspiciously sounds like good Asian values to me, even Confucian values, which were propagated over three decades ago and was met with impolite pushback. If Asia is to be renewed, I believe the time has come for a refresh of its own values which underpinned the region's dramatic

---

[8] Simon Kuper, "What Democrats Can Do to Topple Trump", Financial Times, 9 July 2020.

> *If Asia is to be renewed, I believe the time has come for a refresh of its own values which underpinned the region's dramatic resurgence.*

resurgence. One problem with the 1990s version of Asian values is that they were articulated after the fact, i.e. the emergence of Japan as an economic power and the success of the Tigers. With many of Asia's challenges being here and now, it is good to spell out upfront what the values should *not* be.

As a start, there should be no hint of cultural supremacy or chauvinism in the values. They should be universal, inclusive, and focus on shared beliefs. My second caveat is that the new set of values should not be an excuse to defend the indefensible. This is less about political systems or the virtues of democracy versus dictatorships, since both of them appear to be behaving the same in Asia today. We must speak out against state-sponsored atrocities, public policy failures, and pervasive discrimination and these should not be attributed to the price of development or cultural superiority. My third pre-condition is that values should not be focused exclusively on economic development as the sole criteria to measure progress.

The 2020 version of Asian values should have six defining guideposts.

- The role of government is to deliver progress and prosperity to all citizens regardless of race, religion, caste, creed, sexual orientation, ethnicity, and gender.

- An informed citizenry is well within its rights to exercise oversight and demand transparency and accountability.

- The state has a moral and constitutional obligation to help the poor and disadvantaged groups like migrant workers, minorities, and women.

- Entrepreneurship and billionaires are encouraged but not at the expense of subverting public policy and state capture.

- Societal rights should include the right to education, health, a clean environment, human rights, and access to economic opportunity for all.

- Politics is a meritocracy, not a preserve of the privileged.

I can see constitutional experts and lawyers pouncing on these proposed values and tearing them apart for its naivete, glaring inconsistencies, and how it can actually be implemented across borders and differing political systems. The good news is that I don't expect Asian governments to be standard bearers of these values. The new values should be crowdsourced and carried forward by the region's 4.64 billion citizens, organising as they do through decentralised networks on social media with all of their passion, concerns, and commitment. Only they have the power to force political and business elites to pay attention and be the vanguard of change. There will be winners and losers as we evaluate countries in how they are performing against these values. By almost any economic yardstick, Vietnam is in a sweet spot today and the thought leadership mafia has accorded it the status of an emerging Tiger economy. The country performs less well if measured against a few of the above values.

The new values should be crowdsourced and carried forward by the region's 4.64 billion citizens, organising as they do through decentralised networks on social media with all of their passion, concerns, and commitment.

A final thought about my own motivations in writing this book and what some may regard as its overwhelmingly negative narrative about the region's future. I am an optimist, even an Asia fanatic, and sincerely believe that the region needs to face the future by embracing modernity with a communitarian ethos which made it so successful in the first place. We don't have to reach out to our distant past to find such a successful blend and I am not talking about religion. In maddeningly dense Hong Kong, it is possible to leave crowded Central and be at the feet of the giant *Tian Tan* Buddha statue in less than thirty minutes. On a clear day, you can even glimpse the serene statue when you head to the airport. The statue was built in 1990, in our lifetime, and is meant to symbolise harmony. It is a peaceful place amidst the urgency of modern life in Hong Kong. The Buddha himself was Asia's first, great globalist, whose secular life and teachings on compassion and suffering spread from India to Asia and still resonate 2,500 years after he attained nirvana. This was the original Asian miracle.

I was reminded of Asia's strong traditions when a furniture restorer came to my house in suburban Maryland to fix the Java teak "Suharto" bed, named by a wag because this valuable piece was acquired in Jakarta at the height of the crisis over two decades ago. The bed was wobbly because it had been mishandled during my move back from London. The mover had carelessly placed a nail to hold a piece together. The restorer, who was a young American man who had never been to Asia, gazed admiringly at the bed and gave me a five-minute lecture on its craftsmanship. The beauty about antique Asian furniture, he told me, was that the artisans never used nails. The bed parts were assembled based on a sophisticated understanding of how they locked into the grooves, like a giant puzzle. and the final product was tightened by a wooden wrench. "Asian craftsmanship," he whispered, giving me the perfect hook to end this book. The problem with Asia today is that for every problem, policymakers are deploying multiple hammers and nails, damaging Asia's delicate social fabric. A true Asian renaissance is within reach, only if the region's leaders replace hammers and nails with engagement and empowerment. Pramod would approve.

Acknowledgments

This book is a culmination of several years of work, research, and travels in Asia. My original thesis was more positive, reflecting my own tunnel vision and status quo views on the region. As I write in the book, it took a ride in a three-wheeler in Mumbai to radically challenge my conventional thinking. So, let me start by thanking Pramod and I hope he and his family are safe during this terrible pandemic. A special word of thanks to Chatham House — in particular to Robin Niblett, Champa Patel, Lucy Ridout, Chloe Sagemen and the Press Office — for providing me with the research platform and support to pursue this project. My deep appreciation also to Alejandro Reyes of the Asia Global Institute, who was tenacious in getting me to write for AsiaGlobal Online, where I previewed many of the themes in the book.

I also received strong encouragement and support from a number of friends, mentors, colleagues, and business associates. They include Montek Singh Ahluwalia, Michael Vatikiotis, Bilahari Kausikan, Stanley Fischer, V. Shankar, Edward Bowles, Prakash Loungani, Florence Quirici, Sushen Jhingan, Nick Lovegrove, Nick Greenstock, Caroline Atkinson, Claes Winberg, Salil Tripathi, David Muir, Zaki Cooper, Melanie Ullrich, Marc Uzan, Giancarlo Bruno, Farah Mullick, Zarik Nabi, Manu Bhaskaran, Ravi Velloor, Endy Bayuni, Christopher Johnson, Jeremy Mark, Myron Brilliant, Gary Litman,

Robert Schroeder, Milan Dalal, Heath Gibson, Kate Matthews and Bill Hayton. I would also like to thank a number of senior policymakers in Asia, current and former who prefer to remain anonymous, for their valuable time and insights. The final product is so much better because of their input. All errors and omissions in the book are of course mine.

My agents, Nick Wallwork and Christopher Newson of Newson Wallwork Publishing Services did a terrific job in shepherding the book to prospective publishers during the pandemic. My thanks to World Scientific, my publisher who got the book out at record speed. Thanks, in particular to Chua Hong Koon, Sandhya Venkatesh, Jimmy Low, and the team.

I dedicate this book to my late sister Uma and to my family in Mumbai, Dubai, London, New York, Toronto, Seattle, and Washington D.C., including Zayden, the latest addition to the family. My wife Ferzine and daughter Neha were, as always, strong pillars of support and my deep appreciation to them, including for tolerating my eccentric working hours during the lockdown.

Vasuki Shastry
Washington D.C. and London
December 2020
www.vasukishastry.com

Index